Postcards

REVISTING DISCIPLESHIP

From

BY RICK JAMES

Corinth

Edited by
Rick James and Betty Churchill

Book and cover design by Aaron Martin
www.iamaaronmartin.com
Cover photo by Ugmonk

Cru Press
100 Lake Hart Drive, 2500
Orlando, FL 32832-0100

To order go to CruPress.com

International Standard Book Number: 1-56399-247-7

Table of Contents

Section Five: Briefs & Letters

Section Six: Foundations & History

WRITTEN AND EDITED
Rick James and Betty Churchill

Contributions

WILL WALKER
Learning

BOB THUNE, JR
Gospel

LAURIE MENEFEE
Honest to God

JEFF NIEMAN
It Takes a Village

MARC RUTTER
Transformational Discipleship

BETTY CHURCHILL
Daughters of Eve

DAVID MARSHALL
Raising Men not Boys

NICK DECOLA
Blow Pops

DOUG PALMETER
Deal With It

JANA HOLLEY
Let's Talk About Sin, Yours

JOHN VAMPATELLA
Blind Date

STEPHANIE NANNEN
A Bending of the Will

TIM HENDERSON
You Always Say That
Heading North

DAYLE ROGERS
Window of the Word

TANYA WALKER
Everybody's Different

PAULA SASSER
Seven Kinds of Smart

JASON SEVILLE
Desire for Duty

JIM SAUTNER
Everyone Has Limits

SHANNON COMPERE
The Real Work

ROGER HERSHEY
Selection
Relationship, Scripture
  and Ministry

JIM SYLVESTER
Discipleship Plan
Spiritual Multiplication

RICK JAMES
Remaining Chapters

In the last several decades the Campus Ministry has made significant changes and adaptations to minister to a new generation of students. It has seemed to us that these changes have never reached the level of personal discipleship, and that we disciple students the same way we always have. Our evangelism has adapted, our spiritual formation has shifted, our mission has focused, our scope broadened and yet one-on-one discipleship remains unaltered.

This book is an attempt to update and sharpen our practice of discipleship, and to circulate the flow of change to the outermost reach of the ministry, personal discipleship.

It is not a rewrite but a synthesis: blending the best of what has worked with the fruits of adaptation.

The book is divided into six major sections. The first dealing with the transformation that is the goal of personal discipleship. The second section deals with issues of sin, as do many of the apostle's letters, for it is the enemy of spiritual growth. The third division engages gender considerations as we are growing into either godly men or women, and the forth section is marked off for topics concerning ministry.

Following ministry topics is a series of shorter, quick-read articles and abstracts. Last is the section entitled "foundations and history" which grounds us and brings us back to some fundamental principles of discipleship that are at the core of our ministry and have no expiration date.

We hope that the material will be encouraging and instructive, and help you become more competent disciplers—we've learned a ton putting it together.

Rick James & Betty Churchill

Grace &

Renewal

CHAPTER ONE

The Lost Art Of Making People Feel Stupid

If a disciple is fundamentally a student or learner, then a discipler is fundamentally a teacher. Teaching and learning. That is the raw essence of discipleship.

In Jesus' day there were all sorts of people who gathered to hear Him teach. The ones who liked what they heard and followed Him around were called His disciples. One time He miraculously fed a bunch of them. So they kept following. But they were interested for the wrong reasons, like filling their bellies, so they became disinterested when Jesus told them they had to eat his flesh. They stopped being His disciples and went home.

Then there were the twelve disciples who Jesus chose and to whom he gave special attention. The eating flesh thing was weird to them too, but they were committed to following Him no matter what. Peter said, "Where else would we go? You have the words of eternal life." Their learning led them to belief and trust in Jesus because that was what He relentlessly taught and offered them.

This is what our aim must be as well. We must teach people to believe and trust in Jesus in their actual life and not just in their what-I-believe-because-I-am-a-Christian life. This chapter is about how to do that.

A CASE FOR CUSSING AND THREATS OF PHYSICAL VIOLENCE

I read a great book a few years ago about the Sermon on the Mount so I wanted to teach it to some guys. I asked a student I knew, Ben, if he could round up some fellas for a Bible study. He got six guys: four fraternity presidents and two chaplains. They had all grown up going to church and had probably heard sermons on this passage before.

The first week was introductory and pleasant. At the end I gave them homework—study the first twenty verses and be ready to explain what Jesus was saying. Sensing that they had no reason to do this assignment, I warned them that they better come knowing their stuff because I was going to argue with whatever they said.

They all came back and around the circle we went. Most of them disagreed with each other, but when they didn't I would ask all sorts of antagonizing questions. After thirty minutes, they were so confused about what Jesus was saying, and what they were saying, that they asked me what I thought. My initial thought was that this was the first time a student had actually asked me to tell them what I thought about a passage. I said, "I could give you my opinion, but I'm curious why you think Jesus meant that."

Then Ben blurted out—like we were on Jerry Springer and not at Bible Study—"Okay, tell me what you think this passage means and then I am going to kick your a**." That was the turning point. Until then I had been trying to teach people a bunch of stuff that they only mildly wanted to learn. Now Ben was acting like I hid his car keys and wouldn't tell him where. Think about this for a second: A student was actually cussing at me because I wouldn't tell him what I thought about a passage in the Bible.

I knew I couldn't take him, so I gave my interpretation. They were not as impressed as I thought they would be. They argued with me because they thought it would be cool to see Ben beat up the Bible study leader. At a deeper level they had a genuine hunger to learn the Bible. It never felt so good not to have all the answers. Nobody left with that warm feeling you get when the lesson ties together neatly in the end with clean application points. We didn't even pray.

DUMPING ON PEOPLE STINKS

I know more about the Bible than most of the students I disciple. I could have showed up that day at Bible study and simply dumped everything I had learned about those twenty verses on them, annotated charts and the whole deal. They may have thought I was smart and worth following, I mean, that Jesus was worth following. It could have been neat and tidy with prayer requests and one thing they could do that week to apply what they learned to their lives. I didn't do that because I was tired of pretending that it works.

I figured they would be better off studying for hours only to come up with the "wrong answers." If that makes you uneasy, then you care too much about making sure people have all the correct information about their spiritual life. Just stop for a moment and think about how process-oriented Jesus was with His disciples. He was more concerned that they loved Him, not that they had the right answers. I believe that we generally want what is best for our disciples. It's just that some of our methods do not accomplish what we want.

Take, for example, this group of frat guys. My goal for them was that they would interact with Jesus more relationally. A good beginning, I thought, would be for them to think of him as a person. Well that's easy, right? Just tell them that He was God in the flesh, tempted in every way that we are tempted, and that He wept. But I was not trying to prove a point. I was trying to help them experience a person. So instead of explaining to them what Jesus was saying, I made them wrestle with it. It's the difference between me telling a guy all about a girl he likes and letting him discover her through relational pursuit. He would certainly be wrong and make mistakes along the way, but his attraction to her would lead him to greater intimacy much more than knowledge of her ever could. Come to think of it, having a lot of knowledge about someone you don't know is called stalking.

I should mention that I went home that day and wrote a four-page e-mail to the group in which I clearly laid out my thoughts about the passage. I did it because the unresolved discussion made me nervous. Old habits are hard to break (I'm referring to the one of needing to look smart). In hindsight, I am glad I sent the e-mail. It brought some clarity to the issues of our discussion. So maybe telling people stuff isn't all that bad, but it's always better if they actually want to hear it.

FRUSTRATED PEOPLE LEARN STUFF

I wish you could have been there for our third meeting. They came in like first-year law students, with their scribbled notes and coffee eyes, ready to make their case. We argued less that day, though I didn't escape without being called names that I cannot repeat. I don't know of another scenario where I would boast about such a thing, but this was different. It was frat-tastic.

I have tried all kinds of tricks to get guys to read their Bible: food, cash, guilt, quizzes, you name it. I've never had much success because I'm always giving out all the answers. What I learned with the frat guys is that people are more likely to learn when they have to figure stuff out for themselves. It's kind of like when you have a tune in your head and can't stop thinking about it until you remember the song title. Because we never totally resolved everything in our meetings, our discussions would turn in their heads all week. It's annoying to feel like you don't know stuff. So they would study, not because it was their assignment, but because they actually wanted to learn.

We never prescribed application points. I'm not against it. It just never seemed to fit. I guess it's hard to apply something you don't really understand. After our fourth meeting, a few of the guys hung around after I left and decided to get together at seven the next morning. The guy who told me said, "We decided to meet every week the morning after our Bible study just to pray about what we are learning and talk about how we can help each other apply it to our lives."

I was blown away. I could have done ten lessons on accountability and community and fellowship and not had a response like that. It wasn't about being smart at Bible study anymore. What they were doing was genuine and desperate—learning how to relate to Jesus. Learning is easy. Wanting to learn is not.

We would never tell a non-Christian that all he needs to do to follow Jesus is be faithful to certain activities like Bible study and accountability and prayer. So why would you prescribe that for a Christian? These things are not indicators of transformation. They are only means of transformation.

I was in four honors classes in the ninth grade. Three of them were not hard, and I don't think English would have been either if Satan's girlfriend wasn't my teacher. Realistically she was too old to be Satan's girlfriend, but nobody liked her.

The second week of school was the first open house where parents got the chance to meet the teachers. My classmates and I had told our parents how evil this teacher was for making things so hard on us. And since parents love their children, they all came ready to give this teacher a piece of their mind. She was a no-show.

We found out later she was attending a ceremony where she received a teacher of the year award. This caused our parents to turn on us. She was not going to get fired. Even worse, I began to feel she loved me and wanted to help me become a better person. I worked so hard in that class that I fell in love with English. No teacher ever frustrated me as much as her, but in the end I loved her for what she did for us.

I think the frat guys wanted me to make it easier on them, but in the end I think they loved me for helping them relate to Jesus instead of dumping information on them. And better than loving me, they fell in love with Jesus.

ONE WAY TO STOP TALKING IS TO ASK QUESTIONS

What I learned in the fratmosphere—that tension seeks resolution—is a governing principle in how I disciple people these days. I look for ways to make people uneasy about what they know. I do this by asking questions, and instead of answering them when the silence gets awkward I just keep asking more. I'm not comfortable with silence, but filling it with words about what I believe does not help me understand what my disciples believe. And what they believe is the central issue to their discipleship. Jesus was good at this. He answered questions with questions. He made people think about what they were saying and why they were saying it.

I did it once. It happened a few weeks ago. Two students, Michael and Casey, asked me to disciple them this semester. I did not know them very well, so I planned nothing for our first meeting. The first fifteen minutes were awkward, like a first date. They were expecting something from me—some secret key to the door of their spiritual success, or at least some kind of plan for that meeting. I had nothing. I asked them silly questions such as, "How was your summer?" and "What's God been teaching you?" Then one of the guys set off an alarm. He said something about God was showing him something that he knew intellectually but did not experience. I don't even remember what the particular thing was. I just knew that he had hit on some universal and gigantic problem. Maybe my questions weren't so lame after all. Or maybe it just shows that even lame questions are better than no questions.

Most discipleship materials and discussions I've used are clean and linear. They usually have a subject (Holy Spirit) which may be introduced by some diagnostic questions (which circle represents your life?) to surface the problem (carnal life), followed by some teaching points that explain the subject matter, and then a point of application (pray to be filled with the Holy Spirit). This is painfully general, I know, but this is typically how it goes. Disciples learn something (maybe), but there is no tension, no frustration, no feeling stupid. It's too packaged and pleasant to affect actual life.

PEOPLE ARE GOVERNED BY WHAT THEY WANT

I knew I didn't want to dump on him. Here is where creating tension kicked in. I sat up in my chair, interested for the first time.

> "Yeah, we all know too much," I said. "I had a group of pledges one year that grew up in a really good church, but what they knew and what they experienced were two different worlds. I told them at our first meeting that I thought they were all full of crap. Let me ask you what I asked them."

> I continued. "If Jesus were here physically and were

your discipler this semester instead of me, do you think you would have a better shot at growing spiritually than you do now with me as your discipler and His Spirit living inside you?"

Casey smirked and asked, "What do you mean 'here physically'"?

"I mean here, physically. He could be right by your side as much as you wanted him to be."

"Well, then I'd take that," said Casey.

"Why?"

"Because he would be straight with me, you know. He could see into my heart and just tell it like it is. There wouldn't be any question about what I'm supposed to do."

"So this seems like a no-brainer to you?" I asked.

"I guess," responded Casey, confident but suspicious.

I turned to Michael, "What about you?"

"Well, I know the right answer is the Holy Spirit but since that is what I have had all along, and that hasn't worked out so well, I would honestly say Jesus just to try something new."

They chose the same answer but for different reasons. Michael knew the "right answer." Casey was left wondering why his answer was "wrong" and wishing he hadn't been so sure of himself. Someone was going to look stupid, and nothing creates tension like the potential of looking stupid.

What people know does not impress me anymore. I want to know what they want. In this case, they wanted Jesus as their discipler instead of me, but at the expense of having His Spirit inside them. This scenario has its apparent advantages, but it reveals something about them at the level of their desires. I already knew at this point what it says about them, but again, what I know will very rarely change anyone. They have to discover it. So we continued:

I asked both of them, "If you would be better off having Jesus with you instead of in you, why didn't God establish life that way?" I got blank stares. So I continued. "I mean, the disciples wanted Jesus to stay and He told them at least twice that it was better for them if He left."

Casey, probably sensing that he might be the one to look stupid, questioned, "When did He say that?"

I showed him the verses. "So why is it better?" (i.e. Why were you wrong?) More blank stares.

Let's review. I could have explained all this to them on the front end and avoided hurting anyone's self-esteem. They would know having the Holy Spirit is better, but it would only be head knowledge. Instead, I asked two simple questions and surfaced that deep down they really just wanted Christianity to be easier.

"Okay, Casey, you said you would like it because Jesus would shoot straight with you. He could look in your heart and tell you that you are full of crap. Then what would you do about it?"

"What do you mean?" Casey asked.

"Think about it this way. If Lebron James was your personal coach in basketball, could you play in the NBA?"

"No."

"Why not? You would have one of the best players in the world teaching you."

"But that doesn't mean I could play like him."

"What if somehow LeBron could live inside you and play through you? Then could you play in the NBA?"

Casey gets an epiphany, "I get it. If I didn't have His Spirit in me, I couldn't do what he tells me I need to do. It wouldn't matter that Jesus was here telling me to do it."

Casey was getting somewhere now. I turned to Michael again. "Okay dude, you knew that already. So why isn't that what you want?"
"I don't know."

"Well you said it wasn't working. Why not?"

This is a weird spot to be in. If he doesn't identify himself as the problem, then he is saying that God's way of doing things doesn't work. He doesn't want to believe either one. This tension between what we know to be the right answer and what we really believe gets to the heart of Casey's initial statement, the thing that started all this.

"Okay. We're saying that God has given us everything we need to walk with Him,"

I said. "Everything you need to be courageous, kind, humble, unselfish, etc., is in you. So why isn't our life characterized by those things?"

Michael spoke up, "To use your analogy, I think it's because we don't let God play through us."

"So what keeps us from letting God play in our lives?"

"For me, like even if Lebron lived in me, and even though I am not as good, I might not let him play because I want to be the one playing. It's like I'd rather play badly than let someone else play for me."

I wondered if Michael knew how deep and insightful that statement was. The two of them identified a few more obstacles to letting God play in our lives, such as busyness and laziness.

I asked them what they wanted out of today. I said, "Do you typically just think about getting through the day with as much happiness and as little pain as possible?" They gave a nod of concession. I asked, "Is it safe to say that if you didn't want much of anything today that you also didn't want God to play in your life?"

I explained that I thought a major dilemma in Christian life is that we often have general desires that do not find their way into our day-to-day life. Then I said, "It seems to me that letting God play in our lives has a lot to do with simply wanting him to."

They liked that because it sounded simple. Then Casey asked, "How do I make myself want something?" He had finally discovered the nerve center of everything we were talking about. The answer to that question holds the key to the universal and gigantic problem.

PEOPLE KNOW THEY HAVE PROBLEMS BUT THEY DON'T BELIEVE IT

Michael and Casey did not come to our meeting that day thinking that they had a problem and needed my help to fix it. They came to be discipled, and in their minds, discipleship meant meeting with someone once a week. I could have told them on the front end that they had a problem and that the solution had something to do with what they want. But they wouldn't have cared. Just like non-Christians don't care when we tell them about their problem and God's solution. They only care if they believe it.

That is why our discipleship efforts must be aimed not at what people know, but at what they believe. And the best way to find out what your disciples believe is to ask questions that surface what they want. What they want is what my friend Bob Thune calls heart idols. Once they discover their heart idols, they ask the question, "How do I make myself want something else?

I don't recommend asking your disciples how they can turn from their lame desires to a desire to want to follow Jesus. They need to discover this question at the end of their rope. They need to ask it with a sense of helplessness in their gut.

That is the way Casey asked, "How do I make myself want something else?" Fortunately for me our time was up. "Good question Casey, Why don't you guys think about how to do that and we'll pick it up next week."

CHAPTER TWO

GOSPEL

Or, How I Learned To Disciple A Transsexual

My friend Ryan is a transsexual. He used to hate God, but now he's at least lukewarm toward trusting Jesus. I want to share a few insights into how I've discipled Ryan. That way if you ever disciple a transsexual you'll have some idea of where to begin.

The obvious problem you're probably noticing is that Ryan is not a Christian. At first it was a challenge to disciple someone who hadn't even trusted in Jesus yet! . But the more I did it, the easier it became. You see, evangelism and discipleship are fundamentally the same thing: pointing people toward Jesus as their all-satisfying treasure. So don't get all worried thinking that this chapter doesn't apply to you. It does. Even if you're discipling Christians instead of unbelieving transsexuals.

The reason I met Ryan was because I didn't ask enough questions. Had I been more careful on the front end, I could have avoided the whole messy situation. We have this student in our college community named Amy. Amy is the most Jesus-loving, extraverted, bubbly person I've ever met. And she's extremely hard to say no to, because she says things like, "Jesus told me to talk to this person!" Or, "The Lord is totally working in your life!" Things that make you think Jesus must have ridden in the car with her on the way over. Amy stopped me one week before our Wednesday night prayer meeting to ask if I'd meet with a friend of hers from school – a homosexual who was not yet a believer in Christ, but had been asking lots of questions about faith. I didn't really *want* to, but she was so enthusiastic, so happy in Jesus, so convicting with her "you're a pastor and this is your job" tone of voice. So I agreed.

Then, *after* I'd said yes, she proceeded to tell me the rest of the story. Ryan was an outcast because he dresses as a woman once a week. He'd scheduled a sex-change operation for next spring. He was "married" to a lesbian as a mere formality, to allow the two of them to discreetly pursue their homosexual lifestyles. His parents had disowned him and he hadn't set foot in a church since childhood. I feigned utter confidence in Amy's presence and assured her I'd love to meet with Ryan.

The next morning, I hit my knees and prayed out of my own dire inadequacy. I have never had much success in reaching out to homosexuals. I mean, I come across as harsh and judgmental and arrogant and selfish—to Christians.

That night I met Amy and Ryan at a coffee shop. In those first few minutes, God did a profound work in my life. I was expecting Dennis Rodman in a wedding dress or something. What I found was a human being named Ryan, created in the image of God, with the same wounds and soul-scars and questions as you and me and everyone else.

Don't get me wrong: there was great discomfort on both sides of the table. It was worse than a first date. Ryan was shifty and uneasy. I could tell he was testing the waters, to see if he could trust me. I felt awkward too, afraid that at any moment he would discover that I was Genghis Khan and would stand up and yell obscenities at me and make a big scene. Part of my fear was self interest, but part of it was an honest concern for the kingdom of God. I was sitting across from a guy deeply wounded by Christians. He had finally found one bubbly follower whom he could trust. Now he was risking interaction with a real, live minister one more time. If I didn't win his trust, this might be the last time he thought about Jesus. But if I could show how much God cared about him, maybe he'd hate God a little less. And that would be big.

My goal as I tell Ryan's story is to convince you that discipleship must be centered on the gospel. To see true heart transformation in our disciples, they must delight in Jesus more than money or love or ambition or control or self interest. Remind them of their deep brokenness and sinfulness so that they despair of their own efforts. This is the "bad news" of the gospel. Then rejoice in the powerful grace of God through the cross until they feel and believe God's radical love. This is the "good news" of the gospel. The same gospel that saves sinners also sanctifies the saints.

YOU'RE A SINNER, AND JESUS IS YOUR ONLY HOPE

We tend to think of the gospel message only in the context of evangelism, the door you walk through to get "in." Once you're in, then you move beyond the gospel to deeper biblical principles.

Ryan was pretty sure we were "in" and he was "out." He believed that in the eyes of the average Christian, he was a really bad guy—a transsexual. A pastor had told him once that he was on an express train to hell because of his lifestyle. I wondered if that pastor would say the same thing to a perpetual gossip or a legalist or someone who eats too much. So Ryan consistently steered the conversation toward his lifestyle. He had been to the gay church in town, and they told him that his lifestyle didn't matter. On the surface, he was fishing for me to say something similar: "It's okay to be transsexual. You can still follow Jesus." But underneath, I sensed a much more powerful question in play: "Am I more broken, more sinful, more hopeless than you?"

I moved the conversation away from Ryan's lifestyle and toward the common brokenness and rebellion of humanity. I told him the real issue wasn't his gender confusion. It was his sin. He expected to hear he was worse than the guy next door. I told him he wasn't. Our external sins may be different, but our hearts are all the same. Then I took it a step further: I told him about my own sin.

"Ryan, do you want to know about me? I am a control freak. I like to have everything under my power. I like to put myself in the place of God and manage the outcomes. I am rude and harsh toward my wife and kids. I am judgmental when people don't live up to my standards. I fail to love people the way Jesus does. I love people on my terms, the way I think they deserve to be loved, based on my criteria. I am uncaring and critical and resentful toward those who don't see things my way. I bow down and sell my soul every day to the idol of control. Ryan, I am a sinner, and Jesus is my only hope."

Ryan began to soften. The conversation turned a corner. He began to realize his lifestyle was a secondary issue. Here I was, a happily married minister, telling him that my heart was as dirty and sinful and broken as his. The only difference was that I was trusting in Jesus to make me right with God and transform my heart, and he wasn't.

No thinking follower of Christ would look at Ryan and say, "Change your lifestyle first, and then we can work on your heart." We know that deep, inner change must come first; "make the tree good, and its fruit [will be] good" (Matthew 12:33). So why don't we apply the same truth when it comes to discipleship?

When we forget the gospel, we cheat our disciples. We give the impression that being a follower of Jesus means becoming less broken, less sinful, less hopeless. So we create a caste system of Christianity: there are the really broken people (unbelievers), the fairly broken people (young believers), and the people who have learned to pretend they're not broken (mature believers). Not only is this blatantly unbiblical, it is contrary to common sense. Jesus said that those who are forgiven much will love much (Luke 7:47). Mature Christians are not those who are less broken, but those who realize the depth of their brokenness and cling all the more tightly to Jesus.

THE GOSPEL WORKS FROM THE INSIDE OUT

Gospel-centered discipleship focuses on internal change. We naturally default to external signs of spiritual growth. We do this because it's easier to measure and track. So we suggest our disciples do more. You can tweak external behavior all day, but to change the desires of the heart, you need the gospel. It fuels change from the inside out. It addresses beliefs and desires, not just actions. A truly deep and biblical belief in the gospel will always result in character change. If change isn't happening, there's a heart problem.

This isn't biblical rocket science; it's the principle Jesus used. Good trees bear good fruit. When the people asked him how they could do the works of God, he answered, "This is the work of God, that you believe in him whom he has sent" (John 6:29).

But disciples can be good at faking it, and they become convinced that external solutions are what they need. But just disciple a transsexual or two, and you'll see that Jesus was right. It always comes back to belief.

See, I know that Ryan needs to change his lifestyle. It's not glorifying to God. And every Christian he's ever met has taken the lifestyle change approach to discipleship. They've pushed him to repent and change his external behavior. But why should he? He doesn't want to. He wants to be a transsexual. Until he wants not to be a transsexual, nothing else matters. In the same way, until our disciples want to obey Jesus or pray or reach out to others, nothing else matters.

How do you make someone want to change at this deep level? I don't really know, but I'm good at trying lots of stuff. So that's what I did with Ryan. That first meeting had built some trust between us. He trusted that I wasn't going to hate him or judge him. I began to think and pray about what to do next.

The following week, another student handed me a CD of a lecture she'd heard on homosexuality. It was given by a former homosexual activist who had been radically transformed by Christ. I listened to it, and I thought: maybe this is it. Mike, the guy on the CD, was so refreshingly real. He talked about how much he hated Christians during his gay-activist days, and how it took a strong community of loyal friends to draw him to Jesus. I knew Ryan hated Christians, so I thought he might relate well to what Mike said. I gave the CD to my friend Amy and asked her to pass it along to him thinking it might surface some deeper desires in his soul.

A few days later, Amy called. "Ryan wants to meet with you as soon as possible. He's listened to the CD three times and he has all sorts of questions." I knew that could mean any number of things. So, after putting my kids to bed that night, I rolled over to Starbucks. The three of us sat at a small table in the middle of everything. I was extremely self-conscious. We were going to be using the words *Jesus* and *transsexual* a lot, and that meant every other customer would be trying to eavesdrop on our conversation.

EVERY SIN IS IDOLATRY

Ryan started the dialogue by making it clear that he utterly disagreed with everything on the CD. Mike's statistics were wrong, he hadn't done enough research on gay issues, maybe he was never truly gay anyway, and so on. Had I been trying to change Ryan's behavior, I might have been more apt to defend Mike or to enter into a gay apologetic debate. But none of those things mattered. At this point, I wasn't trying to convince Ryan that his lifestyle was wrong. I was trying to surface some deeper issues in his heart.

> "Okay, so there was lots of stuff that you disagreed with. Did you invite me here to argue about that stuff? Or did you invite me here to talk about some things that you're really thinking about?" With those few questions, I changed the focus of the conversation.

In discipleship, we can talk about behavior and external circumstances all day, but unless we drag some heart idols out on the table, we're just putting a Band-Aid on the problem. As Jesus said: "Out of the overflow of the heart, the mouth speaks." Or as Tim Keller says: "The root of every sin is a breaking of the first commandment." The real question is what god we're worshiping. That's why what your disciples want is much more important than what they *know*.

As we talked, I discerned that Ryan's dominant heart idol was pride. He wanted power, acceptance, love, control. He found these in his sexual identity. Before he accepted his transsexuality, he said he felt weak, unimportant, secretive. Now, he had an identity. He was socially powerful. When he dressed as a woman, he put others on the defensive. He could judge those who disagreed with his lifestyle as being bigoted, unloving, or intolerant. He was in control.

Our heart idols set the trajectory for everything else. I was beginning to see what Ryan loved and worshiped. I could move the conversation in a direction that would address the disease and not the symptoms.

So how do we solve the problem of idolatry? Simple, turn away from idols and turn to Christ. That is the ultimate goal—repentance and faith. But here's the problem: we don't worship idols because we're ignorant or uninformed or bored. We worship idols because we love them. We crave them. They are more important to us than life itself. I worship the idol of control because I believe it will give me more than Jesus will. Ryan worships the idol of pride—manifested in transsexual behavior—because it promises to provide what he needs and wants and craves. Sometimes dealing with our idols is not as easy as repent and believe. Sometimes it requires surfacing the deeper wants in our soul that will pull us toward God, if we will only let them.

Ryan began to talk with Amy and me about some things he did agree with. Mike had said that even during his gay years, he always wanted to be "normal"—to have a wife and kids and a house in the suburbs. Ryan desperately identified with that desire. He felt it would never be possible because he was gay and transsexual. But deep down, the desire—the want—was there.

"Where do you think that desire comes from?" I asked.

"I don't know," Ryan replied.

"Can I offer a possible answer?"

"Sure."

"Understand that I'm going to talk about this from a biblical point of view, because that's my world view."

"Yeah, I know. Go on," he said.

"I think the fact that you desire to be married and have kids proves that God has implanted certain instincts deeply within your soul. If you were born gay, and if there was no God, it would make no sense for you to desire a wife and kids. The existence of that desire testifies to the fact that you are made in the image of God, like the Bible says, and that sexuality is a deeply wired, God-given part of your identity as a human being. That means that it's possible for you to change."

"No it's not. I don't want to change. I'm transsexual. I have been ever since I can remember."

"Then why do you want a wife and kids and a house in the suburbs?" I queried.

"I honestly don't know."

"I think there's more going on there than you're willing to think about."

Ryan sat in contemplation for a few moments. "What do you think it would take for me to change?" he questioned.

"I think you have a heart idol called pride that you are worshiping right now. You are your own god. It will take a work of God's grace to change you. You'll have to come to the point where you decide that Jesus is trustworthy, and you allow Him to reign in your heart instead of yourself. I realize that's going to take some time."

"Bob, let me tell you why I don't trust Jesus..."

THE GOSPEL CHANGES EVERYTHING

This gospel stuff may seem abstract, but I'm trying to convince you that heart idols and belief are the practical things. When your discipleship efforts to revolve around the gospel, you will see profound change, because the gospel changes everything.

Ryan began to tell me the reasons he didn't trust Jesus. They all came back to one common denominator: he didn't trust Christians. He told me how he had been rejected by the students, and even the youth pastor, in a large evangelical youth group because he was small and frail and not manly enough.

But these painful memories paled in comparison to the rejection he felt from his family. His mother and stepfather were both professing Christians. When Ryan had come out and began to live an active transsexual lifestyle, they cut off their support and affirmation. From their point of view, it was a tough love measure, a "love the sinner, hate the sin" sort of approach. But to a sexually broken young man who had been rebuffed by Christians his whole life, it was yet another evidence of Christian hypocrisy. As Ryan spoke about his parents, his whole body seethed with visible rage.

So we talked for a long time about the pervasiveness of sin, and how Christians often fail to live by their own moral standards. And I talked about Jesus a lot, and how Jesus loved to hang out with whores and cheaters and social outcasts. I was trying to get Ryan to see that he could trust Jesus even though he had a hard time trusting Christians. I reminded him that he trusted Amy and me. And I talked about how he needed to forgive his parents, because otherwise he was only rejecting them the same way they had rejected him.

I was utterly unprepared for what came next. "If I asked you to do something for me, would you do it?" Ryan asked.

Now, when you're talking to a transsexual, you naturally get a little uncomfortable with that sort of question. But since I had just been preaching to him about trust, I said, "Sure, anything."

"Would you call my mom and ask her to come here?" Ryan asked.

"Here? You mean Starbucks?"

"No, I mean Omaha. She's never been here. I've asked her to come here again and again, but she won't. She thinks it would be validating my lifestyle for her to come here. But I just want to see her. I want to talk to her. She doesn't have to stay with me or anything. I just want her to come visit. She'll trust you. You can speak her language. She thinks I'm a depraved sex addict. But she'll listen to you. Bob... I can't make any progress with God until I work through things with my mom. You're my friend. Get her to come here."

I felt time slow down, like a movie scene where the outside action is a blur and all you hear are the thoughts in the main character's head. "You're my friend." I couldn't escape the magnitude of that statement. There was not a Christian in the world that Ryan trusted except me and Amy. And now he was asking for my help in overcoming the one issue that clouded the gospel more than anything else in his life: his broken relationship with his family. This wasn't just a step toward the gospel; it was the gospel. Ryan was beginning to want to trust in Jesus. But he would never trust Jesus if he couldn't forgive his mom. And he would never trust Jesus if he couldn't trust me.

So I grabbed a napkin and a pen and wrote down his mom's phone number.

Somewhere along the way, we forget that the gospel doesn't just change eternal destinies; it changes everything. The gospel transforms societies, renews families, and heals relationships. That's why Jesus called it "the gospel of the kingdom" (Luke 16:16). The gospel is all about the rule and reign of Jesus. And where Jesus is rightly honored as Lord, there is more than just personal salvation; there is redemptive action.

The gospel is holistic. For me to say that I cared about Ryan's soul without caring about his relationship with his family would be the pinnacle of hypocrisy. I couldn't tell Ryan to get saved and then we'll deal with his family relationships. The real answer for him was that God wants to heal the wounds in your family. He is a redemptive God.

Now ask yourself: how often do you connect your disciples' life struggles to the gospel? If Ryan were a Christian, we might advise him to read a book on how to honor his father and mother, or we might suggest he do a Bible study on forgiveness. But gospel-centered discipleship asks these questions: How does the gospel need to be expressed in this situation? What heart sin is at the root of the problem? What gospel truth is not being believed or lived out?

This is what distinguishes biblical Christianity from worldly psychology. Any psychologist can say, "Control your anger; forgive each other; treat others with respect." But what gives us the power to love or to forgive or to respect others? It's the gospel. And what is it that keeps us from doing these things? It's our unbelief, our lack of trust in God, our heart idols.

In Ryan's case, I knew two things: his own idols of control and selfishness were preventing him from loving his parents, and his parents had some heart idols of their own that kept them from really loving Ryan like Jesus would. Getting Ryan's mom to fly to Omaha was more than a friendly favor; it was gospel-centered redemptive action. It was incarnating the gospel in a real, tangible way. It was what Jesus would do.

So I found myself engaged in the most awkward phone conversation I've ever had in my life. "Hi, my name is Bob, and I'm calling from Omaha. I'm a friend of Ryan's..."

THE GOSPEL FREES YOU TO RISK

Brennan Manning speaks of having "the courage to accept your acceptance." When we really believe that God is for us, we don't fear rejection by friends, family, and peers. We're no longer living for their approval; we already have God's approval. It's what Paul was talking about when he said, "If God is for us, who can be against us?" The gospel is what enables us to love dangerously, the way Jesus did. And dangerous love is what spurs effective evangelism and social justice and community and mission and reconciliation.

Ryan's parents did come to town a couple of weeks later. It was a great visit. They took the risk of acknowledging their sin and asking Ryan's forgiveness. And Ryan took the risk of beginning to forgive them. Their visit didn't solve all the problems or erase all the hurt. But it was a starting point. And Ryan was right: working through things with his parents helped to remove some of his tension toward God.

Until this point, Ryan had set foot in our church only once. It happened to be the night we were discussing biblical manhood and womanhood, which was either a really bad coincidence or a divine comedy. Could there be any topic more awkward for a man who thinks he's really a woman? What's worse, we had actually split up into two groups that night—men and women. Ryan had come up to me, grinning, and asked which group I wanted him to go to. I was certain he'd never be back. But on the weekend of his parents' visit, they all showed up to our worship service together.

A few weeks later, Ryan and I went out for a steak dinner at one of the finest restaurants in town. It was his way of thanking me for setting up his parents' visit. As I enjoyed my prime rib, Ryan got intensely serious. "Bob, I've got some deep secrets that I've never told anyone, and I think it's time I get them out. You're the only person I trust with stuff like this. If I tell you about them, will you promise to keep them confidential?"

I could tell from Ryan's face that this was no joke. He was deadly pale. So I tried to lighten the moment. "Ryan, sure, man. You know I'll always honor your trust. But if you have dead bodies buried in your backyard or something, I'll have to call the police." He didn't laugh. I choked on my steak a little bit and tried to pretend it was no big deal.

"I'm not going to talk about it here. I'll come in to your office tomorrow."

The following day, Ryan opened a window into his past that had not been opened before. Thankfully, it didn't involve dead bodies, and I didn't have to call the police. But it was deeply serious to him, and getting it out in the open lifted a crushing weight from his soul. As I sat in my office after his departure, I wondered: what made him feel willing to talk about painful secrets from his past? The answer, of course, is that the gospel had freed him to risk. I had spent months saturating every conversation with Ryan in the truth of the gospel. And he was beginning to actually believe the depth of his own brokenness and the power of God's grace. He didn't have to hide anymore.

Ryan hasn't trusted in Jesus yet. But I dare say he knows the gospel better than many Christians. He knows he's a broken person, but not any more broken than the guy next door. He knows that the idols of selfishness and control dominate the landscape of his heart. He knows that Jesus can change everything, including his own desires, if he'll humble himself and surrender. And he knows that being a disciple of Jesus isn't about just getting out of hell or being sexually healthy. It's about the pursuit of a redemptive God who offers a whole new kind of life.

The gospel doesn't just make you right with God; it frees you to delight in God. So saturate your discipleship in the gospel. Because you're a sinner and so are your disciples. And Jesus is your only hope.

CHAPTER THREE

PLEASE COOPERATE

What's Our Part And What's God's In Spiritual Growth?
(excerpt from Flesh)

We need to shed some light on a great mystery of our faith. It is something everyone seems to wonder about, but nobody talks about. When it comes to spiritual growth, what's God's part and what's mine?" For lack of knowledge, Christians seem to fall off on either side of this horse. On the one side, God does all of the work. We simply ask Him to fix us, or we wait for an experience where he takes away our sinful desires. Sliding to the other side of the saddle, we reduce our faith to nothing more than discipline. You stop doing bad things, and you start doing better things. More accurately perhaps, we tend to favor the rodeo sensation of perpetually shifting from side to side.

I was recently watching an episode of Dr. Phil that seemed to exemplify both approaches. The guests had hopelessly screwed up lives (which is always best for network ratings) and they had tried every self-help program imaginable to change their behavior. Sadly, the mother's Satan-spawn offspring still liked torturing furry animals with a darning needle. What's the mom to do? She had come to realize that the depth of their problems could not be overcome by simple discipline. So, completely discouraged, she had come to the omniscient Dr. Phil with an attitude that said, "I've tried everything. I give up. Fix me, Dr. Phil, fix me."

A COLLABORATIVE EFFORT

We would suggest a model called "cooperative sanctification," which views the process of spiritual growth as a partnership. Your job is to help another in the process of spiritual growth so it's rather important for you to understand how this partnership works, lest you ask them to do something, that only God can do, or expect God to do something for which your disciple holds responsibility. The foundation for understanding this partnership is found in the following verse:

> "Therefore, my dear friends, as you have always obeyed—not only in my presence, but now much more in my absence—continue to work out your salvation with fear and trembling, for it is God who works in you to will and to act according to his good purpose." *Philipians 2:12-13*

To get a better look at this collaboration, let's go back in history about 3,000 years. We find the Israelites standing on the east bank of the Jordan River. They've just been wandering in the desert for forty years following their exodus out of Israel. They are poised to take possession of the land God promised them—"the land that God had given them." This taking of the land, or clearing the property, is analogous on many levels (as we will see) to the process by which God makes us holy and rids our lives from sin: clearing or cleansing our souls is like the Israelites clearing of the Promised Land.

Having been promised the land, it must have come as a disappointment when they found out that God had not phoned ahead to the current inhabitants and told them to vacate the premises. But it's not quite so bleak. God promises to give them victory in their battles—to fight for them—though they will need to take the land one battle at a time. In Deuteronomy 20:1 we read:

> "When you go to war against your enemies and see horses and chariots and an army greater than yours, do not be afraid of them, because the LORD your God, who brought you up out of Egypt, will be with you."

Do you see a partnership? God does not vacate the land for them, but neither does He tell them that they must clear it by themselves. It is a project they will do together. So, how does this partnership work? Who does what? Hang on, we'll get there.

THE PARTNERSHIP LOOKS DIFFERENT DEPENDING ON THE BATTLE

As you read through the book of Joshua, you'll notice that in each battle there is a collaborative effort. But, you'll also notice the collaboration can look a little different depending on the battle, or depending on the enemy. The same is true in our battle against sin. In fighting each of our enemies—whether it's greed, anger, jealousy or lust—we must learn the principles of holy warfare and how to fight in partnership with God. In fact, this is exactly what God wants...

> "Praise be to the LORD my Rock, who trains my hands for war, my fingers for battle." *Psalm 144:1*

> "These are the nations the LORD left to test all those Israelites who had not experienced any of the wars in Canaan (he did this only to teach warfare to the descendants of the Israelites who had not had previous battle experience)." *Judges 3:1-2*

GOD'S PART: COVERT ALIGNING

Before the first battle (Jericho) to conquer the land east of the Jordan River, the Israelite army sent spies into Jericho to, well, spy. There, they encountered a prostitute named Rahab who makes the following statement:

> "I know that the LORD has given this land to you and that a great fear of you has fallen on us, so that all who live in this country are melting in fear because of you." *Joshua 2:9*

Unseen and unnoticed, God was already at work causing fear and motivating to action. A similar idea is found in this verse from Philippians:

> "Therefore, my dear friends, as you have always obeyed— not only in my presence, but now much more in my absence—continue to work out your salvation with fear and trembling, for it is God who works in you to will and to act according to his good purpose." *Philipians 2:12,13*

So, God's part in our battle for holiness is to work in us to will and to act according to His good purposes. God leads us into the battle. He tells us what area needs to change. He works in the realm of our emotions to bring about conviction or a distaste for certain sins. He motivates us to want to change. He is at work behind the scenes in our circumstances, and he provides encouragement to fight the battle. The Holy Spirit works at aligning our hearts and minds, as he did with the people of Jericho. But, you may say, "I'm not sure I always feel that alignment taking place."

OUR PART: BEING FILLED WITH HIS SPIRIT

Now we get to a "this is our part" area. The influence of the Holy Spirit in our lives is somewhat contingent on our cultivation of His presence and influence. That influence can be like the slow intravenous drip beside a hospital bed, or like a flowing river.

Let me give you an example. Have you ever been to a party where the atmosphere just seemed to cultivate lust: darkness, the conversations, flirting, what people were wearing, alcohol, music, and, yes, even lava lamps (I'd better stop. I'm beginning to get aroused). There is an atmosphere that cultivates this influence. Now, let me tell you about the Holy Spirit's influence, but first, let's get out of this party.

There, that's better, I couldn't even think in there. We can cultivate greater sensitivity to the Holy Spirit's influence when we do things that involve and co-join us. Spending time with God daily. Praying and relying on God throughout the day. Giving thanks to God throughout the day. Singing or listening to Christian music. Spending time with other Christians. Memorizing Scripture. Praising God for who He is. Getting involved in ministry. These things turn our heart into a spiritual frat party. They cultivate our receptiveness to the Holy Spirit.

> "Do not get drunk on wine, which leads to debauchery.
> Instead, be filled with the Spirit. Speak to one another with
> psalms, hymns and spiritual songs. Sing and make music
> in your heart to the Lord, always giving thanks to God the
> Father for everything, in the name of our Lord Jesus Christ."
> *Ephesians 5:18-20*

So, God works in us to will and to act, but we have a role in cultivating His presence and creating an environment in our heart that heightens His influence.

OUR PART: HABITUAL OBEDIENCE

Now, if we follow the story of Jericho, you will note that the Israelites were given the significant task of doing laps around the city. The laps seem pointless, don't they? But, there is a point in the pointlessness. Faith and obedience are critical to victory, but in the final analysis it is God who provides the victory.

Let's look again at our Philippians passage: "Continue to work out your salvation with fear and trembling, for it is God who works in you to will and to act according to his good purpose."

God is working in us to will and to act. Our role, however, is to make a habit of what God is doing in us through acts of obedience. We work *out* what God is working *in*. It is through willful actions and choices that God changes our character. We cease to be the sort of people who sin in particular areas and we become the sort of people who turn aside from those sins. This is a major role we play in our sanctification—to make "right choices" which act out what God is doing in us. In the war on sin, habitual obedience can take different roles. Here are a few of them:

Spiritual Disciplines
Spiritual disciplines, such as fasting, we could consider "practice" choices (though they serve other functions). When you haven't eaten for several days, your flesh begins to scream for food, Wendy's hamburgers to be specific. But you learn to say, "No" to your desires, and if you give in and have Biggie fries you haven't sinned—practice choices.

Choices to Avoid Temptation
If I were an alcoholic—which I'm not, thank you very much—I might not have the ability to turn down a drink when one is put in my face. But, I could choose not to rent an apartment over a liquor store. We may not have the ability to refrain from making poor choices while on the Internet late at night, but we have a choice of whether to get on the Internet late at night in the first place. Habitual obedience—when fighting particularly vexing sins—will often be fought and won on the choices we make to keep ourselves out of harm's way.

Choices to Be Open and Honest About Sin
Habitual obedience to be open and honest about our struggles and to bring others into them before, during, or after, will play a critical role in seeing victory over specific sins.

Choices to Stop Before Completing the Sin
In the war against sin, the first victories are often partial ones. Yet, over time, stopping ourselves in the act, and ceasing to follow through can be the turning point of the battle. Habitual obedience—choosing to stop—breaks old habits and begins to create new ones. It is the start of a change in our character from being the sort of person who does *that*, to the sort of person who doesn't.

These choices turn God's work in us, into external character change. Like the story of the Israelites at the battle of Jericho, it is God who gives the victory. But, our obedience—like the Israelites walking around Jericho—plays a critical part.

GOD'S PART: THE TIMING

Read these verses that relate to God giving Israel possession of the land:

> "I will send my terror ahead of you and throw into confusion every nation you encounter. I will make all your enemies turn their backs and run ...But I will not drive them out in a single year, because the land would become desolate and the wild animals too numerous for you." *Exodus 23:27, 29*

> "When the LORD your God brings you into the land he swore to your fathers...be careful that you do not forget the LORD, who brought you out of Egypt, out of the land of slavery." *Deuteronomy 6:10-12*

> "You may say to yourself (after you have entered the land), My power and the strength of my hands have produced this wealth for me." *Deuteronomy 8:17*

Haven't you ever thought, "Why doesn't God just change me and make me different?" Well, He doesn't, for the same reasons He didn't give the Israelites the land all at once. We would forget the enslaving power of sin. We would begin to believe that it had been our strength and will power that brought victory over sin. We'd lose our dependence upon the Lord. We wouldn't use our new freedom responsibly. We would never fully appreciate what we'd been delivered from. We would be far less thankful ... and the list could go on.

There is also a principle of ownership. Every acre we've bloodied ourselves to recapture and annex from the enemy carries with it a sense of ownership that cannot be appreciated through any other means. When God says, "But I will not drive them out in a single year, because the land would become desolate, ..." He seems to be saying that if He simply gave it to us, we would never fully possess, or own it. There are important lessons of growth that accompany every battle, so we don't want to fast forward through the process. Actually, we would all love to fast forward through the process, but God loves us too much to let us have the remote control.

YOUR PART AND GOD'S PART: A COMMITMENT TO FIGHT

As the Israelites took possession of the land, there was a tendency, over time, to grow weary of fighting, especially when victory was elusive. It became tempting to say, "Okay, since we're never going to get rid of you, why don't you just take a tiny portion of the land, and not bother anyone." They sought a truce. Likewise, over time, and in the face of many defeats, it can grow tempting to allow sin to set up camp in our life: we call a truce and accept that we will always be a certain way. Look at Numbers 33:55:

> "But if you do not drive out the inhabitants of the land, those
> you allow to remain will become barbs in your eyes and
> thorns in your sides. They will give you trouble in the land,
> where you will live."

God required them to persevere in the fight for the land. Likewise, He requires us to persevere in our fight for holiness. Through a variety of means, God motivates us to this end. He gives us encouragement, a fresh motivation, renews our hearts and minds, and restores our zeal. Our part is to repent when we have settled for mediocrity or become apathetic. We are to confess and ask for a renewed heart to keep fighting. Our part is to persevere in pursuing God. Repentance, confession, humbling ourselves, and pursuing God are the vehicles to renewed zeal, not mustering more effort in a battle (an important nuance of the collaboration).

GOD'S PART: DISCIPLINE

> "Again the Israelites did evil in the eyes of the LORD, and for
> seven years he gave them into the hands of the Midianites.
> Because the power of Midian was so oppressive, the Isra-
> elites prepared shelters for themselves in mountain clefts,
> caves and strongholds." *Judges 6:1-3*

One would assume that having entered the land, Israel's days of bondage and slavery were gone forever—em, no! In fact, due to a failure to fully take the land, Israel is turned over to bondage. God disciplined Israel, and this discipline often took the form of enslavement.

One of my favorite ads that I think brings out the enslaving nature of sin, was put out by MADD (Mothers Against Drunk Drivers). The visual is of a half-poured drink sitting next to a bottle of alcohol. The copy runs behind the glass, in a list, finally disappearing into the drink, reading:

> This drink cost: $2.95, a marriage, a car, two children,
> a house...

As we are His children, God's part in the holiness process is discipline. Just like with a child, discipline and consequences help us to move beyond certain behavior. Unlike most parents, God's discipline is never done in anger but always out of love and for our growth. God disciplines us in a variety of ways, but a major way can be allowing a certain degree of bondage to a sin.

Bondage carries with it some important lessons. It is a prerequisite for a deep understanding of God's grace. That deep understanding can mean knowing, really knowing, that without Christ we are bound by sin. It can be the key that unlocks the dynamics of the "Spirit-filled" life—learning to depend on God's resources to fight against sin. And, it causes us to despise sin as our master, leading us to forsake certain sin.

SUMMARY

The fight for our holiness is a partnership. Each battle is different, but we have tried to look at some of the major ways this partnership plays out using Israel's struggle for the Promised Land as a paradigm. There are other nuances to be sure, but if you can get your mind around these, it will help you to explain a great deal of what your disciple is experiencing in their battle for holiness. Like learning to dance, as we grow we pick up the rhythm of the partnership. Eventually, we learn to stop stepping on God's toes as He leads us to where we need to be led.

CHAPTER FOUR

HONEST TO GOD

The Psalmist's Argument For Emotional Authenticity

Meeting with [*insert your student's name here*] has become such a drain. Frankly, I dread our appointments. She is so completely depressed! I understand that this is a hard time with [*insert life crisis here—parents' divorce, relationship break up, financial stress, etc*], but I feel like we re-hash the same things every time we meet.

"Where is God in this mess?"

"I have prayed and prayed. What happened to that promise about asking in faith?"

"How can I ever trust God if He never shows up?"

"Why can't I get over this and go on with life?"

We're all familiar with this student. We've all watched enough Dr. Phil to know better than to let anybody stuff their emotions. We need to let people be authentic—provide a safe place to process questions and feelings. I can listen, empathize and point to biblical truths to help them regain some perspective, but to move through a life crisis they need some honest conversations with God.

Most of us also know the student who seemed to have it all together spiritually, but upon graduation and hitting a few hard bumps in life, decided that God is not applicable in the real world and left Him along the side of the road somewhere. If we're committed to building Christ-centered laborers who walk with God for a lifetime, we have to equip our students to handle disappointments and heartaches. They will come just as Jesus promised (Matthew 6:34).

Believe it or not, there is actually a biblical model for complaining. It's a great way to equip our students to live an authentic life before God and others, whatever their lot in life may be.

PURGING THE PUS

Somewhere along the way everyone actually does come to terms with the reality that "life is hard." I'd wager you've even said it when at a loss of other words of comfort, but one day—you *really* get it. And honestly, it's not comforting. In that moment I'm left with a sense of anxiety or hopelessness that leads to passivity and cynicism—and, as they say, it ain't pretty. When I get in this funk, I become self-consumed with my autobiography: *Life as It Ought to Be* by Laurie Menefee. This leaves little time or energy to give to others who may have far more significant and valid complaints. Does this sound familiar? Do you recognize this pattern in your life or those you're trying to build into?

As adopted children of God the Father, we need to learn how to bring these feelings of disillusionment into the presence of our loving God who commands us to "cast all our anxieties before him, because he cares for us" (1 Peter 5:7). The Greek word for anxieties in that verse is *merimna*, which roughly means "pre-occupations." Vine's describes it as that which causes us "to draw in different directions, distract ... especially, an anxious care." God knew we would have burdensome cares in this fallen world. He asks us not to ignore, hide or judge those feelings, but rather bring them out into the open so that they can be part of our relationship with Him.

Often in our orderly Christian world, we are not as honest as we need to be with God and ourselves, not to mention others—even those we're trying to disciple or for whom we're trying to model an authentic Christian life. We would rather suck it up, focus on serving others or watch reality TV until our negative emotions are anesthetized. We often avoid negative emotions associated with disappointments, broken hearts, rejection, tragedies and failures. We are afraid to embrace these emotions because we may find that maybe we don't have as much faith and trust as we thought. Or worse, maybe God is not who we thought He was.

Just like our physical bodies need to purge the pus of a flesh wound in order to heal, we need to purge the emotions and thoughts around our heart wound. A gross analogy, I know, but you get the point. It's a fallacy that expressing our emotions appropriately will somehow overwhelm us and throw us off course. On the contrary, expressing real emotion in real time in healthy ways has proven to be emotionally and even physiologically healing.

PART OF THE PACKAGE

As Genesis reminds us, we are made in the image of God. Part of being made in His image is that we have emotions—even strong, negative ones. God communicates that He is jealous for His people's affections (Exodus 20:5). It's a righteous jealousy, as are all His emotions, but an emotion He admits to possessing. Jesus covered the gamut of negative emotions, even being called "a man of sorrows, familiar with sufferings" in Isaiah 55:3. In John 13:21, it says Jesus was "troubled in spirit." The text employs the Greek word tarosso, which is often used in reference to people when they are anxious. Likewise we are warned of "grieving the Holy Spirit" in Ephesians.

The Holy Trinity is emotional and therefore, so are we. This does not to imply that our emotions are always based in truth and therefore always righteous. Our emotions are often based in self-consumption and wrong thinking, but that does not invalidate or negate them. And certainly those based on real heartache and loss are very real. The point is that emotions are a God-given and God-created part of how we relate to Him and others.

THERE'S A RIGHT WAY AND A WRONG WAY

So what is the right way to complain? We know that Paul warns the church in Corinth "not to grumble, as some of them (the Israelites) did—and were killed by the destroying angel" (1 Corinthians 10:10). However, the first three times that the Jews grumbled against Moses for water and food, God graciously gave them what they wanted (Exodus 15:24; 16:8,12; 17:3-6). It wasn't until much later in the journey, that the Israelites responded in fear rather than faith to the spies who returned from viewing the Promised Land and God punished them (Numbers 14:2-35). Paul refers to this event in his Corinth letter. Their complaining and God's response did not lead to an increase in their faith.

The history of the grumblings of God's people begs the question: Are we to complain when we feel that angst in our guts or are we to suck it up and pretend that everything is okay?" Fortunately, the book of Psalms is filled with examples of the right way to complain. The Psalms were used for both public and private worship. They were at the heart of the community gathered together to declare their faith in God. Within the book, there are at least seven categories of psalms, the most common of which is the lament psalm.

Biblical scholar and commentator Tremper Longman writes, "The lament is the psalmist's cry when in great distress and he has nowhere to turn but to God." He further states that the psalmist may be troubled by his own thoughts and actions, he may be complaining about the actions of others against him (the enemies) or he may be frustrated by God Himself.

This type of psalm usually begins with the author saying, "I need help." Or "Something is not right." Then the psalmist expresses his fears and what he hopes God will do to solve the crisis. Then, with the lone exception of Psalm 88, the psalmist ends with either a confession of trust in God or a vow to praise Him or both. The hope in these psalms is that the author is still in communication with God in the midst of his disappointments.

The shift in the emotional mood within these psalms has been perplexing to scholars but I would make the following suggestion. These biblical complaints are swaddled in two protective blankets. One is the continuance of faith. Even in doubt and despair there is an abiding cord of faith, laid down like the base track in a song. The emotional vocals, guitar, and drums create all kinds of havoc while the calm, cool, bedrock of the bass plays under it all. Coming to God with complaints is an expression of faith. The second blanket is the continuance of obedience: regardless of the outcome, the psalmist has purposed in his heart that he will continue to praise God.

Now, back to our complaining. These psalms can teach us how to express our negative feelings toward God. They can also free us to let our students process and experience their emotions. Sometimes we're tempted to talk others out of their negative emotions instead of letting them grieve. We don't need to manage their emotions to make life more controlled for us or to make us feel like we're really helping them grow in some way. Ironically, this may actually impede the process of helping them connect deeply with God.

Wouldn't it be better to teach our disciples to complain to God and deepen their relationship with Him at the same time? I think Psalm 90 is a perfect example of a lament psalm. Grab a Bible and read it through a couple of times and then let's walk through it. This is what I share with the women I disciple.

The complaint of Psalm 90 is that our days pass away too quickly and they're filled with trouble. Then the psalmist pleads with God, who is eternal, to help him see his life with wisdom, to make the most of the time he's given.

The psalmist starts out with praise and acknowledgment of God's everlasting nature, but then quickly gets to the point of his complaint: "You turn men back into dust... You sweep men away in the sleep of death... We are consumed by your anger and terrified by your indignations... All our days pass away under your wrath... We finish our years with a moan." Verse 10 drives the point home: "The length of our days is seventy years—or eighty, if we have the strength; yet their span is but trouble and sorrow, for they quickly pass and we fly away."

The prayer in verse 12 shows how he begs for help: "Teach us to number our days aright, that we gain a heart of wisdom ... have compassion on your servants!" Then the transition: "Satisfy us with your unfailing love that we may sing for joy and be glad for all our days." He goes on to ask God to make him thankful for all his days and years and to show His deeds and His splendor to his children. Seeing life from God's point of view reminds us of who He is and who we are. It gives our years on earth meaning, even if they are but few.

Like many of the psalms, the writer uses metaphors to make his points more vivid and palpable. Look at verses 5 and 6: "You sweep men away in the sleep of death; they are like the new grass of the morning—though in the morning it springs up new, by evening it is dry and withered." Like me, you may be more familiar with the kind of grass that stays green. But in the arid climate of the author's day, it was common for grass to grow in very shallow soil. It was therefore vulnerable to bouts of drought and could quickly be green when it had moisture and just as quickly turn brown when it lacked moisture. Thus, for this song of complaint, withering grass becomes a suitable metaphor. Using this type of imagery can be a powerful form of emotional expression.

The difference between the Israelites' grumbling and the psalmists' lamenting is that the psalmists confess their honest emotions, faith and trust. They make the shift in focus from themselves and their circumstances to what is right and true about the nature and character and God.

YOUR OWN LAMENT

We've all felt vulnerable toward circumstances in life that we cannot control. A family member was just diagnosed with cancer. Another college student dies in a binge-drinking incident. A tragic accident takes the life of a friend. Do you think about the fragility of our lives and become disheartened? Perhaps it is not a life-threatening situation you face, but rather the loss of a friendship, dissention with a family member or lack of direction for your life. If so, a proper way to express these helpless feelings is to be honest with God. He is listening and He cares. He wants to enter into the everyday experience of His people for He asks us to "pray continually" (1 Thessalonians 5:17). Henry Nouwen wrote this about prayer in his book *With Open Hands*: "When you want to pray, then the first question is: How do I open my hands? Prayer is a way of life which allows you to find a stillness in the midst of the world where you open your hands to God's promises, and find hope for yourself."

If you opened your hand to God right now, what would be there? Is there disappointment, frustration or just plain discontent? Anyone can write a lament psalm as a catalyst to being honest with God. Pour out your heart to Him; empty it of everything that's there. In time, allow Him to bring you the assurance of His presence with you in the midst of your pain. As you experience the power of this healing in your own life, I encourage you to share it with those you're building into. Discipleship is modeling an authentic relationship with the Lord and this is one means toward that level of intimacy.

All of Scripture is meant to engage our hearts and minds in the wonder of God—even the psalms of complaint. Although I cannot explain the intricacies of how it happens, expressing our complaint to God in an attitude of faith can make a difference in our daily experience of life. It renews our mind in truth; it cultivates hope; it relieves pressure; it reminds us that we are not alone. We are not abandoned as orphans, but are sons and daughters of an involved Father who loves us dearly.

In my own lamenting with the Lord, one image that comes to mind is that of my 2-year-old nephew, Evan. He lives in New York City in a brownstone building, which means that to enter his apartment requires walking up 44 steps. When Evan was too young to go down the stairs, but old enough to know their purpose, he would sit on the top step after getting his feelings hurt and say repeatedly, "Daddy ... home?" He was confident that his daddy would eventually come up those stairs to give him the kind of comfort he was longing for. No matter how long he had to wait, he was going to sit at the top of the stairs and voice his lament. I often feel like Evan and tell the Lord that, "Like a child I'm waiting for you, but I have no idea where you are, when you'll be here, or what you're doing. I just want you to get here! I'm waiting for you!"

What are you distressed about today? In what areas are you waiting on God to move or change or even show up? How can you apply this form of voicing your emotions to God? Then, how can you use it to help your students process their emotions in a healthy way with the Lord? How can you help move them to a place of trust and see a right and true perspective of who God is?

In most of the lament psalms, it is difficult to discern the challenges and circumstances that the writer was facing. I think that's a good thing, by God's design, because it allows us to pray along with the song, connecting someone else's words to our own situations. Since we don't know exactly what the psalmist was facing, we cannot compare our woes as more or less difficult. Each of us has individual burdens that will affect us uniquely as a result or our own family background, our personal preferences, our goals, dreams, desires, and a myriad of other factors. Pain is only relative to our own experience, no one else's.

FOR EXAMPLE

Recently I spent time with Christine who was going through a tough time. On the verge of graduation, she thought she had her life mapped out and yet it just wasn't working out like it was supposed to. All of her life she had wanted to be a doctor, like her mother. As a pre-med major, she had scored reasonably well on her M-CAT, yet her rejection letters denying her entrance into medical school seemed to come daily.

When we met she was distraught and confused. I asked, "Christine, how are you processing your disappointment of not getting into med school?"

She looked away sheepishly and said, "Not so well, actually. It's so infuriating! I might be in the verge of a big fat depression. I can't seem to shake it. I can hardly pray."

I continued to dig a little deeper. "Not surprising really. Do you feel that God has let you down?"

"I guess so," Christine admitted. "I almost feel tricked by Him. I mean, why would He give me a desire to be a doctor all these years and then leave me hanging in the most crucial step? I just don't get it."

"Do you realize that God knew you were going to feel exactly like this—disappointed in Him? I've felt deeply disappointed myself, especially as I watched my Dad suffer so much from his fight against cancer. But I've found He left us with an incredible example of how to communicate our feelings of distress directly to Him. It's been really good for my own soul and my relationship with Him.

I continued. "Have you ever written a formal complaint to God? He gave us the whole book of Psalms as evidence that being honest with Him about our negative feelings is not only appropriate and welcomed but God considers it a form of worship."

"That's cool! Can you tell me how to do it then?"

"Sure. Let's look at Psalm 90 as an example."

EXPERIENCING IT FOR YOURSELF

We can experience a great deal of comfort by inviting the Lord to wait with us. Will you be like my nephew Evan and wait in confidence for a God who is so kind and confident to absorb our unfiltered, raw emotions? Will you invite Him to put His arms around you even when you know He has the power to change the situation that brings you dissonance or pain? And will you help those you disciple learn how to do the same?

There is one final aspect I need to address. In our day and age, it's essential that as mature believers we help our students who have experienced grave sins against themselves find hope and healing. The percentage of women who have experienced some form of sexual abuse is astronomical; and the number of men who have experienced the same is also growing. Helping these men and women properly express their anger and grieve in a healthy way will free them to walk with God in the depths of their soul for a lifetime. Often professional help is needed, but I believe this tool can also be powerful in helping them process their emotions with others.

My hope is that we will be so real in our relationship with God that our authenticity will attract those who do not yet know Him. We have the risen Christ living within us. He provides the strength we need to live in a broken world. Give Him a new place of intimacy in your life by incorporating your negative emotions in your worship of Him. The lament psalms are a great place to start.

CHAPTER FIVE

TRIAL LAWYER

Coaching A Disciple Through Adversity

> "In fact, when we were with you, we kept telling you that we would be persecuted. And it turned out that way, as you well know." *1 Thessalonians 3:4*

For the apostle Paul the benchmark of success was preparing his disciples for ministry but also for trials and persecution. The spiritual foundation one builds is best measured by what it takes to topple it. Trials, like rain, must eventually fall upon the life of your disciples and you play a crucial role in helping them to integrate and interpret their circumstances. Effective coaching can make the difference in how they persevere through them, or if they do at all. Paul obviously felt the burden of this responsibility, desperately hoping through his letters that trials and persecutions had not thrown his disciples off course. What follows are teaching points and coaching tips to help you, help them, weather the storms.

GOD'S ANGER

One of the bitter seeds of trials is the nagging sense that what we are suffering is directly related to God's displeasure with us. This has the effect of removing from us perhaps the only thought of available comfort: that God loves us and is on our side. We are indebted to the writer of Hebrews for uncoupling this fatalistic chain of logic: I am experiencing hardships, therefore God must be angry with me.

> "And you have forgotten that word of encouragement that

addresses you as sons: "My son, do not make light of the Lord's discipline, and do not lose heart when he rebukes you, because the Lord disciplines those he loves, and he punishes everyone he accepts as a son." Endure hardship as discipline; God is treating you as sons. For what son is not disciplined by his father.

"Moreover, we have all had human fathers who disciplined us and we respected them for it. How much more should we submit to the Father of our spirits and live! Our fathers disciplined us for a little while as they thought best; but God disciplines us for our good, that we may share in his holiness." *Hebrews 12:9-10*

This passage also brings us to the foundation of those nagging feelings: childhood baggage. Most of us remember being disciplined by our parents and through imperfect parenting we come to associate discipline with anger. The law of the adolescent jungle is: you disobey, and disobey, and disobey, until your parents finally loose their temper and then you get punished, unless you can pin it on a sibling.

The Bible tells us that God doesn't parent this way. He is not yelling at us in the backseat, "So help me mister, if I have to pull over this car." God's discipline comes from His heart not His fist. The passage also suggests that God's discipline (which takes the form of trials) is actually an indicator of God's approval and demonstrates the reality of our adoption into God's family. Granted I would have chosen a nice bedroom and an X-box, but I long for the affirmation. Trials can be a sign, not that we've been doing something wrong, but something right, and as a result God is preparing us to move up a grade in our spiritual schooling.

Your disciple in the midst of a trial is going to feel rejected by God, or feel that God is angry or disappointed with him. If God were visibly there, He could clear up the matter. But He's not, so He would like you to do that. Communicate that God is not angry, that He has not deserted them, that they haven't failed and that they haven't necessarily done anything wrong. Your strength in discipleship may not be cheerleading, but you're going to have to grab a set of pom-poms and give it a go. Your team is getting beat up out there and morale is low. It is not your personal support, per say, that makes the difference but showing them that God is in the audience actually rooting for them, and not booing them. This passage in Hebrews is extremely helpful in accomplishing this.

TRIALS: GAS STATIONS NOT ROADBLOCKS

Most trials present themselves as obstacles preventing us from living a godly life. We think, "If only I didn't have to deal with this, then I'd be free to love and live for God." If perceived this way—as an intruder—your disciple will never learn from the trial. Trials are not obstacles (though they often feel that way) that keep us from getting to the goal; they are the fuel we need to get there.

Have you ever prayed for greater holiness only to find the world cave in around you, and actually observe that you'd become at least 30% more evil under the pile of adversity? While trials might provide momentary setbacks to our visible progress in the faith, they ultimately provide the fuel we need to get to our destination—greater godliness. They build into our lives passion, perseverance, and deeper character change that go far beyond the surface behavior change we were trying to manifest in our lives.

If you have ever played a sport and received private lessons from a pro, you understand how this dynamic works. The local "pro" checks your fundamentals and realigns your swing, stance, or posture: your approach was somehow flawed. Now, upon leaving the lesson you are thrilled to find that you've paid $40 an hour to get worse. (It's now clear to you why your instructor is not currently on the pro tour but giving lessons and running the snack shop.) Your new foundation is awkward and it seems your game has taken a step back. But this realignment has now postured you to make progress because your game had gone as far as it could without professional help.

Often God answers our prayer for greater holiness, not by providing better circumstances that help us perform better, but by providing trials. These trials will often bring out the worst in us. In the midst of this, encourage your disciples that they should not expect to be at their peak performance and that patient, godly perseverance is the new definition of success. Identify with them: "I'll tell you, when I was going through (fill in the blank), I considered it a good day if I hadn't sworn at anyone." You have the ability to take enormous weight and guilt off their shoulders. Do it.

OLD SIN HABITS

> "Therefore, prepare your minds for action; be self-controlled; set your hope fully on the grace to be given you when Jesus Christ is revealed." *1 Peter 1:13*

Peter, wonderful shepherd that he is, is concerned that in the midst of difficult trials, his disciples will return for comfort to old habits of sin. This is a concern. When I meet with men going through trials I always ask, "How are things going with the Internet?" Because men often medicate pain with lust, I know that difficult trials can send them scurrying back to these familiar filthy waters to get a drink. If you know the person well, you can often guess at what fire hydrant they've been sniffing.

I identify with what they are doing, because I've done it myself. I give them the freedom to come clean in the ways they've been seeking comfort. I do not wag my finger in their face but rather I look to create an environment of grace and empathy. If I say anything it is simply, "I'm so sorry," because usually they feel awful about whatever they've done.

As we move along in the conversation, I simply ask questions, seek to understand, and empathize. Then, toward the end of our time, I go back to the issue (I hadn't forgotten) and now I gently say, "Listen, as God is doing this good—but painful—work in your life these choices are simply going to bring guilt and confusion into an already difficult situation. I know you don't want to be there. How can I help you make good choices in this area as you persevere through these difficult times?" It is a gentle reminder that grace is not license, and that God desires holiness in the midst of trials—"*So let's not return to that swamp. Agreed?*"

What I want to communicate is that I, and God, are concerned about how they are doing in and through this trial, not simply the sin it has manifest—but, by the way, that's not OK.

DOUBT

In the Gospels, Jesus' absence is as conspicuous as His presence, and often accompanies a major trial or testing—you definitely don't want to be sent across the lake without Him. And so with every season of trials comes the unmistakable sense that Jesus is either asleep in the back of the boat or has chartered a sturdier vessel. It's just you and an angry sea. With the deterioration of our circumstances and this sense of being orphaned comes a natural weakening of faith: doubt sets in.

It's instructive to see faith as a muscle, and trials like bodybuilding. The weights of Jesus' absence and the world-gone-wild form the resistance, whispering daily, "God isn't there, and He doesn't care." Each day your disciple must lift that weight, by faith clinging to the promises of God, for it sure is heck is not by sight. The more difficult the trial, the heavier the weight, and the larger the faith muscle must become to lift it. Through the trial, faith grows and expands, but it doesn't feel strong because it is constantly exercised to its exhaustion point. Paradoxically through trials, you are most prone to doubt and it is through such that faith actually grows to meet the heavy resistance. At the end of the trial, circumstances change, God comes out of hiding, the resistance is removed, and the experience of spiritual strength returns, but the muscle of faith has grown larger through the process. Peter describes the process in these words:

> "In this you greatly rejoice, though now for a little while you may have had to suffer grief in all kinds of trials. These have come so that your faith—of greater worth than gold, which perishes even though refined by fire—may be proved genuine and may result in praise, glory and honor when Jesus Christ is revealed." *1 Peter 1:6-7*

However you illustrate the process, it will aid your disciples in the translation of an experience that is both foreign and unintelligible. It also helps relieve the guilt of doubt, which is best viewed, not as a failure of faith, but the vehicle by which faith grows. I always find it a source of encouragement to look at the doubting moments of John the Baptist whom Jesus gives this endorsement: "Among those born of women there is no one greater than John."

> "When the men came to Jesus, they said, "John the Baptist sent us to you to ask, 'Are you the one who was to come, or should we expect someone else?'"

> "At that very time Jesus cured many who had diseases, sicknesses and evil spirits, and gave sight to many who were blind.

> "So he replied to the messengers, 'Go back and report to John what you have seen and heard: The blind receive sight, the lame walk, those who have leprosy are cured, the deaf hear, the dead are raised, and the good news is preached to the poor. Blessed is the man who does not fall away on account of me.'" *Luke 7:20-23*

BUT I'VE CAUSED IT

Some trials are a natural result of mistakes we've made or our own failings as people. The rub is that it's difficult to experience God's comfort in a trial when we trace the source and find that the breadcrumbs lead to our own backdoor. Somehow, in our minds, this puts the trial outside of God's sovereignty: "God didn't cause this, I did."

Trials are rarely alien circumstances imposed on our life, but are organically grown out of the fabric of our lives. I teach my children through the natural hardships that arise in their lives; I do not import foreign ones. A trial arisen from my own life and choices does not mean God didn't have the ability to shield me from the consequences, or that it is any less purposeful, or that God is any less compassionate for my struggles.

Your disciples need to be assured that what they are suffering still abides by all of the same properties of a trial: God has allowed it, He could have prevented it, He felt it was necessary for them to go through, it has a divinely appointed ending, God will use it for good in their lives, and He cares deeply for the struggle they are experiencing. The plan hasn't changed just because the root cause of the trial isn't Satan but ourselves.

RANDOM THOUGHTS

In 1 Peter 1:6, it says that, "you may have had to suffer grief in all kinds of trials." The key phrase, "you may have had to," could be translated "it may have become necessary" for you to suffer trials. The verse discloses that there is design and intent behind trials. God has looked at your life and decided that it was necessary for you to go through a trial for the sake of spiritual growth. God looked at your life, looked at the upcoming trial, and said, "Yep, bring it on. She needs this."

Often Christians fail to persevere in trials because they believe that they are random happenstance, and therefore have no point or benefit. Right now if you were to go into a hospital and listen in to conversations taking place between friends and family with sick loved ones you might hear phrases such as, "You'll see, it will all work out," "You'll come through this a stronger person," or "Every cloud has a silver lining." These people need hope, and loved ones reflexively provide it by explaining that their pain has purpose. Unfortunately, without God, these can be nothing more than shallow platitudes, because there really is no guarantee that their pain will be redemptive. However, as Christians we always have hope because there is nothing random, unplanned, or unforeseen in any of the trials that come into our lives.

1 Peter 1:6 is a helpful verse to share with a disciple in the midst of trials because it affirms the truth that nothing about a trial is random: its beginning, intensity, purpose, and duration have all been thoughtfully planned and foreseen by God.

REDEFINING SUCCESS

In Edith Schaeffer's book *Affliction* she gives a profound illustration to a person suffering through a difficult trial. Schaeffer draws out two playing fields on a piece of paper—one representing the world of ministry, and the other representing the world of trials. She goes on to explain that we all want to glorify God in the arena of ministry and good works but forget that it is equally possible to glorify Him in the arena of trials.

To give thanks, patiently endure, and praise God in the midst of a trial is of eternal value. Even if our personal ministry has dried up, we will be equally rewarded for how we have glorified God in the midst of trials. Trials, like ministry, provide an opportunity to accrue heavenly reward, as we witness in the life of Job. A choice to praise and give thanks while afflicted can echo through heaven as loudly as preaching the gospel. Schaeffer's point is that trials do not prevent us from competing on the playing field of ministry, but are a separate playing field altogether, offering the opportunity to win or loose, gain or suffer loss.

Seeing our faithfulness in the midst of a trial as a performance separate from, but equal to, ministry can provide motivation for your disciples to embrace and endure the peculiar race course God has set before them.

SICK AND TIRED OF BEING SICK AND TIRED

"And we urge you, brothers, warn those who are idle, encourage the timid, help the weak, be patient with everyone."
1 Thessalonians 5:14

Paul teaches what we have all experienced in ministry: that different people require different tactics to move them onward in their walk with God. Some sheep need a hug, some a cattle prod. There are people who seemingly never emerge from under the rock of trials, and take a posture of self-pity or resentment toward God. And there are those, you learn, for whom life in general seems to be a trial.

As you progress down the path of encouragement and patience, there will come a time when you will realize that what your disciple really needs is to get on with their lives—to get sick and tired of always being sick and tired. Knowing when to gently encourage and when to insert your foot onto someone's rear is a finer nuance of discipleship. Those who are lousy cheerleaders need to learn how to gently encourage their disciples, while on the other hand, born encouragers and comforters need to learn there is a time for a good kick, and the place is the backside.

A good tact to take is to move them in the direction of thankfulness and a posture of embracing their hardships.

In James 1:2, it says, "Consider it pure joy ... whenever you face trials of various kinds." This passage encourages a positive outlook in the midst of trials for the many reasons we've already looked at. There are many reasons to be both thankful as well as embracing of our trials.

If your presentation of these reasons over successive weeks has not brought about an attitude change, prescribe a steady diet of thanksgiving: "I want you throughout the day to take time to give thanks for the smallest of provisions, for how God is using these circumstances in your life, etc." Thanksgiving changes our perspective to see what God is doing, not what He isn't. It is preventative medicine for heart disease that can develop through prolonged trials or a cynical, pessimistic attitude that may be endemic to your disciple's personality.

Teach them to be thankful and hopeful.

BETWEEN THE VERSES

"I still had no peace of mind, because I did not find my brother Titus there. So I said goodbye to them and went on to Macedonia." *2 Corinthians 2:13*

"But God, who comforts the downcast, comforted us by the coming of Titus..." *2 Corinthians 7:6*

Between these two passages (anxiety tied to the absence of Titus, and the "coming of Titus") is a thoughtful detour where Paul describes what keeps him pressing on in the midst of trials, anxiety, and suffering. Look for the repeated phrase, "therefore we do not loose heart."

Within these chapters, Paul shares some mind-bending (bordering on hallucinogenic) perspectives, allowing you to see what kept him pressing on amid staggering pressures. Try walking a disciple through these chapters, asking him to pull out what enabled Paul to keep focus in the midst of overwhelming trials and opposition. And while in 2 Corinthians, don't forget the powerful first chapter which describes the flow of God's grace between the positive and negative polarities, affliction and comfort.

Most often I hear people remark to someone going through a trial, "Remember, trials produce perseverance." Perseverance is not a particularly motivating goal. The progression described in James 1:4 is actually that trials produce perseverance, and perseverance in trials, maturity. The motivation to persevere under trials is mature character, life transformation, and a powerful faith. It is in these chapters that you are exposed to the motivating results of perseverance.

ENDNOTE

The productivity of evangelism and discipleship can seem to compete with the patience needed to comfort and coach a young Christian through their trials. The struggle exemplified in the conflict between Paul and Barnabas over whether to take John Mark along on the next missionary journey. The apparent evidence, in that John Mark ultimately produced an important gospel, is that Barnabas was right to patiently wade through the troph of John Mark's ministry. I'm not sure if that makes Paul wrong, but it does make Barnabas right.

CHAPTER SIX

IT TAKES A VILLAGE

The Primacy Of Community In Raising A Disciple

America today is a nation of individuals, and this impacts the way we live, think and believe. This worldview deeply affects our faith, for individualism is an understanding of the world that has as its epicenter the individual soul. In other words, for Americans the most important thing is the individual, not the community, which is perhaps why Mother Teresa referred to America as the most socially impoverished country in the world. She could see no visible community.

There is nothing inherently wrong with individualism. But like all worldviews, individualism impacts our relationship with God, in both good and bad ways. American Christians correctly understand the importance of a relationship with God being personal, and that growth comes through personal study, prayer and worship. But our individualism can blind us to the importance of a community, leaving us lonely and disconnected from one another.

We see the impact of this lack of community every day. The family has broken down. Neighbors see each other only when they take out the garbage. Kids only play during play dates scheduled by grown ups, or during organized soccer or t-ball. Surprisingly, the technology we hoped would have connected us, has left us even more detached: instead of visiting in person with friends, we call on our iPhones while driving somewhere; instead of writing letters or talking, we email or send instant messages. We are more accessible, but less interconnected. As a result, we live in a world of many acquaintances, but few deep relationships.

This individualistic mindset profoundly impacts how Christians approach discipleship. Churches and ministries often define discipleship as hierarchical systems of one-on-one meeting times, where a more spiritually mature person meets regularly with a less mature person to help mentor the disciple in growth and development. I am not saying that individual discipleship doesn't have its place, but as I look at the Bible, I see a pattern for growth that is even more powerful and effective than just one-on-one meetings. The picture I see is a village, an interconnected community.

The village is a place where groups of believers freely involve themselves in each other's lives, and challenge each other to take those next steps of faith. The village includes believers both mature and young, mentors and peers, and is a place where the lost are welcome to join. The village is a home with an open door where your presence matters, where truth goes forth with grace, and where friends together pursue Christ-likeness.

Now I must admit I am a little biased toward this idea of a village. As a student many years ago, God allowed me to experience true biblical community, through a group of close-knit friends who were challenge me constantly in my relationship with Christ. To this day I keep in touch with many of these friends (I even married one of them). While there were many godly individuals who discipled me, the biblical ideals I learned from them were fleshed out through countless interactions in my village of dear friends. I feel we need more of this: to get back to this ideal or to forge ahead to find it. In reclaiming this vision we'll begin with what the Bible has to say about this idea of a village.

A BIBLICAL OVERVIEW OF COMMUNITY AND DISCIPLESHIP

Let's begin with a basic definition of our village. A community is a place where believers connect with each other on a soul level and in doing so, spur each other on to a deeper relationship with God. A community is more than just individual friendships; it is an atmosphere of deep relationships, a synergistic place where friends connect in grace and truth. In such a community, believers can authentically challenge each other through words and deeds toward being like Christ.

Another word for this atmosphere of relationships is *interconnectedness* which has its foundation in the very nature of God: the Trinity. God the Father, God the Son, and God the Holy Spirit eternally subsist as one God in three persons, forever relating and loving one another. In creating us in His image God has put this communal need in the soul of every person. Look at the story of humanity's creation. "Let us make men in our image, after our likeness" (Genesis 1:26). People were created with an inner need to connect with each other. God makes this clear about Adam. "It is not good that the man should be alone" (Genesis 2:18).

This human need brings out one of the tragedies of the Fall. Sin broke our community with God (Genesis 3:8), and it devastated our ability to build community with one another. What happened at the Garden? Adam and Eve shifted blame (Genesis 3:12-13), their sons Cain and Abel quarreled, and brother killed brother (Genesis 4:5-8): a graphic picture of how sin hinders our ability to create true community.

Despite the impact of sin, the Bible relates that God's redemption of our falleness always involves the building, or rebuilding, of communities as places of growth. The nation of Israel serves as an example of a community and its impact. The people worshiped together as a community (Deuteronomy. 26-27). They celebrated holy days as a community, such as Passover in Exodus 12-13 and Yom Kippur in Leviticus 16. God promised blessings if they obeyed God and curses if they did not (Deuteronomy. 28). To help foster interconnectedness, Moses organized the people of Israel first by tribe, then by family (Numbers 26). The community was held responsible for Achan's sin, and his entire clan paid the price (Joshua 7:24). We'll stop at Joshua, but suffice it to say that God structured Israel's entire society around the idea of an interconnected community.

The New Testament expands the concept of community even further. Jesus demonstrated the value of interconnectedness with His disciples. Seldom did Jesus spend time with just one disciple. He spent significant time with the multitudes, with the twelve, or with three, or even by Himself to pray and be with the Father. Even in Jesus' most significant moments, such as the Transfiguration and the Garden of Gethsemane, Jesus brought with Him not one, but several disciples.

This was the model of interconnectedness that the apostles brought into the early church. At Pentecost "there were added that day about 3,000 souls" (Acts 2:41)." Now one thing is clear – with 3,000 new believers the apostles could not have individually meet with each person on a regular basis. Very few ministries today could accommodate such rapid growth.

So how did they do it? The story in Acts provides a few clues. "They were continually devoting themselves to the apostles' teaching, and to fellowship, to the breaking of bread and to prayer" (Acts 2:42). Few (if any) buildings in ancient Jerusalem could house 3,000 people. So these new believers must have spent time together in smaller communities. The apostles most likely traveled from house to house, from community to community teaching the Word. The communities themselves must have contributed greatly to the growth of new believers: "Everyone kept feeling a sense of awe … and all those who believed were together, and had all things in common" (Acts 2:43-44). No structure could accommodate such supernatural growth. Only a village of authentic believers could disciple the early church.

So how did the apostle Paul disciple the many new believers around him? He traveled with groups of disciples. When Paul went on his missionary adventures, people came with him: Barnabas, Luke, Titus, Timothy were all among those who traveled with him. Just look at the beginning of many of his letters. He often mentions the names of others that had been with him. Even his personal letters to Titus and Timothy were not just for individuals, for they were collected and made available to the church at large. While Paul may have spent individual time with men such as Titus or Timothy, he clearly invested his time to create a community of disciples. It takes a village to make a disciple.

THE IMPACT OF COMMUNITY DISCIPLESHIP

In order to comprehend the relationship between community and discipleship, let's first clarify what we mean. Discipleship is the process where believers help one another become better followers of Christ. Let's look at the impact a village plays in developing disciples.

First, community helps bring the Word of God alive and make it real. No one disputes that God's Word is essential for personal growth. Prior to the Reformation, the Word of God was spoken in communities to the detriment of the individual's spiritual growth. However, the pendulum has swung perhaps too far in the other direction. Our primary focus today is the study and meditation of the individual in some form of quiet time or personal devotion. While individual times in the Word are important, believers should not neglect processing God's Word together in the village.

From the beginning, God wanted His Word to play a vital role through community. After Moses wrote the Law, he commanded the people every seven years to "read this law before all Israel in their hearing" (Deuteronomy 31:10). Why did they emphasize reading as a community instead of individually? Moses wanted Israel to "hear and learn to fear the Lord your God, and be careful to do all the words of this law, and that their children who have not known it may hear and fear the Lord" (Deuteronomy 4:12-13). Throughout the Old Testament, when Israel neglected this command, God brought revival through the reading of His Word. Look at the examples of Josiah in 2 Chronicles 34:29-33 and Nehemiah in Nehemiah 9. The New Testament also shows a focus on community times of teaching the Scriptures (Acts 2:42, Acts 19:9, etc.). Paul exhorted Timothy to "devote yourself to the public reading of Scripture" (1 Timothy 4:13). The Bible shows clearly the impact of God's Word read and taught in communities.

Like many Christians, I grew up thinking the sole key to my spiritual growth came through spending individual time reading the Bible.

I struggled to read it every day, but did not fully understand or apply what I read. When I started college, I began attending a Bible study led by a fellow student. It was an amazing time. Through the group, God's Word ceased being archaic stories and began to come alive. Together we read, discussed, and applied God's Word. I heard insights I never would have noticed through my own limited study and understanding. Together we processed and made applications into our lives. The village helps make disciples by helping God's Word come alive in the context of community.

A second way discipleship occurs in community is through prayer. Once again, individual prayer is absolutely vital. Jesus often withdrew to pray alone. However, it is not enough, for prayer ignites in the context of community. Throughout the Bible, prayer in communities of God's people often brought about significant life change. For example, Joshua along with the elders of Israel (a community of leadership) together sought God's favor after the sin of Achan (Joshua 7:6). The book of Judges shows a pattern of God's people sinning, then corporately crying out to God. Only then does God bring forth a judge who restores His people and brings revival.

Jesus often modeled the value of community prayer (Matthew 18:19-20). Perhaps the clearest New Testament example comes in Acts 4. After Peter and John's arrest and release, the early church met together to pray. "They lifted their voices together to God" (Acts 4:24). Together they asked God to give them boldness, and God answered dramatically. "When they had prayed, the place in which they were gathered together was shaken, and they were all filled with the Holy Spirit and continued to speak the word of God with boldness" (Acts 4:31). Prayer ignites in the context of community.

I remember the first time I experienced the power of community prayer. I came to college believing that prayer was a personal obligation. A friend in my dorm challenged several of us to meet to pray. Every night we met for half an hour to pray, and to my surprise praying with friends wasn't boring. We prayed diligently for each other, for our needs, and for our concerns. We prayed for friends to come to Christ, for our parents, and for our futures. Our non-Christian friends began to notice what we were doing, and sometimes joined us. We began to see God move. Friends came to Christ. Our faith began to grow. Our relationships deepened. Praying together actually encouraged us to pray more as individuals. Prayer ignites in the context of community.

Christians usually view the third area of discipleship, evangelism, as an event for individuals. However, evangelism too explodes in the context of community. The early church understood this power, for as a community they preached the gospel with boldness, and people responded. "The Lord added to their number day by day those who were being saved" (Acts 2:47). Paul commended the Thessalonian church saying, "not only has the word of the Lord sounded forth from you in Macedonia and Achaia, but your faith in God has gone forth everywhere" (1 Thessalonians 1:8). Evangelism explodes in the context of community.

Evangelism can be contagious. It is far easier to share your faith while surrounded by others who share their faith. I once led a group of student leaders who together embraced the need to reach the lost. These young men had a desire to see every student in their area of campus hear about Christ, and together they began talking with their neighbors about Jesus. Each week they would share stories over dinner about the conversations they had about Christ. We would rejoice over new believers, pray for lost students we had met, and all of us would leave more motivated to talk with others about our Savior. We became a community that shared our faith. Evangelism explodes in the context of community.

A fourth aspect of discipleship is character growth. The village is a powerful place where life change can occur in many ways. Community can impact character growth by spurring on group revival. God can inspire people as a group to seek changed lives (2 Chronicles 34, Nehemiah 9, Jonah 3). The community challenges individuals to seek after God, transforming the entire community.

Community can also be helpful in correction and reconciling relationships. Jesus challenged His followers to involve several others, or even the entire church to win over a brother who "sinned against you" (Matthew 18:13-17). God can also use individuals known in a community to help encourage Christlike behavior. For example, the death of Ananias and Sapphira reminded their entire fellowship of the need for holiness and integrity (Acts 5:1-11). A true community can also embrace individuals in need of correction, for a group of people can have significant influence in the life of an individual. A great example is how Aquila and Priscilla gently corrected Apollos, making him more useful for the gospel (Acts 18:24-28).

The village also can play a significant role in helping individuals see victory over sin. James challenges believers to "confess your sins to one another, and pray for one another that you may be healed" (James 5:16). There is healing power in confessing our sins to caring friends. While these character issues should also come to light in individual friendships, a loving community can more effectively embrace a struggling believer. "We who are strong have an obligation to bear with the failings of those who are weak, and not to please ourselves. Let each of us please his neighbor for his good, to build him up" (Romans 15:1-2). True character change happens best in community.

APPLICATIONS OF DISCIPLESHIP IN COMMUNITY

So how can we build a village? Let me conclude with some user-friendly ideas from the frontlines of campus ministry in developing a disciple-making community.

Before we begin with practical suggestions, we must first recognize that community involves a mindset that impacts every aspect of ministry. True community is not another ministry activity that we do, rather, community is the context in which all of ministry activities take place. Many ministries focus heavily on the relationship between the leader and individuals. Instead, we need to create a series of interconnected relationships independent of the leader, which pull the person closer to the community and to Christ. The immediate picture that comes to mind is that of my family. Lisa and I are the proud parents of ten children, and our kids enjoy a tremendous amount of interconnectedness between them (independent of mom and dad). As a result, we have a family identity, a sense of what it means to be a Nieman.

Before a ministry can make changes to strengthen community, they must first change their mindset to recognize the central role that the village plays in disciple-making. That said, here are some practical suggestions that have flowed out of this emphasis in our ministry. This is not a step-by-step manual and can be contextualized for your ministry context.

First, I would recommend that any ministry, whether on campus or in the church, create a form of community groups. These are more than just one-hour weekly Bible study events. These are open groups of people dedicated to learning together about God. Studying and discussing the Scripture is still important, and still happens weekly but a true community group goes beyond discussing the Bible. Community groups pray for each other, talk about life together, reach out to their lost friends, and provide true friendship. Together they challenge each other to walk more closely with God.

A second way to develop community discipleship is to give each person a specific role. If you are building a true community, why should the leader do everything? One member could bring snacks, another organize outreaches, while a third could focus on prayer. Giving people responsibility creates ownership, develops leadership, and builds an environment for growth and. I should also note that community groups can share some natural affinity. It could be men in the same fraternity, women on the same floor of a dorm, or members of ROTC or a marching band. This helps build community more naturally, as the group lives life together.

Third, develop mature leaders who can create these disciple-making villages. One of the biggest mistakes ministries can make is failing to develop their leaders. Leaders need to experience community among themselves, to know how to foster community among those they lead. At the University of Michigan, we bring our leaders together two hours a week for Family Night. The first hour we share what God is doing, pray, worship, and give vision and training. The second hour we break into smaller leadership groups, look into the Scriptures and create a more intimate forum for growth. We want these leaders to first experience together the interconnectedness we want them to build in the community groups they lead.

Fourth, parties and other social events play a large role in building community. Most ministries attempt to bring people together socially, because shared experiences enhance community. I would suggest building a community team of students to help strategically plan these social events. There are many examples of parties that help build a sense of family. Here in the Midwest, our culture offers a great example—a barn dance. We hire a square dance caller, rent a barn, get some cider, apples and donuts, and have fun. People come as strangers, and often leave as new friends. That is the heart of community. Community groups can also intentionally put together social events that build deeper relationships. A few years ago, a gifted leader struggled with getting students to attend his group—until he invited them to go canoeing. Another great memory maker can be inviting a community group of the opposite gender on some form of group date.

A fifth idea unique to the university environment involves building a class identity. In campus ministry, this need is essential for freshmen who typically come to campus knowing very few people. Building a freshmen class identity is vital because these freshmen will be your leaders in two years. One simple way to develop class community at the outset is to invite the freshmen in your ministry over for dinner. A home is a warm, inviting environment. In a home you eat real food. In a home everyone knows your name, takes your coat, and asks how your day has been. Homes are where the family comes together. Jesus knew the value of a meal in building community.

Social events are not the only way to build class identity. Three years ago a group of about twenty freshmen went to the Ground Zero memorial in NYC. Through this overnight ministry trip they bonded deeply. Today they comprise one of the strongest senior classes we have ever had. We also hold meetings for each class (not just freshmen) at our fall retreat. We have a sophomore lead the freshman time, a junior lead the sophomore time, a senior lead the junior time, and one of our staff lead the senior time. The idea of a class identity is a powerful tool for campus ministries in building a village.

But perhaps the most important thing is for leaders to model true community themselves. They need to take the lead and initiate praying with others and sharing their faith. Leaders need to model vulnerability and authenticity. They need to resolve conflict with one another in positive ways, curbing petty disputes and personality conflicts, and modeling true community to those they lead.

In conclusion, the Bible shows that the idea of a village is a powerful platform for discipleship. These communities help followers of Christ grow in their understanding and application of the Word, in prayer, in sharing their faith with others, and in true character growth. As ministries, we need to be more focused on building communities, not just Bible studies. This is what occurred in my life. That's why I'm in ministry today.

CHAPTER SEVEN

FAITH HILL

The Foundational Role Of Faith In Spiritual Growth

Everyone knows that faith plays a significant role in our spiritual growth, but practically speaking it either occupies too much or too little of our understanding. If our conception of spiritual growth is nothing more than self-effort we will not experience life transformation. But if every spiritual pothole is paved with "just trust God," we will also miss out on true spiritual growth. This is not to detract from the centrality of faith in becoming more like Christ, only to understand its role, so we can better coach those whom we disciple.

In the Christian life there are certain truths that are either so formative, or so fragile, that your disciple may require special assistance in learning to hold them in the shopping cart of faith. As a mature Christian we are used to toting these truths around like a handbag (such as the security of our salvation), but young Christians need to develop the spiritual muscles that we take for granted. What follows is a partial list of these foundational truths that require the exertion of faith, and may require your assistance. It is in these areas that the need for faith is most acute and where the lack of it will have the greatest ramifications.

FAITH AND FORGIVENESS

Few of the great battles in life are ever won overnight, so it is safe to assume that your disciples will see many spiritual failures before they finally see the flag raised, hear the national anthem, take their place on the winner's platform and the world is joined together under the Nike swoosh. It might be a small failure or a stunningly gross one, but in either case they will desperately need to experience God's forgiveness.

The problem with many sins is that even after we've confessed them, it is difficult to feel cleansed, to not berate ourselves, and not suspect that God's still fuming over the incident. When we sin we instinctively feel someone must pay a price: no one gets off easy. What we need to decide is who is going to pay. Your disciple will therefore move in one of the following directions:

- *Alternative #1*
  "I am pig swill." This is one of the terms I use when beating myself up for having fallen into the same trap of sin, yet again. I've not copyrighted the phrase so feel free to use it. In essence, I'm crucifying myself for the sin. Yes, what Jesus did was nice, but I'm going to cover the tab—check, please. Someone must pay and rightfully it should be me so I pound myself for my stupidity.

- *Alterative #2*
  "You, you made me sin." That "you" could be a person, Satan, or even God, but either way someone needs to take the fall for the sin I've just committed and I'll be darned if it's going to be me.

- *Alternative #3*
  "Now that you mention it, I'm not sure that really was a sin." Recognize that phrase? It's called justification. As the word implies, we decide to make a judgment over and against our conscience, declaring that what we did was actually right, or at least not that wrong. Why go to the effort? Because someone must pay for sin, unless of course there is no sin and that's what we're shooting for in this approach: to eliminate the offense.

- *Alternative #4*
  "I couldn't help myself, it's just my personality." Let's call this rationalizing, which is equivalent to the courtroom plea of insanity. What I'm saying is, "Yes, it was sin, but I didn't have the moral capacity to say 'no.'" My personality was such, and circumstances were such, that I could do no other than what I did. The effectiveness of this strategy lies in how good you are at convincing yourself that it's really not your fault. I'm pretty gullible, so I usually believe me.

Of course what makes this all unnecessary is that someone has already paid the price, Christ. What is needed is confession. The problem is that we can confess our sins while failing to employ faith. Faith involves a choice of the will to believe that God has forgiven us through Christ's death, while turning a deaf ear to doubts. We reckon that God is more merciful than we can imagine and believe that through Christ's death we are completely forgiven, and "as far as the east is from the west, so far has he removed our transgressions from us"(Psalm 103:12).

We often ask our disciples to scribble out their sins on a piece of paper, and have them write the verse 1 John 1:9 across the list, and tear up the list. I see no expiration date on this exercise. It is effective because it develops the faith component of confession: a visual aid to under gird a young and underdeveloped faith muscle. It might be useful to walk your disciples through the different responses listed above to help them see where in the process of confession, they are failing to exercise faith. You must teach them confession, but you must also teach them that confession involves faith.

FAITH THAT GOD CAN MAKE YOU HOLY

> "Being confident of this, that he who began a good work
> in you will carry it on to completion until the day of Christ
> Jesus." *Philippians 1:6*

Most of the great heroes of the Bible share two things in common: they all wore sandals, and they were all required to persevere in their faith, though final victory was often years in the future. We, too—no matter how many setbacks we encounter—must never waiver in our belief that God can make us holy, and, if we persevere, will ultimately lead us in triumph.

Every disciple is willing to trust God for victory over sin at least once. The problem is when the war turns into Vietnam, with infrequent victories, heavy losses, and no foreseeable exit strategy. It is at this juncture that they need to know that faith is a long-term struggle and holiness a lifelong battle. Point to the many battles of faith in scripture fought and won over years, and not days. Show them how the Promised Land was taken one battle at a time. When victory is elusive they will need someone to help make sense of it and prepare them for the long war. Without a proper perspective, they may resolve the conflict with a ceasefire, and an acceptance of behavior far from godliness. Help them persevere in the battle believing God will, in time, bring victory.

> "No temptation has seized you except what is common to
> man. And God is faithful; he will not let you be tempted

beyond what you can bear. But when you are tempted, he
will also provide a way out so that you can stand up under
it." *1 Corinthians 10:13*

Here is another truth into which faith must sink its teeth: we must
choose to believe that our temptations and struggles are not unique
and therefore never insurmountable, unfixable, or unforgivable. It is a
lie to believe that any temptation is irresistible, or that we are unique in
any of our struggles. God always provides what we need to remain holy,
even if it's simply an escape hatch. Every disciple is tempted to believe
that in some area of their lives, they deviate from the norm. Satan
desires for us to feel alone. You might ask your disciples if they have
ever felt this way or in what area they tend to think of themselves as
having unique trials or temptations. Forfeit faith in this area and you've
dangerously increased the power of sin.

FAITH THAT ALL THINGS WORK FOR THE GOOD

"And we know that in all things God works for the good of
those who love him, who have been called according to his
purpose." *Romans 8:28*

The next battle of faith is for all those who have experienced damage in their lives, or within themselves, due to sin. God can take any
manure and from it grow a garden, as you participate in this promise
by faith. While it may be impossible to imagine how God can bring
good out of our train wreck of past and present failures, this is hardly a
limiting factor. For God can do "immeasurably more than all we ask or
imagine" (Ephesians 3:20).

There is no limit to God's capacity to redeem evil. Everything in our
past can be taken and used for good. Every failure (like Peter's failures)
can be transformed by God's mercy. Every weakness (like Paul's weaknesses) can be a vehicle for God to demonstrate His strength. Though
we must persevere in faith, and sometimes for years, the equation will
always add up: crap + God = life. And faith is the means by which God
enters the equation.

Through the examples of biblical characters such as Peter and Paul,
and through examples from your own life, you must help your disciples
strap on the shield of faith against the lie that anything in their lives is
unredeemable, gratuitous, or random.

FAITH IN OUR REWARD

"Now, there is in store for me the crown of righteousness,
which the Lord, the righteous Judge, will award to me on
that day—and not only to me, but also to all who have
longed for his appearing." *2 Timothy 4:8*

Some years ago I was in China and like any tourist I visited the Great
Wall. Along the bottom of the wall, a worker of this communist country
was picking up trash. I clocked him at one piece of trash a minute,
which at that rate would have taken him longer to clear the grounds
than it took to build the Great Wall. Where we visited included a maze
of concession stands, tons of them—Great Concession stands. Someone
told me that those who operated the stands employed principles of
the free market, meaning that the more they sold and the more they
charged for what they sold, the more they profited. One of the women at
the booths actually grabbed my coat and dragged me to her counter. It
would be an understatement to say that it was a motivated workforce.

The difference between these two workers was a chasm. Let's call it
the Great Chasm. One worked like a sluggard because he knew that he
would always make the same amount no matter what he did (communism). The other worker knew that her effort would be rewarded (the
free market).

The doctrine of eternal security (that we can never loose our salvation) was never meant to negate the teaching of rewards. In many places
in the Bible, God makes it clear that our obedience and faithfulness will
be rewarded. We are called to exercise faith in future rewards, choosing
to believe that our actions or inaction will be compensated. When our
minds move down the trail of "what difference will this really make?"
the response of faith is—a lot. We are not told what these rewards will
be, but simply given the assurance that it will be worth our while.

Teaching our disciples to maintain an eternal perspective, or to live
for eternity can cultivate their faith toward this truth, provided that our
definition of what is eternal encompasses far more than evangelism, for
Jesus states that even a cup of water given in his name will not fail to be
rewarded.

FAITH IN GOD'S GOODNESS

"'For I know the plans I have for you,' declares the LORD,
'plans to prosper you and not to harm you, plans to give you
hope and a future.'" *Jeremiah 29:11*

If you go back to the Garden of Eden, (which is probably now a parking lot in downtown Baghdad) you will notice that the first sin was a distrust of God's goodness. Adam and Eve became convinced that God was holding out on them. Eating from the tree was in their best interests. The foundation of most sin is a lack of faith in God's goodness, and disbelief that His plans for us are really best.

When things are going wrong, we justify our sin with self-pity. We find ourselves thinking, "Well, I'm going to do this because God isn't taking care of me anyway, and rather than helping, He's allowing my life to disintegrate." Such reasoning is designed by our scheming mind to bring us to a sense of entitlement to sin.

More innocuously, many of us fall prey to pessimism and distrust that what lies in wait over the time horizon is anything but good, often brought on by a nagging suspicion that God never did forget our sin, and payday is right around the bend.

We must fight the battle to deny or disbelieve God's goodness, with faith, never giving an inch. Everything God does in our lives is motivated by love, and any minor deconstruction of that truth is a lie that can have serious ramifications.

In helping your disciples with this struggle, you might ask some questions to discover if their mind has a proclivity to move down this path. You might also share in what ways you tend to doubt the goodness of God. Intimacy with Christ is the best answer to any and all doubts of His goodness. When we feel close to Christ, we sense that He is on our side, and when we feel distant, we come to suspect that He is not.

Memorizing scripture is great, but passages of scripture are animated by our intimacy with Christ.

IDENTITY: IDENTITY THEFT

In a series of ads for Citibank's identity theft program, the viewer sits and listens to the thief who, having stolen the person's credit card number, recounts their various bizarre purchases and exploits. What makes the ads humorous as well as memorable is the thief's story is told (lip-synced) through the identity theft victim, sitting forlornly mouthing the words.

In some way we are all victims of identity theft. Having trusted Christ, we are heirs with Christ of all that is in Him. Most of us never fully grasp what God's Word says is true of us in Christ, or worse, we simply don't think about it. We are children of God, chosen before time to be in the family of God, yet these concepts don't make it to the starting line-up of thoughts that propel us into the day.

In the movie *Cheaper by the Dozen*, the youngest child is treated as the family outcast. The other kids call him "FedEx" because they suspect he was adopted and simply delivered to the family, not born into it. Over the course of time he begins to believe it, rumors become a lie, and the lie grows in power until he runs away from the family believing he has no place within it. There's a message from an otherwise boring movie: our identity matters.

Our faith in our identity in Christ is absolutely foundational to our lives. Faith is fed by reading the Bible. "The Daily Affirmation of Faith" was written to provide a concise, clear statement of the truth of God's Word as it applies to our victory in Christ (what is true of us in Him). Commend it to your disciples for daily reading particularly during times of deep trials and temptation when they are most prone to forget who they truly are, and believe things about themselves and God which are not true.

THE DAILY AFFIRMATION OF FAITH

Today I deliberately choose to submit myself fully to God as He has made Himself known to me through the Holy Scripture which I honestly accept as the only inspired, infallible, authoritative standard for all life and practice. In this day I will not judge God, His work, myself, or others on the basis of feelings or circumstances.

One
I recognize by faith that the triune God is worthy of all honor, praise, and worship as the Creator, Sustainer, and End of all things. I confess that God, as my Creator, made me for Himself. In this day, I therefore choose to live for Him. (Revelation 5:9-10; Isaiah 43:1,7,21; Revelation 4:11)

Two
I recognize by faith that God loved me and chose me in Jesus Christ before time began (Ephesians 1:1-7).

Three
I recognize by faith that God has proven His love to me in sending His Son to die in my place, in whom every provision has already been made for my past, present, and future needs through His representative work, and that I have been quickened, raised, seated with Jesus Christ in the heavenlies, and anointed with the Holy Spirit (Romans 5:6-11; 8:28; Philippians 1:6; 4:6,7,13,19; Ephesians 1:3; 2:5,6; Acts 2:1-4,33).

Four

I recognize by faith that God has accepted me, since I have received Jesus Christ as my Savior and Lord (John 1:12; Ephesians 1:6); that He has forgiven me (Ephesians 1:7); adopted me into His family, assuming every responsibility for me (John 17:11,17; Ephesians 1:5; Philippians 1:6); given me eternal life (John 3:36; 1 John 5:9-13); applied the perfect righteousness of Christ to me so that I am now justified (Romans 5:1; 8:3-4; 10:4); made me complete in Christ (Colossians 2:10); and offers Himself to me as my daily sufficiency through prayer and the decisions of faith (1 Corinthians 1:30; Colossians 1:27; Galatians 2:20; John 14:13-14; Matthew 21:22; Romans 6:1-19; Hebrews 4:1-3,11).

Five

I recognize by faith that the Holy Spirit has baptized me into the body of Christ (1 Corinthians 12:13); sealed me (Ephesians 1:13-14); anointed me for life and service (Acts 1:8; John 7:37-39); seeks to lead me into a deeper walk with Jesus Christ (John 14:16-18; 15:26-27; 16:13-15; Romans 8:11-16); and to fill my life with Himself (Ephesians 5:18).

Six

I recognize by faith that only God can deal with sin and only God can produce holiness of life. I confess that in my salvation my part was only to receive Him and that He dealt with my sin and saved me. Now I confess that in order to live a holy life, I can only surrender to His will and receive Him as my sanctification; trusting Him to do whatever may be necessary in my life, without and within, so I may be enabled to live today in purity, freedom, rest and power for His glory. (John 1:12; 1 Corinthians 1:30; 2 Corinthians 9:8; Galatians 2:20; Hebrew 4:9; 1 John 5:4; Jude 24).

OUR SALVATION

We'll conclude with the most fundamental of truths, and ground zero for faith. All things build upon this.

"Yet to all who received him, to those who believed in his

name, he gave the right to become children of God." *John 1:12*

"I write these things to you who believe in the name of the
Son of God so that you may know that you have eternal life."
1 John 5:13

In describing our spiritual armor, Paul uses a helmet to illustrate the
truth of our salvation: that which protects the mind, and protects us
from a fatal blow. We make it a critical part of basic follow-up, because
scripture affirms that it is. Let your disciples doubt that Iraq had weapons of mass destruction. Let them doubt that the Cubs will ever win a
World Series. But, rehearse this with them until that helmet cannot be
pried off their head.

HOW FAITH GROWS

Faith is like a muscle; it grows by lifting weights. Weights are the resistance—the doubts, mental whispers, and circumstances that tell us the
opposite of what faith must believe. When God seems absent and hor-
rible circumstances swirl around us, everything seems to shout, "God
isn't here! And if He is, He certainly doesn't care." In those circumstances, faith curls the barbell toward the heart and says, "No, God is
good. He is for me. He has a plan." Thus, it is the circumstances adverse
to our faith that become the vehicle for our growth—they are the weight
on the barbell.

And so all disciples are periodically tossed into a boat and sent out
into a raging storm, where God is conspicuous by his absence. We
are not trying to rescue our disciples from the situations and circumstances that will cause faith to grow. Our role is to come alongside them,
strengthen their feeble arms and help them to curl the heavy weights
that will cause their faith to bulk-up. (I think I just described a steroid.)

God provides the weight (adverse circumstances and trials), but they
must continue to lift the weight. We must spot them helping them push
out more repetitions than they thought possible while making sure the
barbell doesn't pin them to the bench-press.

Alternatively faith grows through new challenges and we serve our
disciples well by calling them into circumstances where they will
need to trust and rely on God. They take courageous steps, God shows
Himself faithful, and their faith grows.

Through the stress and strain of faith development, the truths discussed in this article are the most common fracture points, and the
places your disciples may most need your encouragement to wind their
way up the hill of faith.

CHAPTER EIGHT

TRANSFORMATION DISCIPLESHIP

The Gospel As Fuel For Discipleship

Over the years I have had the privilege of introducing many students to Jesus Christ and helping them grow as His disciples. I have witnessed the vicissitudes of great growth and the valleys of defeat and failure in the spiritual development process.

There are things now that I would do differently, focus on more, sweat less, and leave in God's hands more readily. I want to share a little of what I have learned over the years about the gospel and discipleship.

Above all else, I have seen that spiritual growth requires establishing a solid foundation and building on that foundation. It is living and breathing the basics. The word *disciple* means that we are people who spend our lives apprenticed to our master, Jesus Christ. We are discipling and being discipled to be lovers and learners of Jesus. He is our foundation and our focus.

Yet spiritual growth is a marathon not a sprint. This reality leads me to what I now emphasize with greater fervor in my discipleship. In recent years, I have had a paradigm shift as a disciple and discipler with some ah-has and an uh-oh. The ah-ha: the gospel is the fuel and path to transformational growth. The gospel is not just something I share with the lost, but it is what I apply every day to my life as well. The uh-oh: as Christians we often misunderstand it, misapply it or even neglect it in our spiritual journey.

How can we enhance the ah-has and lessen the uh-ohs on our discipleship journey? I invite you to consider what I see as four significant areas of discipleship: the divine portrait, the potential pitfalls, the powerful provision, and the practices for growth.

THE DIVINE PORTRAIT

The context of our discipleship has to be placed in the bigger picture of God's story. God is in the restoration business. He is recovering lost people and lost lives—including yours and those you disciple. To grow, we must first understand the way our lives with God were designed to look, how sin destroyed that relationship and how restoration is available through redemption. We must know the divine story to see where our stories fit.

Paul tells us in 2 Corinthians 5:18-19, "All this is from God who reconciled us to himself through Christ and gave us the ministry of reconciliation: that God was reconciling the world to himself in Christ, not counting men's sins against them. And he has committed to us the message of reconciliation." The heart of the gospel and discipleship is God reconciling all things back to the way they should be.

In *How People Grow*, Drs. Henry Cloud and John Townsend note that the essence of spiritual growth is about returning to the life God created for people to live. What is the life God created people to live? His story in Genesis reveals that God is our Creator. He is the source of life and giver of good things. Second, God created us to be in relationship with Him and with each other. We were not intended to be alone. Third, God created humans to submit to Him so that they could experience life. Fourth, God's role and the roles of man were distinct in His ordering of creation.

Initially, there was no confusion in these roles. God's role was to be our source and provider and we were to depend on Him. God as Creator was to be in control, we were to yield to His control and have self-control. God was the judge of life and we were to experience that life, intimacy and relationship. Ultimately, God made the rules and designed reality and we were to obey them and live in that reality.

We were created to live in this beautiful portrait. However, the fall of man reversed God's created order. Genesis 3 reveals that man became independent from the source of life, lost his relationship with God and with each other, and tried to usurp God's design and become his own lord.

In essence, man reversed the roles and now reaps the consequences. First, our tendency to be our own source has resulted in dependence on ourselves. This leaves us hungry and empty, turning to lust and idolatry instead of real life. Second, our desire for control has made us try to control our world and each other, while losing control of ourselves. Third, our desire to be the judge of life has resulted in judging others and ourselves. Fourth, our desire to be God has resulted in creating our own rules and reality.

Life was lost, yet God did not allow things to stay that way. God in

Christ is reconciling all things back to the way it is supposed to be. In redemption, man is brought back to God through Jesus as the source of life. Man is brought back into relationship with God and one another. Finally, our roles are restored back to the way they were designed to be under His lordship.

Redemption through Christ results in a growing heart and redeemed life. First, we give up our independent posture toward God and become dependent on Him. Second, we cease trying to control things and yield, trust and rest in God's control and sovereignty. Third, we give up the role of playing judge with others and ourselves and instead receive grace and minister grace. Finally, we stop trying to redesign life our way and return to living the life God designed us to live.

Discipleship is essentially following Jesus in this life of redemption and restoration and helping others walk that road too. It is living out God's design for life so that He is glorified, as we are satisfied in Him.

PITFALLS TO PROGRESS

So if that is the way God designed life to work, why might there be so little transformation? Let's look at some potential holes in our discipleship process.

For several years I was involved in a group that studied leaders at risk—individuals in ministry who had major moral failures. We identified the common denominators or red flags in their lives that contributed to their falls. The main red flags included issues of power and control; an extreme focus on ministry success to the neglect of the heart; and a tendency to be isolated and disconnected from the life of God and people. These leaders were not experiencing the gospel that they had been called to preach.

What were some of the pitfalls to avoid? First, over time there was a subtle neglect of the heart. This could be seen in an inordinate focus on ministry success, leadership position, and power. God warns us in Proverbs 4:23, "Above all else, guard your heart, for it is the wellspring of life." Our ministry flows from our heart. Paul in 1 Corinthians 13 indicates we can have great success in ministry and yet have no love or grace in our hearts.

Second, there was a failure to understand and apply the portrait of God's design for life. This could be seen in a tendency to be involved in ministry activity, yet isolated from the life of God and relationship with others. Also, there was the leader's need to be in control and not be dependent on others for ministry or life.

Third, familiarity can breed unfamiliarity. C.S. Lewis in *The Great Divorce* comments, "There have been some who were so occupied in spreading Christianity that they never gave a thought to Christ."

Fourth, we use phony remedies for growth. In his book *The Spirit of the Disciplines*, Dallas Willard makes the point that spirituality wrongly understood or pursued is the major source of human misery and rebellion against God. A professor and friend, Steve Childers, cautions us to beware of "counterfeit remedies" in our pursuit of heart and character growth. One must guard against an unbalanced or deficient approach to growth.

There are three counterfeit remedies: intellectualism, emotionalism, and moralism. Intellectualism dismisses transformation of heart and places an inordinate focus on what one believes. Emotionalism or passivism places an extreme focus on affections or experiences. Moralism or legalism places inordinate focus on one's behavior and willpower. Faced with a lack of transformation the moralist may "just try harder." This leads often to cycles of despair and denial. This is what Paul notes in Galatians 3:3 as "works righteousness." Each of these approaches misses the critical element of the transformational power of the gospel and the cross.

Though Jesus calls us to be holy and pursue righteousness, He cautions us to beware of the counterfeit approach of the Pharisees (Matthew 5:20). Paul notes,

"They have a zeal for God, but it is not enlightened. For, being ignorant of the righteousness that comes from God, and seeking to establish their own, they did not submit to God's righteousness. For the Messiah is the end of the law, that every one who has faith may be justified" (Romans 10:2-4).

What is wrong with this kind of spirituality? It is not enlightened. Rather than seeing our great weakness and enormous debt of sin, it relies on our moral strength and standing. It does not receive through faith in the Messiah, but instead tries through effort and willpower. In all his preaching on the kingdom, Jesus did not look for moral achievements in His followers, but for faith in Him. That is foundational to spiritual growth.

POSTURE OF A HEART THAT GROWS

Believers cannot afford to neglect the heart. What is the posture of a heart that receives Christ and grows? The heart that grows is characterized by poverty of spirit. There is an admission of total need and dependence. God honors humble hearts and opposes the proud (1 Peter 5:5-6). He declares in Matthew 5:3, "blessed are the poor in spirit." He applauds the posture of the tax collector who declared, "God, have mercy on me, a sinner" while condemning the proud posture of the Pharisee (Luke 18:13). "Poor in spirit" refers to a heart attitude of empty-handedness, which is the opposite of spiritual pride or self-sufficiency.

One Friday evening, I pulled into my driveway, entered my home and had hardly dropped my computer bag when there was a knock at the door. It was my neighbor. With tears rolling down his face, he said, "Marc, I need help. Sherry is divorcing me." I was shocked, not so much about his message but that he was there. In the five years we had lived next door, he politely resisted any dialogue about family, life or spiritual things. Now his vulnerability and open hearted were striking as he wept before me.

He began to open up to me about his failure and concluded by saying, "She says she doesn't love me and hasn't for a long time." He was a picture of poverty of spirit, which proved to be the beginning of my friend's growth in Christ.

How does a leader cultivate a heart that is humbly postured? First, we must get reacquainted with our lostness. Richard Lovelace notes, "The shallowness of many people who are 'saved' may be due to the fact that they never known themselves to be lost." Jesus said, "I have not come to call the righteous but sinners to repentance" (Matthew 9:13).

Second, we need to learn to beg. Martin Luther said, "We are all beggars." We need to pray that God would grant us a fresh awareness of our need for the gospel and that we would come to Him continuously like little children in need of His love and grace.

Third, we are called to surrender. Surrender means coming to a place where we agree with God that what He says about us is true. We were meant to live by His system and design: dependent on Him for life, for righteousness, and resting in His control. Each day we need to return to His design and prayerfully surrender to it.

PROVISION AND POWER FOR A GROWING HEART

John Owen realized that the essence of sanctification is "nothing but the implanting, writing, and realizing of the gospel in our souls." As followers of Christ we must discover the gospel's power each day. Perhaps the familiar has become unfamiliar to you. The gospel is for the lost and the found. It offers salvation not only from sin's penalty (past), but sin's power (present) and sin's presence (future). The goal of the gospel is not merely to forgive repentant sinners, but to change them into true worshipers of God and authentic lovers of people.

Tim Keller coined this definition of the gospel: "The gospel is that you are more sinful and flawed than you ever dared believe yet can be more accepted and loved than you ever dared hope at the same time because Jesus Christ lived and died in your place."

PRACTICES OF A GROWING HEART

Jonathan Edwards declared, "The secret of the Christian life is to allow the gospel to filter into your life both rationally and experientially."

Let's look at the words of Paul to see how the gospel gets filtered down into our lives. "So then, just as you received Christ Jesus as Lord, continue to live (walk) in Him, rooted and built up in him, strengthened in the faith as you were taught, and overflowing with thankfulness" (Colossians 2:6-7).

First, the heart that grows believes and walks in the gospel. The gospel is not just a gate I walk through once but a path I should walk each day. Remember the timeless blessings of the gospel.

- *I AM FORGIVEN!*
  God canceled my debt I am not in jail. I am released (Colossians 1:13).

- *I AM ACCEPTED!*
  God is for me. To be accepted means all of who you are, good and bad, is received by another without condemnation. "There is now no condemnation for those who belong to Jesus" (Romans 8:1). Christ's perfect righteousness has been credited to my account through Him (2 Corinthians 5:21). God is truthful with me. He reveals my sin to me but He is not angry with me. As a result, I can be honest with God without fear of rejection. I can rest in Him and trust Him.

- *I AM UNITED!*
  Because we are united to Jesus through faith, God accepts us each day as whole and complete, even though our lives may still be full of inconsistencies.

- *I AM ADOPTED!*
  I am a child of God with all the rights and privileges of a son (1 John 3:1-2). I do not have to control life, trying to make it work. I have access to the Creator and the source of life. I have entrée to the lap of my father, His provision and His discipline for my growth.

- *I AM FREE!*
  I have a new master and the gospel has the power to change me. There is hope for change. I am free from the bondage to the law. I do not need to prove myself

worthy. The law tutors me to Christ and replaces bond-age with an appeal to living on the basis of relationship rather than performance and good works.

- *I AM NOT ALONE!*
  I have His presence through the Holy Spirit. He is able to counsel, comfort, and empower me to live the life God designed for me (John 16:5-15). As I live by and de-pend on the Spirit, I will not gratify the desires of the sinful nature (Galatians 5:16).

The gospel is the fuel of a redeemed life. The gospel moves me to God, life, and back to his His divine design. We fill our tanks with that fuel by believing and walking in it. As believers, when we "rehearse and delight in the many privileges that are ours in Christ," we are in effect preaching the gospel to ourselves.

In the daily grind of life, I remind myself of the gospel. When I am feeling like a failure and hearing words of condemnation, I remind myself that I am accepted by Christ's perfect obedience. When I feel fearful that my financial needs will not be met or that God wants to punish me, I cling to my adoption, recognizing I am a son, not an orphan. When I feel like I am held in bondage to lust, I embrace my redemption. I have been delivered, am not alone and have others to run to with my needs.

As the gospel filters into our lives, it will expose sin and idolatry, which leads us to a second practice of a growing heart. The heart that grows repents and believes the gospel. Jesus announced, "The time has come. The kingdom of God is near. Repent and believe the good news!" (Mark 1:15). Martin Luther notes that when Jesus said to repent, "He willed that the whole life of believers should be one of repentance" (first of Martin Luther's ninety-five Theses nailed to the Wittenberg Door in 1517).

What are we to repent of? One of the greatest threats to a cohesive heart is idolatry. Idolatry can be defined as seeking something other than God as the source of life and depending on something other than God and His provision for life. Paul believed a primary reason hearts are not transformed is that the affections of people's hearts have been captured by idols. These grip them and steal their heart's affection away from God (cf. Ephesians 5:3-5).

How are we to deal with idols? Jesus says we are to apply the practice of repenting and believing. Paul sees repentance and faith as two sides of the same coin (Ephesians 4:22-24). Repentance is a change in direc-tion, moving away from the destructive path back toward God's ways of life. Paul does not tell people to do the right thing because it is right, but so they will live (Romans 8:13; Deuteronomy 6:20-25). Repentance is always a move away from death to life.

To drain its power, one must recognize that the idol's path is one of death, hunger, and emptiness. Idolatry is driven and perpetuated by being cut off from the life of God (Ephesians 4:18-19). When separated from the life of God, we seek to fill the vacuum in idolatrous ways. The life of God includes: support, connection, honesty, healing, confession, repentance, correction, discipline. So when people are hurting (and stuck in idolatry) they need to find healing through God and His people.

I am learning to ask myself: In what ways am I disconnected from the life of God and His people? In what ways can I rest in Him to fill my emptiness? The bottom line is that "the just shall live by faith." By faith we believe God is the source and rest in Him.

Yet, the practice of repenting and believing the gospel is not just an individual practice. Sanctification always happens in a family setting—the body of Christ (Hebrews 10:24-25). It has been said, "If you want to go fast, go alone; but if you want to go far, go together!"

I recall an incident where during a special family time I said some hurtful words to my wife. Though I confessed my sin to Jesus and to my wife, I still felt bad as a dad and husband. My youngest daughter, sensing my need for grace, quickly reminded me: "Dad it's okay. You are forgiven and Jesus really loves you anyway!" That simple act freed me up to say thanks to her and truthfully acknowledge my need to grow in my speech and love. When you have grace, it allows you to bring the real you into the light without being rejected. God is not put out by our sin, nor is He surprised. In fact, He yearns for honesty and for us to bring it into the light.

God designed us for relationship with Him and others. God wants to minister His grace to us from others. Those who only study the facts of the grace of God and do not experience other people loving and forgiving them will fall short in their realization of grace. James 5:16 and 1 John 1:9 show the importance of confessing our sins to both God and others to experience healing. Hiding only hinders the healing process.

The body of Christ is critical in the healing of addictions and idolatry. Often alienation drives addictive behavior. Paul calls it the "continual lust for more" caused by being "separated from the life of God" (Ephesians 4:18-19). Henry Cloud notes,

> "As people are cut off from others and their souls are starved for connectedness, the need for love turns into an insatiable hunger for something (idolatry). It can be a substance, sex, food, shopping, or gambling, but these never satisfy, because the real need is for connectedness to God and others, and to God through others. When

people receive that, the power of addiction is broken."

The practices for discipleship are clear: Preach the gospel; emphasize repenting and believing; stay connected to one another; don't hide but face the truth and confess sin; give and receive grace and forgiveness; tell and celebrate how God is redeeming and restoring you.

CONCLUSION

Keep the gospel the main thing in your discipleship. It is easy to forget that the gospel is not just for the lost but for the laborer as well. The gospel is simple and yet powerfully promotes growth and spiritual formation. Perhaps our familiarity has bred unfamiliarity. Isn't it time to taste again and delight in the Lord and the gospel?

The Christian life is nothing more than grabbing hold of the gospel every day and finding that it is not only true, but also it works. We never outgrow our need for the gospel of Jesus Christ.

Cloud adds, "There are no new ways of dealing with sin, for God gave us the Way a long time ago. There is no rocket science, only the gospel. But what a gospel it is! It is the medicine for the sickness we all possess, and that really is good news."

Disciples of Jesus should be the most repentant people of all and the freest. Why? Because we know the gospel.

John Bunyan, the author of *Pilgrim's Progress* penned a simple poem for himself that captures what I have sought to write about:

"Run John Run. The law commands.
But gives neither feet nor hands.
Better news the gospel brings:
It bids me fly and gives me wings."

Let's fly and help others fly with a renewed emphasis on the gospel in our discipleship.

Men &

Women

DAUGHTERS OF EVE

The Case Against Androgynous Discipleship

I've never really discipled a guy, at least technically speaking, but here are some classic observations about the differences between men and women when it comes to ministry.

A guys' Bible study is scheduled for an hour and is typically over in 45 minutes, while a women's group scheduled for two hours will inevitably go three.

Success in a guys' group is measured by actual number of words exchanged. A women's group measures success in tears—both from laughter and heartache.

For women, group bonding happens over soul-baring conversation. For guys it happens via blood-drawing contact sport.

A guy's dad is diagnosed with terminal cancer and he mentions it in passing three weeks after he finds out. A girl calls in a panic at 2 a.m. to process which dress to wear to the spring formal

The points are obviously exaggerated stereotypes, but you can probably make some connections to your own experience.

These are just the surface level manifestations of hard-wiring differences. God created us uniquely, men and women, but both in His image. I want to explore the unique aspects of how women experience life-change and growth. How are we motivated? What struggles are unique to women? What are the ramifications of Eve's gene pool in our soul and spirit?

WHITE NOISE

It's been said that the core need of a woman is to be wanted and pursued, as opposed to men, whose core need is for respect (from *His Needs, Her Needs* by Willard F. Harley Jr.). Some would say that's a result of the fall and the curse of Eve to "desire after [her] husband" (Genesis 3:16). Others would say that it's because God created us with that need - to be wanted, pursued, and treasured, in order that He might draw us to Himself by meeting that need. I think it's probably both. Regardless if it is by design or default, the result is that women in almost every culture and age have a greater felt need for emotional connection and intimacy in relationships, and apart from the ramifications of sin in the world and their lives, most are motivated to find that connection with a man.

That need is the white noise of a woman's life. It's always there. This is especially true for women ages 18 to 24. It's what we think about when there's nothing else to think about. It affects how we hear everything else. It's the backdrop against which all other life factors are measured, experienced and tried.

The presence of, lack of, hope for, rejection by, bitterness toward, fear of, scars from—men or a man—is the context in which we live. For some the white noise in the background is a definitive hope—a tall, dark handsome husband, 2.5 children and an SUV. For others, it's a much more abstract idea of "happily ever after." Whatever the backdrop, it is tainted and colored by our family and life experience. For almost every woman there is this ubiquitous and overarching assumption that whatever else life may bring, it will fit into the context of a life partner. No matter how independent and self-sufficient a woman is, the idea of who she will share her life with is somewhere in the mix. In most cases the "who" far outweighs the "what" of life.

Before you get on your feminist high horse, I acknowledge that most women expect and desire a career. But very few, if any, pursue that career to the exclusion of at least the hope of a husband and family. Granted it does sometimes cost a woman that, but I'd say rarely is it a conscious choice. We want *both* and if one has to choose one over the other—apart from the consequences of sin in the world or in the lives of women scarred by abuse, divorce or any other number of factors—at the most gut level, women first long for a life companion.

Ironically, even as I'm working on this article, the *Today Show* just did a story on a recent study measuring "happy quotients" for women. The overwhelming result was that "women measure happiness by company kept rather than money made." Certainly there is enough evidence in the secular world that this is a driving factor. Often it's been said that what pornography is to men, romance novels are to women—again, the longing to be wooed and wanted.

And why is it that in the history of music, 82% of every song ever written is about a romantic relationship? OK, I totally made up that statistic, but it has to be close to the truth. Take out hymns, nursery rhymes, national anthems and college fight songs and you're at least at 98%. We can all relate to a sappy love song.

Even within Christian circles nothing draws a crowd like a relationship talk. I happened to attend Denton Bible Church when Tom Nelson first taught the Song of Solomon series. Attendance went from averaging 400 to more than 1,200 by the end of that series and that was only limited by actual space. There were people sitting on cushions on the stage every week, because there were not enough chairs. Recently at my church in Austin, we showed the extremely outdated video version of that series to our singles group and consistently drew 300 singles each week, in spite of the big hair, bad suits and the VHS quality of the tape. Anyway, you get the point.

What few people say out loud is that this longing or desire is perfectly normal. Kudos to Liz Tuccillo and Greg Behrendt, the writers of *He's Just Not that Into You*. They are one of the few popular secular voices who make such a blatant statement, "There is nothing wrong with wanting to get married. You shouldn't feel ashamed, needy or unliberated." Often such a desire is perceived as a weakness. But that is how God made us—with a real and valid need to be wanted, to be pursued, to be treasured, to live in tandem with a soul-mate.

However, where this longing goes awry is in the why. Women both in the secular world as well as within the confines of conservative Christendom have come to believe, either consciously or unconsciously, that marriage is the purpose of life. Everything else is icing. It's one of the many manifestations of the all-about-me gene innate to all humanity.

IT ALWAYS COMES BACK TO THAT

You're probably thinking what does any of this have to do with discipling women. It is and has been my experience that it has everything to do with it. Regardless of the topic you're teaching, the application of the principles will come back to men, dating, relationships and marriage, whether it's women who have been married for 30 years, a group of newlyweds or singles young or old. That's where we live, as much as we hate to admit it.

Nothing has the potential to stop a woman who is growing in the Lord like a new relationship. We've all had a woman in our Bible study who showed promise and then the guy comes around and we never see her again. There's something about the immediate gratification and tangibility that is so much more satisfying, apparently. As frustrating as it is after years of working with women, I can't say I don't understand it. What woman hasn't cried herself to sleep mumbling something about wanting "Jesus with skin on him."

Because this backdrop influences our perspective and value of everything else, then it's the one thing we need to hold in a right and true perspective. It affects our view of God, our view of our own body, soul and spirit, our willingness to trust God, and our willingness to be obedient. At the most practical level it can determine whether or not a woman is motivated to go to a weekly meeting or go on a project and leave her could-be-the-one boyfriend at home or if she's willing to settle for the not-so-godly guy.

The good news is that God does work all things together for His good, even our poor motives. I know many a staff person, both men and women, who as students showed up at a weekly meeting solely for macking rights. And look at them now.

TO KNOW HIM IS TO LOVE HIM

God created us for a purpose—to know Him. The Old Testament is filled with God pursuing His people. Repeatedly we see some variation of the phrases: "I've done [this] so that you will know that I am God" or "know that I am the Lord" or "that you will know me." The Psalms are filled with great promises for those who "know Him."

One of my favorite passages is Isaiah 43:10, "I have called you to be my witnesses so that you will know me and believe me." We evangelize so that others will know Him, but we also go deeper in our own relationship with Him when we do so. The book of Ezekiel is a long list of warnings of what will happen to God's people if they don't return to Him. More than 50 times He says that such and such will happen and then "they will know that I am the Lord."

The New Testament is a revelation of Jesus drawing us into a relationship with Himself. The book of John is an excellent picture of Jesus revealing who He is. He wants us to know Him as Paul describes, counting "all things to be loss in view of the surpassing value of knowing Christ Jesus, my Lord" (Philippians 3:8). That's the whole point of life—"to know Him and make Him known." (Who was the first to say that? Very clever.)

Marriage is one of the most profound means to that end. The bride/

bridegroom and husband/wife relationship is one of the most common metaphors in scripture for our relationship with God. The books of Song of Solomon and Hosea are examples. Psalm 45 is all about the king's wedding and Isaiah 62:5 promises that "as the bridegroom rejoices over his bride, so your God will rejoice over you." Jesus refers to Himself as the bridegroom in Matthew 9 and then there is the parable of the virgins waiting for the bridegroom in Matthew 25. John also refers to himself as the rejoicing friend of the bridegroom in John 3:29. Paul writing to the Corinthians expresses his godly jealousy "for I betrothed you to one husband, so that to Christ I might present you as a pure virgin" and in Ephesians 5 there is the direct comparison of a husband loving his wife as Christ loves the church. Not to mention, the grand finale of Revelation and of the age is the ultimate wedding feast.

A marriage relationship is the most intimate of any, and it is just a taste of the intimacy that God desires to have with each of us. I think it's His greatest gift by which we begin to understand His love for us, but certainly not the only means. Unfortunately, as the ramifications of sin in the world grow exponentially, the idea, purpose and context of marriage has been warped and distorted—undervaluing the vow and overvaluing having one's needs met. So many are missing out on the fullness of what God intended in marriage.

Part of thinking about it rightly is to place it in right relation to God's purpose—knowing Him. If we truly value that as the purpose of our lives, then marriage is not the focus, but a very fun and challenging means to that end—a fabulous by-product. But not everyone will take that route. Most will, but some won't. And for those who do marry but believe it to be the end rather than the means, I guarantee marriage will be painfully disappointing. But amazingly God uses that, too, to draw us to an intimate knowledge of Himself, just as He can use singleness to do the same.

DEAD END TO DOORWAY

Frankly, being single and 38 and having worked with single women from college to middle age for the past 20 years, I'm more than a little tired of talking about men, or the problems with men, or the lack of men, or the wonders of men. There is nothing new under the sun. I have my share of cynicism about well-intending friends forwarding me that "valentine from Jesus" email. I continue to wrestle with it personally, as well as with the women I work with. I wish it weren't the white noise in my own head and heart, but it is. Certainly there are seasons that it's louder than others, but it is always there at some level.

Sometimes it's a resigned acceptance of the reality of singlehood that means deciding if I can trust this car mechanic or not, or thinking about a 403(b) plan that will take care of just me. Or sometimes it's really loud, an acute loneliness when I sit alone at church or spend another night in the silence of my own apartment. (Pathetic, I know. Allow me some melodrama!) Sometimes I'm so grateful for my singlehood. It is so obvious that God has protected me from choices I would have made in the past and I'm grateful for the wealth of friends that fill my life. That too influences my perspective of life factors. The white noise is not always a negative influence, it's just always there as part of my reality. I've realized that often the nature of the white noise is indicative of the health of my walk with the Lord.

I'm finally beginning to see this ubiquitous issue as a doorway to spiritual growth, rather than a distraction or dead end. Talking about guy relationships is a fast track to connecting to the heart of a woman. Just like in my own life, the attitudes and perspectives around that issue can be indicative of where a woman is spiritually. How a woman talks about men or the relationship she has with her boyfriend or husband usually gives some clues to her views of God and her relationship with Him.

In the past few months, I've had two significant conversations with women—one with a non-believer and the other with a very young believer. Both conversations began with guy trouble, but led to great discussions about God's heart for an intimate relationship with them and a clear gospel explanation. We talked about God's intent for marriage as a reflection of our relationship with Him. We discussed the hopes and needs they're expecting men to meet that only God can. We talked about God's idea and purpose of marriage versus the world's ideas. It is not about having needs met, but rather fulfillment is found in giving yourself for the life of another. The parallels between marriage and the Christian life are extensive—that's a whole chapter in and of itself. But the point is that by talking about this very real felt need with these women, they were able to begin to comprehend God's heart and redirect some of their longings and expectations toward Him. Both have made some significant decisions to start walking with the Lord.

A friend who is a mature believer is in the midst of a dating relationship for the first time in awhile. It's brought up all sorts of issues about fears and her view of God and ability to trust Him. These issues would have otherwise gone untested were it not for her relationship with this guy. In my own life, God has used relationships with men to bring me to the most broken places I've ever been, but so needed to be, in order to know more fully how good and faithful and kind and secure He is.

NO MORE ROLLING OF THE EYES

Instead of fighting the inevitable, run with it. Instead of trying to get back to "the topic at hand," connect it to where we live. Learn the pas sages about God's desire to know us and the marriage metaphors. Use them to get at the root issues for the women you work with—their view of God and longing for Him. Asking the right questions and making the connections can be a doorway to growth, whether it's a one-on-one discipleship relationship, leading a small group, or in sharing your faith with a woman.

I confess to being one of those who mock the popularity of Beth Moore by responding to almost any trivial problem with a sarcastic, "Have you done the Beth Moore study on that?" But I also have to confess that I gave in and actually did one of her studies on my own, *Breaking Free*. One of the chapters talks about the longings of a woman to be a bride and to be fruitful and to live happily ever after. I confess I started the week with dread and cynicism, but I ended up weeping everyday. The study forced me to deal with these longings in my own soul and experience how God really can meet them.

I don't want to communicate that every small group should be about addressing guys and dating. But the topic can be a doorway to talk about other issues of the Christian life or a point of application from other topics. However, with a college women's group, sooner or later you will have to throw them a bone and do an actual study on dating.

There is a whole litany of relationship books out there. Henry Cloud's *Boundaries in Dating* is always one of my first recommendations. Then there is *Every Woman's Battle* by Shannon Ethridge or Paula Rhinehardt's *Sex and the Soul of a Woman*, and of course the classics, *Passion and Purity* by Elisabeth Elliott and *Lady in Waiting* by Jackie Kendall and Debby Jones.

I also recommend *Lies Women Believe* by Nancy Leigh DeMoss. She's not one to mince words and you may even disagree with some of her conservative viewpoints, but she offers great insight and conviction for putting these longings in proper perspective with God's intent. And as one friend said, "I suspect she's probably right on the controversial issues, but I don't really want to study it for myself, because that will only confirm that she is right and I'll have to change."

Speaking of Nancy Leigh DeMoss, at a recent Winter Conference, she was one of our keynote speakers. At the beginning of the women's time she did an informal survey. Like all good staff, my friends and I sat in the back of the room and looked through the results. In response to the question, "How important is marriage to you?", literally every response was a 4 or a 5, the highest values of the fifty or so cards perused out of 500. On the back of the card, Nancy asked the audience to list their greatest struggle. Perhaps as many as half the women responded with "knowing that God loves me." That is a frightening combination. It's not surprising, but I guarantee if we don't help our students find and experience the security of God's love, then they will look for and expect a man to meet that need and the ramifications of sin will be multiplied in another generation.

Life-change and growth for anyone happens at the heart level, where strong emotions reside. Nothing is closer to a woman's heart than the need to be wanted, loved, valued and treasured. It's common to all of us. Instead of fighting the ever present, I encourage you to use it as a doorway to her spirit, connect it to what God wants to do in her heart and introduce her to the Bridegroom that will not disappoint.

CHAPTER TEN

RAISING MEN NOT BOYS

The Wisdom Of The Men's Movement

Discipleship is a sexual issue. By this I mean it cannot be blind to gender. Our spiritual growth takes place within a male or female body so at some point we are led to consider the question: What does it look like, not simply to be a godly individual, but a godly male or female? What follows is a general overview of some of the current principles being taught in male discipleship as well as my own thoughts and synthesis from years of discipling men.

A few years ago, I had the opportunity to speak to some men in our region. There were more than 250 guys in the room. We were seated in a coliseum setting with a table strategically placed in the middle. Many were in groups from their schools wondering what was in store for them. Most were expecting a talk of some sort, but few were ready for what took place.

I stepped into the middle of the coliseum as an announcer does, preparing to describe the fight. With a loud, booming voice I called out to the men, igniting their passion to compete with one another, and I placed forth the challenge. "Perhaps there are guys in here that have a grudge against another guy. It could be that you're tired of getting spooned in the conference bed you've been sharing, or another guy stole the eye of the girl you were checking out. Maybe there's a school that you've wanted to conquer for some time." My intent was to get them ready to battle. I wanted them to challenge each other at the arm wrestling table I had prepared for them.

Schools tested schools, pitting their gladiator against another. Roommates brought their "issues" to the table, while friends dared each other. As they competed, the roar of the crowd escalated. In that moment I remember thinking how great it is to be a man. I laugh about it today as I reflect back to the moment two of the skinniest guys in the room tore off their shirts and made their way to the table. No concern for their physique, no embarrassment, just satisfaction in being able to go at it with one another.

I barely remember what I spoke on that evening. What I do recall is the moment we shared in competition and I'll never forget the end of our time together. I invited the men to stand up and lock their arms around one another, shoulder to shoulder. There we all stood in a giant circle, I gazed into the eyes of every guy in that room and I made this comment, "Some of us are athletic, others gifted in different ways. Several are good looking, and some of you aren't. A number are intelligent. Some are wealthy, while others have little financial means. It doesn't matter; what all of us have in common is that we are men and we need to be proud of that."

I once heard it said that we live in a culture where manhood seems more like a problem to overcome. *Reader's Digest* published an article by Tucker Carlson where he addresses the issue of how television portrays manhood. It was titled, "You Idiot! If you believe what you see on TV, all men are morons."

Spend some time with the guys on our campuses or take a good look on the inside of ourselves to see that there is some confusion about what it means to be a man. In the book *Raising a Modern Day Knight* Robert Lewis quotes a poem written by a young man who wrestled with his own personal manhood vacuum. He wrote:

> "What is a man?
> Is he someone who is strong and tall,
> Or is taut and talented as he plays ball?
> Is he someone who is hardened and rough,
> Who smokes and drinks and swears enough?
> Is he someone who chases women hard,
> With a quest to conquer, but never dropping his guard?
> Is he someone with a good business mind,
> Who gets ahead of the others with his nose to the grind?
> Or is he someone who tries his best,
> Not really caring about any of the rest?
> What is a man? Does anyone know?
> TELL ME!
> Who is the prototype? To whom shall I go?"

These students are going to come to us as they wrestle with these issues, and what an awesome responsibility and privilege we have to raise up men not boys. I love the passage in 1 Corinthians 13:11 where Paul talks about putting childish ways behind. He says "When I was a child, I talked like a child; I thought like a child, I reasoned like a child. When I became a man, I put childish ways behind me." In Paul's days I think it was clearer what those steps to manhood were. But I believe we can restore a sense of understanding to our culture and call them to a clear vision of what it means to be a man.

WHAT IS A MAN?

I get so frustrated when I read the trash that is out there about men and what our society is doing to undermine who we are. At times we buy into the lie that we are shallow and insensitive. Raymond from the TV show "Everybody Loves Raymond" captures well what our culture thinks about us. Some would say that all we think about is food, sleep and sex. As true as that is, there is so much more to who we are.

Peggy Noonan wrote a remarkable article on October 12, 2001 called, "Welcome Back, Duke" where she captured well the significance of being a man and what we bring to the table in times of crisis and pain. You would do well to take some time to look it up and read it. She talks about masculine men and draws upon the pictures that are forever etched into our psyche from September 11, 2001.

When I am coming alongside of the guys on our campuses, I work hard to connect them with images of true manhood. On my shelf at home are movies like *Apollo 13, Braveheart, Gettysburg, Glory*, and *Saving Private Ryan*. The pictures that I have in my mind are of those men who made a difference. It's the men coming off a landing craft, the door dropping down, bullets taking lives as the soldiers storm the beach. It's Eric Liddell standing on principle as he drops out of his Olympic race to honor the Sabbath and then later traveling to China to be a missionary. It's Derek Redmond's dad coming out of the stands to help his son, supporting the injured man, swatting the official away and taking his boy across the finish line. With all the negative stuff that's out there, men need a positive vision of what a man can do—what a man can be.

The greatest place we can take our men to see what authentic manhood looks like is God's Word. 1 Corinthians 15: 45-49 introduces two masculine identities—Adams and Christ. We fall under one of them. Robert Lewis in his series "Quest for Authentic Manhood" describes it this way:

The First Adam
Manhood is set on a natural course. At his core is the idea of getting all you can.

Manhood is based on instinct and reaction. At his core is selfishness.

Manhood is without Transcendent meaning. A finite, temporal existence with a temporal perspective on life.

The Second Adam
Manhood is set on a heavenly course. You are able to see life as bigger than what is in front of you.

Manhood is based on revelation, not on instinct and re-action. Jesus was a man under authority and so are we.

Manhood is life giving. Masculinity is best expressed when it is here for others.

As I work with men on the campus, above all else, I want to point them to the person of Jesus and how manhood played itself out in His life—He is our ultimate model.

Most of my life has been spent trying to achieve a certain level of success. Early on, life centered on basketball and my relationships with the opposite sex. In marriage and in ministry, life revolved around what I could accomplish. Although many around me would not have perceived me to be selfish, at my core, I wanted what felt good and looked good. I reacted to life around me instead of looking at life as bigger than just me. When I began to look at the life of Jesus, I saw that in every situation He brought life to those around him. Whether He was with the woman at the well, a prostitute, or whoever, He gave them life and they were never the same.

Over the past few years I have been working with my three sons, helping them to know and understand the manhood definition that has been passed onto me. It is the same definition that I've had the privilege of sharing with college-age men through the "Quest for Authentic Manhood" material by Robert Lewis. A while back I walked into the bathroom of one of the guys that I worked with and there hanging above the toilet for every man to see was Lewis's definition:

An Authentic Man Rejects Passivity

Accepts Responsibility
- A will to obey
- A work to do
- A woman to love

Leads Courageously
- Over Feelings
- Gives Direction, Protection, Provision

Expects the Greater Reward
- God's reward

REJECTS PASSIVITY

According to Robert Lewis, and I would agree, men have a natural tendency to avoid social and spiritual responsibility. A friend of mine who directed Cru at a school in our region once told me that the majority of those stepping up to the tasks of the ministry were the women. They saw the need and were willing to fill the gap. One male student shared with me that he would often sit back and wait for someone else to initiate instead of stepping up to take responsibility. Sounds like Adam in Genesis 3:6, doesn't it?

"When the woman saw that the fruit of the tree was good for food and pleasing to the eye, and also desirable for gaining wisdom, she took some and ate it. She also gave some to her husband, who was with her, and he ate it." (Genesis 3:6)

I have the same potential to be like Adam. I have to fight passivity in the spiritual and social areas of my life: as a husband, a father, and as a member of my church and community. At 6'6", 230 pounds I hardly think of myself as passive and if you ever played basketball with me you'd understand why. I love contact, as a matter of fact; I had a good friend say to me one time, "You're the only person I know that can make fly fishing a contact sport."

But, there are many times when I just want to sit on my butt and pretend that I haven't a clue what is going on in life around me. Like when I'm at home and the three boys have my wife, Cristi, tied up in knots (literally), and I quietly close the door of my office. Or when I place the burden of the kids' problems at school on my wife, expecting her to check the homework and deal with the teachers. And then there's the Sunday school class of boys that needs a male presence and once again I hesitate at just the right moment and let a woman meet that need. I've had to be reminded at times what it means to reject passivity.

ACCEPTS RESPONSIBILITY

I want the young men that I spend time with to understand what it looks like to accept responsibility. I want them to know what it means to have a will to obey God. I help them see that their work and responsibility goes far beyond their major in school and into the work that Jesus has called them to: in ministry, in their families, and in their community.

Finally we explore the mysteries of loving a woman and what that looks like outside and inside of marriage. I want to help them understand a sense of duty. I seek to model how I lead my wife, my boys and my ministry, so they can see what it looks like to step up to the plate in these areas and what it looks like to fail miserably. My goal is to give these men a sense of vision; I want to challenge them to walk with Jesus, to desire spiritual transformation, and hunger to take responsibility.

A few years back, there were three guys that I was discipling at Rutgers. We sat down together and began to unravel this definition of manhood—rejecting passivity and accepting responsibility. Initially the guys felt uncomfortable because much of what we discussed went against current cultural thinking. As we met together and wrestled with the tension of our feelings placed up against the principles of God's Word, I began to see these men step up and take responsibility within our movement on the campus. They led and inspired others to lead. They took the initiative in their relationships with the women that they were dating as they saw that the responsibility and direction of those relationships rested on them. Today, they continue to walk with Jesus and lead in their homes and in their church.

LEADS COURAGEOUSLY

We were created to lead and that leadership requires courage—the third principle. It's the same courage that it takes to charge into a burning building when everyone else is leaving. As men we have the ability to muster up that courage to give direction, protection and provision when we are able to master our feelings and lead out of principle. Robert Lewis says, "That in order to do this we have to come under the authority of a power you respect more than yourself. That is called conversion to the lordship of Jesus Christ."

A GREATER REWARD

Finally I lead the guys I work with toward the greater reward. One of my favorite set of verses in the Bible is from Hebrews 12:1-3.

> "Therefore, since we have so great a cloud of witnesses
>   surrounding us,
> let us also lay aside every encumbrance, and the sin which

> so easily entangles us,
> and let us run with endurance the race that is before us,
> fixing our eyes on Jesus, the author and perfecter of faith,
> who for the joy set before Him endured the cross,
> despising the shame and has sat down at the right hand of
>   the throne of God.
> For consider Him who endured such hostility by sinners
>   against Himself,
> so that you may not grow weary and lose heart."

These verses capture how we are able to go after the greater reward. I want the guys that I am working with to learn to come to grips with their sin and go soul to soul with other guys in the areas in which they struggle. One of the greatest satisfactions in my life has been helping create an environment where a college-age man is able to get his sin out into the open and experience forgiveness from his peers. How wonderful it is to finally look beyond the temporary satisfaction of our sin and seek the greater reward—God's reward.

CONTENT DRIVEN – I DON'T THINK SO!

We've all been doing ministry long enough to know there are a thousand ideas and tons of materials on discipleship and men related issues. I've gotten a lot out of the David English's "Quest for Authentic Manhood" material and would encourage any of you to check it out if you haven't. But I'd be the first to admit that there are other resources out there that are equally good.

What I've learned in my years of working alongside of men is that success comes from relationship and not the content. Content is secondary because my greatest concern is for them and their walks with the Lord. There is a great scene in the movie *Antoine Fischer* where Antoine challenges the Navy psychologist. He gets in the doctor's face calling for him to get involved in his life and not just jump in for a moment and leave.

I realize that if I tried to get into the life of every guy I've worked with, I would fail. So what I do is, create an environment where they are learning how to connect with other men, those in the same life-stage who that can help them process life spiritually and emotionally. In this way, they don't become dependent solely on me. One of the tools that I've used to help guys process life together is a series of studies on very predictable, emotional, and developmental phases of life that men experience.

In his series, *Quest for Authentic Manhood*, David English encourages men to process with each other the various life stages that they go through emotionally and the spiritual implications of those struggles. The idea is to get guys to connect with each other to process life. One of the things David has shared is that often we have a high drive on our campuses for competence in the ministry. Within that drive to conquer it is possible to lose out on authenticity and relationship. It's great to be effective, but what we really want and need is intimacy with the Lord and each other. We need to be pulling back and asking what is really going on in our walks with the Lord and how can we lead out of that relationship. Connectedness with the Lord and with other men really helps foster that environment.

I try to use common experiences that men enjoy such as competition, food, and outdoor activities to get them connected. Within those opportunities, I teach them to be transparent with others.

On summer projects, our staff do an activity called Soul to Soul, where we help the guys create an environment in which they get to know each other quickly and as naturally as possible. Each of the guys shares their personal life story as deeply as they feel comfortable in a small group atmosphere of affirmation and confidentiality. They may incorporate their family background, spiritual background and anything important to getting to know them better. Then the rest of the guys in that group ask questions about that individual's story. Following the question time, the men gather around and pray for that guy and give him affirmation.

Most of the guys I've worked with have never experienced this kind of acceptance. I've discovered that the more vulnerable I've been and the more I've been able to share from my own struggles as a man, the more they have been willing to open up and share things that they've never put on the table before. As a result of connecting and processing together, the content we cover has purpose and consequently growth occurs.

SEX AND PORNOGRAPHY

Early in my staff career I realized how difficult it is for most of us to have deep conversations about sex and pornography with guys. I was sitting across from a student on a summer project and had spent a significant amount of time trying to tap into his life. Finally, with all the courage he could muster, he shared his struggle with homosexuality and the battle that he'd faced for so many years. It was apparent from the student's application that those who knew him had never gone below the surface in this area of the student's life.

That's not a huge shock. It's not like you and the guy you're hanging out with are playing x-box in his dorm room and you naturally transition into a question, "Have you been playing with anything that you shouldn't be lately?" Most of the applicants I review for summer project have seldom talked extensively about this subject. In the years that I've been working with men I've made the attempt, in the context of relationship, to ask the clarifying questions like, "By struggling, what do you mean?" or "What are the bad choices that you've made?" This helps men to talk about the Internet, pornography, and other areas that might be difficult.

Alcoholics Anonymous has been one of few programs that has actually seen success in healing addiction. Many who come through the 12-step program cite step 5 as the turning point: "Admitted to God, ourselves, and one another the exact nature of our wrongs." Step 5 is powerful because it's predicated on James 5:16, "Therefore confess your sins to each other and pray for each other so that you may be healed." This is not the end of the battle, but it is a turning point. In my role as a discipler, I seek to ask the questions that will surface the exact nature of the wrongs. Only then does the healing begin.

CONCLUSION

Manhood isn't a problem to overcome. I love being a man and wouldn't trade it for anything. It's the joy of conquering a mountain top in the midst of a hail storm, the simplicity of quietly sitting around a fire with your friends and poking the embers. It's walking into your son's room while he's sleeping and praying about how you're going to lead him. It's holding your wife securely and providing an environment for her to flourish and feel safe. It's never taking your eyes off of Jesus and always expressing dependence upon him.

I could never do it alone and God never intended me to. I have those in my life that have challenged me to move from being a boy to becoming a man and I'd never want to go back. And as a man I take responsibility for helping others make their rite of passage.

Sin &

Consequences

BLOW POPS

Finding Life And Growth Out Of The Ashes Of Destructive Sin

Let's start with a story. Rocky is "the man." You've met few students like him. He has great potential as a student leader. He is truly seeking to grow in his faith and has a strong desire to influence others. He is socially adept and well liked. This kind of key leader only comes along once every few years.

Despite his leadership capabilities, Rocky has one seemingly minor problem. It's really a bad habit that he can't shake--Rocky is addicted to Charms Blow-Pops. While it started as a harmless pleasure, his habit is starting to extract a toll on his life. The cost of eating two-dozen Blow-Pops a day is adding up. A trip to the dentist reveals six cavities, which are not only painful, but expensive. Physically, his once chiseled frame is turning *sloshy*.

What is more alarming is how his habit is beginning to affect his relationships. His roommates are getting increasingly annoyed at finding used Blow-Pop sticks all over their room. Every time Rocky tries to quit he gets irritable and angry. His friends notice that he is spending more and more time alone.

Things hit rock bottom when Rocky is caught rummaging through his roommate's Green Bay Packer piggy bank looking for change to support his fix. Humiliated, deflated and disillusioned Rocky comes to you for help. He relates to you that he's been keenly aware that his habit has become a real problem but he's been too embarrassed to talk about it with anyone. He says he's asked the Lord countless times to remove his compulsion, tried to memorize Scripture and even promised God he would completely swear off his sweet sensations. But while he might get a few days of freedom, nothing he's tried has brought lasting change.

David prayed, "Keep your servant also from willful sins; may they not rule over me" (Psalm 19:13). Unfortunately, this tongue-and-cheek story about Rocky illustrates an all too real experience for sincere believers. Like Rocky, many seeking Christ are frustrated, disillusioned and perilously close to despair because they are lumped up by habitual sins "that rule over them." And often these areas are kept hidden because of the fear of judgment and rejection.

Let's step back and use Rocky's experience as an example. Rocky's got a problem. In this case, his Blow-Pops represent an area of a person's life where one has lost control and feels a sense of powerlessness, defeat or unmanageability. Hebrews 12:1-2 offers us some insight here. In light of the great cloud of witnesses and those who have demonstrated exemplary faith in the past, the author exhorts his readers to "throw off everything that hinders and the sin that so easily entangles."

Let's look at one's Blow-Pops through this grid. Sometimes a person's Blow-Pop is an obvious manifestation of sin (the sin that so easily entangles)—lust, using pornography, alcohol and drug abuse, fits of rage, lying, gossiping. Other times it's a little less obvious (that which hinders)—dependency relationships, addiction to work or academic success, use of movies, video games, or soaps, food addiction, sports, online chatting, etc.

Regardless of the form of the destructiveness, several common characteristics are often true of people struggling with habitual sin. First, there is a sincere desire to stop but an inability to do so despite their best efforts. They feel trapped in the behavior. Think about it in terms of addiction: they are powerless to stop the controlling behavior.

Second, the sin and extent of the destructiveness of the behavior remains in the dark. Consequently they experiences tremendous shame and guilt. It begins to define their walk with Christ and becomes THE ISSUE of their lives.

Third, there may be a Jekyll and Hyde quality to their lives. When the behavior and sin pattern kicks in, they become someone else. In addition, they may do really well in achieving victory and then have a sudden slip or relapse seemingly out of nowhere.

Fourth, the behavior almost always isolates people from true relationship. And, both the cause and the solution of the behavior has, at its root, a relational component. Thus the solution *has to* focus on the relational and not just the moral. But, more about that later.

Finally, acting out the habitual sin has an idolatrous dynamic to it. Whatever they use in seeking to get their needs met is taking the place of God in their lives.

Yet, in the midst of the mess and heartache flowing from this failure there is hope for change—not just in the way one behaves, but deep, lasting heart change. Let's look at a fresh view of habitual sin. To be sure, God has a holy hatred for sin and is never responsible for directly tempting anyone (James 1:13). However, isn't it just like the Lord to use Satan's insidious schemes as an actual opportunity for His outlandish grace and power to be displayed? As disciple makers, we have precious few windows into the hearts of people. Our Blow-Pops represent one window God can use for His glory as it relates to long-term heart and character change.

The following are some principles for us to apply as God makes a way for us to move into people's lives and join them on their journey. For these principles to work, it is assumed that the person in view here—the grower—has a desire to change. Many aren't convinced that what they are doing is sin or that their seemingly innocent habit is becoming a destructive force in their lives. We can love those folks, be available to them, share our own story with them, but God needs to work in their heart before they are ready to do the hard work necessary to truly change. There is a saying in Alcoholics Anonymous that fits here: "Half measures availed us nothing."

However, in this context, we're talking about people who truly want to change. They are sick and tired of being strangled and suffocated by habitual sin. They have tried to be free but have not found lasting answers. It is to these people we have the privilege of offering hope.

ADDRESS SINFUL BEHAVIOR BUT KEEP YOUR EYE ON THE BIG PICTURE—RELATIONSHIP

First, by way of perspective, habitual sin needs to be addressed. But, the behavior itself isn't the main issue. In other words, the struggle this person faces is not primarily moral but relational. As John Ortberg has stated, ultimately, we are to be growing in love for God and others. This is the essence of maturity and godliness, not whether we "acted out" last week. The behavior is important, not because it is a moral failure but because it hinders and even cuts off relating with God and others in holy and intimate ways. And, as Henry Cloud relates, the behavior must be dealt with otherwise there is no hope of getting to the deeper issues of relational sin and need that will lead to more lasting and profound heart change.

HELP STUDENTS DEVELOP A STRATEGY FOR GROWTH AND CHANGE

Recognizing that one needs to keep relationship primary, the person also must have a strategy to deal with the behavior. Successful plans for lasting change always include these actions:

- Come into the light with God and others (1 John 1, James 5:16)
- Understand that we're powerless and weak and have no chance to overcome our habitual sin if left to our own devices and strength (John 15:5, 2 Corinthians 12:7-10, Matthew 5:3-4)
- Community—going beyond accountability. More on that below.
- Acceptance and direction (synonymous with grace and truth)
- Addressing issues of the heart and not just of behavior
- Renewing of the mind, which includes submission to Scripture, worship, and experience of love *from* God and *from* others. When we read in Romans 12:2 that we are to "be transformed by the renewing of (our) mind," it is easy to focus on memorizing and meditating on Scripture so that our minds might be made new. This is undoubtedly important. But ask yourself: "In what ways has God renewed my mind?" For most it is through a myriad of means—Scripture, worship, prayer, service, and through the love, acceptance and honesty of others. Apply these principles to the discipleship relationship and as it relates to helping students see freedom from habitual sin.

These ideas are clearly not exhaustive. In fact there may be some issues beyond your training and experience to handle. That's okay. One of the things that's important for you to become familiar with is the other resources for growth available in your geographic area—pastoral, counseling and support groups.

THE BATTLE IS WON ONE DAY AT A TIME

Emphasize the one-day-at-time nature of the struggle. And, avoid calling students to dramatic one-time commitments. It is unwise and unrealistic to encourage them to commit to such things as purity (whatever that is) or not masturbating ever again (or this month). Most of the time people who sincerely want to walk with Christ have made countless commitments in areas of habitual sin. These can often be counter productive in that they ultimately lead to disillusionment and despair. A more effective approach is to help students take things one day at a time. This is a biblical concept. Remember God's provision of *manna* for the Israelites on a daily basis? (See also Matthew 6:11;

Hebrews 3:7; 4:7). This perspective also highlights the relational nature of growth. We invite God into our daily struggles and temptations and receive moment by moment His gracious power and presence. Rather than thinking in terms of victory, think of it as a process of growth and change and the benefits of the journey.

YOU'RE NOT ALONE

Encourage students that they aren't alone. So many think they are the only ones who struggle. Do you know of some mature students who are honest with their struggles and are walking in the light? Give them a platform and access to others. This is a huge opportunity to bring students into light and relationship and out of isolation.

Think about ways you can connect students with one another, especially in small groups. Existing Bible studies are an excellent place to start. One reason 12-step recovery groups are successful is the fellowship shared over a common experience and brokenness. Thus, the meetings and group members become a major component God uses to break people of destructive habits and set them on a course of developing more mature and healthy relationships.

Let's talk about a specific Blow-Pop at this point. There are an increasing number of resources to help people ensnared by sexual sin and addiction. For group and campus settings, two excellent resources are the companion books written by Rick James called *Flesh* (for men) and *Fantasy* (for women). They are available through Cru Press and will help move students out of isolation and into community with one another.

LEAD FROM WEAKNESS

This principle goes far deeper then simply how you lead others. Perhaps the heading should read "Live from Weakness." Some reflective questions at this point are in order: Am I living in "the light" myself (1 John 1)? Am I embracing my own weakness and brokenness so God's power might rest on me (2 Corinthians 12:7-10)? Am I embracing the fact that apart from Christ I can do nothing (John 15:5)? Am I appropriately opening up my life and my heart in my daily experience with others? Thus when it comes to leading others I am simply living out *who* I am. Ultimately it's not an issue of thinking about how I can get others to share their "uglies" with me but rather a natural dynamic borne out of a lifestyle of authenticity.

Obviously there is need for some Spirit-directed discretion here. It is inappropriate for us to share things that would unduly damage a relationship or compromise other relationships in which we are involved. I'll trust you'll be able to make those distinctions as the Spirit directs and guides.

However, as we practice authentic living, God will naturally give insight into how to enter into another's life. Then, we simply take advantage of opportunities to go deeper. Practically, it means looking for ways to empathize with our disciples and how they are feeling. Over time, you earn the right to enter in.

BEYOND ACCOUNTABILITY

Elements of what we commonly refer to as accountability are helpful in dealing with habitual sin. Accountability offers us the opportunity to come into the light and confess our sins to others. However, accountability groups or partners can take on the component of simply becoming a "tracking device" for sinful and destructive behavior. They can easily focus on the negative—avoiding certain behavior—and not on the positive of moving out of isolation and into authentic, real relationships. Accountability relationships can become somewhat artificial in nature. We might come to the group meeting, confess our sins, and yes be accepted, but there might be little interaction or connection outside of the meeting itself.

Perhaps a new paradigm is needed here. Ask yourself some tough questions: Am I willing "to do life" with this person(s)? That means understanding their dreams, passions, and calling. Am I willing to speak the truth and hear the truth from these people? Am I willing to call them in the heat of the moment and not just give a report after the fact? Am I willing to explore how my emotions often drive my behavior and what I think about God and others? Who is God calling them to be? Am I willing to walk the journey of life together? Is my heart changing? Am I growing in my desire and ability to love God and others? And, of course we need to help the people we are working with ask these same questions. This might be setting the bar high, but, again, we need to think relationally not just morally.

Finally, never give up when it comes to seeking grace/truth relationships. There may be a few false starts in developing intimate connections that will last. Sometimes group members don't mesh well. Sometimes people start strong but lose focus and commitment to the group. People graduate or move away. We need to convince others, and be convinced ourselves that it's worth the risk, and the blood, sweat and tears. As a wise campus director once said to me, "Even if the group doesn't work, you can still grow because you've trusted the Lord in stepping out of isolation and toward relationship with others."

MAKE CONNECTIONS TO EXISTING BIBLICAL MODELS OF GROWTH

Before offering a specific application let's look at how we view growth within Cru. We emphasize many facets of a person's growth strategy—the importance of God's Word, prayer, God's love and forgiveness, and worship. But, two models are at the forefront when it comes to what it means to walk with Christ and grow in our faith: the Spirit-filled life and what's been labeled as the Growth Model.

Here is a brief sketch of what these mean. First, the foundational principles of the Spirit-filled life are:

- God has given His Spirit so that we can enjoy intimacy with Him and enjoy all He has for us (John 14:16-17; 1 Corinthians 2:12)
- The believer is incapable of living the Christian life in his own strength (John 15:5). To attempt to do so leads to an inability to experience the power and presence of God on a moment-by-moment basis and an inability to consistently overcome sin and temptation (Romans 7:14-25; 1 Corinthians 3:1-3; Galatians 5:16-21).
- The Spirit-filled life is the Christ-directed life by which Christ lives His life through us in the power of the Holy Spirit (John 15)
- By faith we invite the Holy Spirit to control us thus experiencing God's presence and power moment-by moment (Romans 8:1-17; Ephesians 5:18-20; Galatians 5:22-23)

Second, in recent years we have begun to talk about heart change and character development in terms of the "Growth Model." While there are many facets to the Growth Model, its basic principles include the recognition that a person grows best in an environment of grace and truth over time (John 1:14). Thus, in our struggle we desperately need grace (acceptance) and we desperately need truth (direction). And we need to see heart and character change as a long-term journey, not an overnight fix. Our model for growth places a heavy emphasis on moving out of isolation and into *relationship* with others.

Now, let's make some connections between our discussion about our Blow-Pops and these two models for growth. The Spirit-filled life is the essence of admitting our powerlessness before God and our need to surrender to Him moment by moment. Consider a model from the world of addiction recovery. First, notice the first three steps of *Alcoholics Anonymous* adapted for our purposes:

- Admitted we were powerless over our Blow-Pop(s) and that our lives had become unmanageable
- Came to believe that God could restore us to sanity
- Made a decision to turn our will and our lives over to the care of God...

Compare these steps to John 15:5: "I am the vine, you are the branches. He who abides in me and I in Him bears much fruit, for apart from me you can do nothing." The two key words that a person hears upon entering the "Program" are that they are *powerless* ("apart from me you can do nothing") and that they need to *surrender* ("abide in me") to God on a moment-by-moment basis. Isn't this the essence of what it means to walk in the Spirit? In order for people to see behavioral change as it relates to their Blow-Pops, they need to embrace that they are utterly powerless to change on their own. God must be invited into each temptation in order for the behavior to change over time and the heart and mind to be renewed.

Admitting powerlessness actually becomes a blessing for it is the only way for God's power to be manifested in a person's life. Recall Paul's boast in 2 Corinthians 12: "He said to me, 'My grace is sufficient for you, for my power is perfected in weakness.' Therefore I will boast all the more gladly about my weaknesses ... so that Christ's power may rest on me."

Second, as mentioned above, the Growth Model emphasizes the relational dynamic that must be present for a person to grow and change. In AA participants are told that their only hope for recovery and healing is to attend a lot of meetings, make a lot of phone calls to other members, and get immersed in "The Fellowship." Developing relationships with other recovering people is essential to putting aside the "drug" (our Blow-Pops).

One of the most powerful dynamics of a healthy recovery group is the recognition that there is a level playing field. It doesn't make a bit of difference whether one enters the door of a meeting as a CEO of a Fortune 500 company or as an ex-con recently released from the local penitentiary. There is a connection between participants that everyone is powerless and our lives are a mess because of the addiction. There is a tremendous amount of acceptance based on a common struggle.

A person also receives truth, or direction, in two forms. First, there is honesty that flows from truth. If we hope to recover, we must be brutally honest about our Blow-Pop and our "sin history." In AA, people are told upon entering the Program that their chances of recovery are good if they are willing to be brutally honest about their addictive behavior and their sinful attitudes. Second, people receive the truth by "working the Program." They must work through each of the 12 steps with a sponsor (loosely compared to a discipler) who can help them navigate what it means to recover and learn to live in a healthy and mature lifestyle. They do not get coddled and told they are okay but they are presented with a strategy and the tools to grow and mature.

The goal of making comparisons to AA is not to convince you to start a 12-step group, but rather to show how a relatively successful program of recovery actually mirrors in many ways biblical principles such as walking in the Spirit and moving into relationships of grace and truth. We need to show how to apply the Spirit filled life and the Growth Model directly to a person's Blow-Pops.

PUTTING IT INTO PRACTICE

In closing, let's look at how you can take at least one practical step toward leading your group out of isolation and into relationship. First, read Rocky's story together, either in a small group or one-on-one. Feel free to embellish and edit it as needed. Then, take some time to think through some questions to help students break the ice and begin living in the light. Here are just a few suggestions:

- How would you counsel Rocky?
- What is he doing right?
- In what ways might his thinking and strategy for change be wrong?
- Can you relate to Rocky's struggle?
- Would you be willing to take the risk of coming into the light with at least one of your Blow-Pops?
- What's the most challenging thing about your struggle?
- What's the most frustrating thing about your struggle?
- How does it feel to share about your Blow-Pop?
- What one step can you take to move toward freedom and growth in this area?

At the conclusion of your discussion suggest an exercise. Give them each a Blow-Pop. Invite them to put the Blow-Pop in a conspicuous spot—next to the computer, night stand, bathroom sink. Suggest that each time they look at the Blow-Pop it would serve as an opportunity to quickly express their powerlessness to God over their named Blow-Pop and offer a brief prayer of surrender. In the morning when they look at the Blow-Pop, have it be a reminder to ask the Lord to help overcome sin and temptation *just for that day*.

Most importantly suggest to them how the Blow-Pop is not a reminder of their sin but an invitation into relationship. First, let it serve as a reminder that as they are tempted throughout today they can invite God into the temptation and into relationship with them. Second, the Blow-Pop can serve as a reminder to move into relationship with others who are walking the journey with them.

As we share the gospel, we will be most effective when we experience the reality of the gospel ourselves. What a privilege to help students embrace the gospel's power in areas where they've felt the greatest failure. What profound evidence of God's power being manifested in weakness and in the most unlikely "places."

CHAPTER TWELVE

DEAL WITH IT

Requiring Others To Take Responsibility For Their Choices

Being a mature disciple of Christ includes being responsible for our lives; living in light of eternity, and being good stewards of what God has given us. In discipleship, our disciples take more responsibility for their lives and owning their mission of seeking and saving the lost. It is a turning process from self to Christ, from self to others.

But, there is a tendency for us to short circuit growth and maturity by taking responsibility for what we are not responsible for. We have a responsibility *to* those we build, but not for them. Helping others to be responsible for their life and mission has more to do with the discipler than the one being discipled.

ALLOWING PEOPLE THE FREEDOM TO CHOOSE

It was a warm afternoon. The shadows were starting to grow longer. The sharp edges of the rough plastered homes cast zigzag shadows on the pathway. A rich young man made his way down the path seeking an ordinary man who had no home. He was looking for Jesus, an iterant teacher loved by some and loathed by others.

The rich man was a ruler, well known and well connected. He was a person of influence, a potential leader, and an insider to the Pharisees. He was seeking answers to the important questions of life, such as, "What must I do to obtain eternal life?"

The ruler was a good man. He obeyed the laws of man and God and that was his problem. He didn't realize what a failure he was. In the discussion that followed, Jesus asked him to sell all he had and give the money to the poor. The first commandment is to have no other gods.

Giving away his wealth would demonstrate he has no gods, not even money, before God. The young rich ruler was not willing to uphold the first command.

The rich young ruler came to Jesus seeking answers. But what did Jesus really offer him? Jesus said, "Sell all that you possess … and come follow me." In Matthew 4:19, Jesus said to Simon and Andrew, "Follow me." In Matthew 9:9, Jesus says to Matthew the tax collector, "Follow me." It seems that Jesus was offering the same opportunity to the rich young ruler that he offered to those who would be his intimate disciples. He offered this man an opportunity not only for eternal life but to be mentored by the Master, to be in His close circle of friends. What an opportunity.

"But when he had heard these things, he became very sad; for he was extremely rich." This potential disciple turned and walked away. Do you know the most amazing thing? Jesus let him walk. The ruler was a man of character, an insider to influential groups. But Jesus let him walk.

I suspect that most of us who seek to build disciples would not have let the rich young man walk away. I would have chased after him. I would have made excuses for him, given him some slack, not been so hard on him or tried to help him understand what he was missing. But we have no record of Jesus doing any of that, and as far as we know, this young man never came back.

Jesus never forced himself on anyone. We see this principle throughout the Bible. In the garden, Adam and Eve were about to lead all mankind into rebellion, and God let them choose. He knew the pain that would ensue from their decision—that death was to come to creation. God respected His creation so much that He allowed them to make their own decision, one that brought pain and suffering to billions of people. God respects the decisions we make. This is not an attempt to debate free will and predestination. My desire is to illustrate that when people want to sin, God does not always stop them.

Jesus respected the rich young ruler's decision to not follow Him. When we chase after potential disciples, and fail to give them a real choice, we insult them by not respecting the choices they make.

When we coerce others in the discipleship process we actually inhibit their growth. Part of God's design is that we grow by trial and error. He gives us His law, which is good. I try to keep it but fail. I learn I need a savior. He gives me instructions on how to live. I then choose to disregard God's ways. This brings pain and suffering and heartbreak into my life. The next time around I might make a better choice.

I remember helping my oldest son Zac to realize that he is responsible for himself. We live in Maine and it was a cold winter day, but not too cold. I think Zac was about three-years-old years old. All three of our sons have always loved playing outside, no matter what the thermometer says. This particular day was no exception. Zac wanted to go outside, but did not want to put his coat on. I told him, "Sure, if that is what you want to do." He was outside for about all of five minutes before he came running in complaining how cold he was. I knelt on the floor with him and held him close to me to warm his chilly little bones. I agreed with him—it really was cold out there. Then with love and compassion in my heart and voice, I said, "What do you think you could do next time?" Never, and I mean never again has he walked outside and into the cold without his coat. In fact he is more responsible than I am when we go places.

The principle is one Jesus taught and modeled—give people a choice, respect that choice, and allow natural consequences to be implemented. Then show compassion and ask what they could do differently the next time. Our disciples are responsible for their growth, not us. When we step in and take responsibility, we short-circuit God's plan for maturity.

Just recently I was working on remodeling my wife's kitchen. When the work goes well the kitchen is mine, and when it goes poorly it is hers. (Can you see how responsible I really am?) Anyway, the phone rang. It was a former student who I had discipled. He had been making some poor choices concerning alcohol and was paying a heavy consequence. I did my best to show compassion and listen. Eventually I asked, "So what do you think you need to do?" He talked about his church involvement and the need for other guy friends. I told him his solution sounded like a great idea, that he always seems to know the right thing to do and that I am proud of him. He wrote me later and thanked me for my advice. My advice? His plan for change was all his idea. Growth has a longer lasting impact when we allow others to make those connections themselves.

We have good intentions. We desire to help others grow. The problem is we want it so much that we don't accept the fact that not all Christians want to grow. We refuse to do what God does and accept no for an answer. We can see our own folly in how we recruit others to a conference, a short-term missions project, or a small group. We can love, teach, and build relationships, but the choice to participate, to be committed, to say yes and no to God is theirs.

NOT ASSUMING RESPONSIBILITY THAT BELONGS TO THEM

We not only fail to allow our disciples the opportunity to say no, but we take responsibility for them. We do or say things to pick up the slack for their own lack of engagement and responsibility. We think, process and set standards for them. Our over responsibility comes out in the age old sex and dating question, "How far should I go (sexually) with her or him." This is a no win question. I used to answer it but now I never do. If I tell them how far I think they should go, they will either use it as an excuse to go that far and when they blow it they blame me, or they write off what I say as being unreal and then do what they want anyway. To even answer the question is to start taking responsibility for their behavior and growth.

Dan was on a short-tem missions project with Cru. He built deep relationships and grew in wonderful ways. Upon return to campus he experienced a let down. The relationships were not as intense, the mission less focused. By Christmas break he had about had it with Cru. As Dan rode with me to the pharmacy one day, he poured out his heart to me about his discontent. I listened, I understood and I could have solved his problem. But I didn't. I looked over at him and said, "Dan what you said really stinks. What do you think you could do about it?"

For the next ten minutes he gave solution after solution. Finally he said, "Well it's like you said I just have to ..." I reminded him that it was not I but he who said it. He drove on with a big grin and a determination to be responsible for his life and do something about his problem.

HELPING THEM TAKE RESPONSIBILITY

> "And he said, 'Who told you that you were naked? Have you
> eaten from the tree that I commanded you not to eat from?'
> The man said, 'The woman you put here with me—she gave
> me some fruit from the tree, and I ate it.' Then the LORD
> God said to the woman, 'What is this you have done?' The
> woman said, 'The serpent deceived me, and I ate.'"
> *Genesis 3:11-13*

The attitude of irresponsibility is rampant in society. I cannot keep count of the number of male students who say to me in reference to moral failure, "God created me, He knows I am weak, He understands." Without realizing it, they are making God responsible for their sin. They might as well say, "God it's your fault I slept with this woman because you gave me these desires. You blew it God, not me." Can you imagine? Sounds like Adam in the garden. That person will never grow as long as they blame God for their choices and sin.

Whether it's God, others, circumstances, or faulty DNA, the list of reasons somehow makes one the victim with no responsibility for ensuing consequences. We need to help our disciples see, like Adam and Eve in the garden, when they are not taking responsibility for their actions and choices. This is of greater value to their growth than dealing with any specific sin or failure.

A RESPONSIBLE LIFE IS NOT LIVED BY FEELINGS
AND CIRCUMSTANCES

An increasing number of Christians live by feelings. They equate being led by the Spirit with being led by how they feel. It's difficult to disagree because feelings are subjective. Telling them that their feelings are only feelings is like saying God does not lead them.

Understanding where feelings come from helps others understand the role of feelings. Imagine two people who are dating. The guy asks the woman out for a Friday night. She says she's busy and gives no further information. He feels left hanging. Friday night he goes to the movies with the guys and sees her walk in with another man's arm around her. What does he feel now? Monday morning he bumps into her in class. She acts as if nothing is wrong. As they chat, she says, "My brother is a marine and he was in town this weekend and we went to see..." Now what does he feel? What generated the feelings?

The point is, feelings are often generated by how we interpret circumstances. When choices are made based on feelings, it's really the circumstances that are leading us and not the Spirit. Thus, circumstances become responsible, and not us. The individual escapes responsibility for growth and ends up blaming God for the life they lead.

Furthermore, we know Satan too generates circumstances. This should be enough warning for us to live by faith in the present and base our choices on what God says, not on our feelings about circumstances.

IMPARTING RESPONSIBILITY REQUIRES THAT WE GIVE UP CONTROL

Helping others become responsible for their life and mission is not all that hard. But we pay a price. We are forced to give up control of that person and their future. We must run the risk of loosing that person. We also risk being hurt. On the other hand, we gain great freedom in ministering to others. We are free to speak the truth in love and others' decisions. We are free from manipulating behavior. We are free to be ourselves. And conversely, we free those around us to grow. We free them to be real. We free them from performance, which they usually get tired of sooner or later and quit any way. We free them to experience life's consequences. And best of all we free them to grow to maturity and experience all the fullness of a life surrendered to God in brokenness and humility.

CHAPTER THIRTEEN

LET'S TALK ABOUT SIN, YOURS

The Loving Confrontation Of Sin

I have a friend who has a problem. She's struggling with a particular sin. Unfortunately she doesn't know she's struggling. She's living unaware of her sin. But I've witnessed the struggle. I've watched her and seen the ill effects it's having in her life. And I know others who've witnessed her struggle. It's been subtle and slowly built over time, but it's there. The Holy Spirit has confirmed in my spirit that she has a problem. The hard part is not knowing what to do about it.

At some point, we will observe our friends and disciples in some sort of sin. We all have blind spots. The hard part is that in true biblical community it's our job to sharpen each other just like it says in Proverbs, "As iron sharpens iron" (Proverbs 27:17, NIV). If we care about our friends, we desire for them to live in holiness. Living out biblical community is speaking the truth in love, addressing the sin we see in the lives of friends and disciples.

To be honest, I'm not sure what this would look like. I know few people who live this out, or at least live it out well. I have several personal examples of how not to do it: times when I completely botched it and came off a little self-righteous and, for lack of a better word, bitchy. Like the time in college when my friend Lisa was being driven by her emotions, not seeking truth in a particular situation. She was in a mode of what I later nicknamed "emotions in motion." So I put my arms around her and lovingly and gently listened to her pain and when the time was right, I spoke some gentle truth to her. Not quite. Remember, this was long before "WWJD" so I was left to my own walk with the Lord and spiritual maturity from which to draw. Though it's been several years, I'm pretty sure the conversation went something like this:

Lisa (crying): "I can't believe he said that to me. And then he dumped me. What do I do? I want to get him back." She cried and lit some cigarettes. She smoked when she got upset.

Me: "Lisa, get your crap together! Oh my gosh, you're driving me crazy and acting stupidly! Snap out of it and pull yourself together. Life goes on and so must we. I'll see you tomorrow morning at prayer!"

Door slamming.

Obviously, it wasn't one of my finest moments. But I have learned since then that gentleness and sensitivity go a long way. I learned to speak the truth in love or else I sound like the clanging symbol talked about in 1 Corinthians 13. Lisa recently told me that had she not known I loved her, she would have "gone all WWF on me."

That was several years ago and hopefully I've grown and matured in some areas, but I still struggle when faced with a confrontation. The question becomes, "What did Jesus do?" In this case, that actually is the right question to ask.

Let's look at an example from the life of Jesus. My favorite story in the Gospels is the one about the Samaritan woman at the well in John 4. I don't know why it's my favorite. Perhaps because I feel I can relate to the woman. She's seen as a prostitute. She's had several husbands and is still living in sin. Though I've never been a prostitute, I've no doubt spiritually prostituted myself and have replaced God temporarily with people or things that make me feel good in the moment. In some ways, I'm just like her.

In this account of the woman at the well, she is not a believer when Jesus confronts her and most of the people we would confront are believers. However, there are still a couple of lessons we can learn from Jesus' interaction with this woman.

Let me set the scene. The Samaritan woman comes to draw water at the well at a time of day when no one else would be there. Maybe she's ashamed. Maybe she's tired of being judged and scorned. Whatever the case, she chooses to draw water when she can do it alone, even if it means enduring the physical sacrifice of going to the well at noon (the sixth hour) in the hottest part of the day. The temperature could have been as high as 120 degrees.

Then there's Jesus. He's traveling from Judea to Galilee and has chosen to pass through Samaria instead of going around it like most Jews at this time would do. The Jews and the Samaritans didn't get along. After a time, Jesus got tired and decided to rest by the well while His disciples went into the city to get some food. That's when the woman walked up.

(The following passage is from *The Message*, a paraphrase translated by Eugene Peterson.)

> "Jesus said, 'Give Me a drink.'

> "The Samaritan woman, taken aback, asked, 'How come you, a Jew, are asking me, a Samaritan woman, for a drink?' (Jews in those days wouldn't be caught dead talking to Samaritans.)

> "Jesus answered, 'If you knew the generosity of God and who I am, you would be asking me for a drink, and I would give you fresh, living water.'

> "The woman said, 'Sir, you don't even have a bucket to draw with, and this well is deep. So how are you going to get this "living water"? Are you a better man than our ancestor Jacob, who dug this well and drank from it, he and his sons and livestock, and passed it down to us?'

> "Jesus said, 'Everyone who drinks this water will get thirsty again and again. Anyone who drinks the water I give will never thirst—not ever. The water I give will be an artesian spring within, gushing fountains of endless life.'

> "The woman said, 'Sir, give me this water so I won't ever get thirsty, won't ever have to come back to this well again!'

> "He said, 'Go call your husband and then come back.'

> "'I have no husband,' she said.

> "'That's nicely put: "I have no husband." You've had five husbands, and the man you're living with now isn't even your husband. You spoke the truth.'

> "'Oh, so you're a prophet! Well, tell me this: Our ancestors worshiped God at this mountain, but you Jews insist that Jerusalem is the only place for worship, right?'

> "'Believe me, woman, the time is coming when you Samaritans will worship the Father neither here at this mountain nor there in Jerusalem. You worship guessing in the dark; we Jews worship in the clear light of day. God's way of salvation

is made available through the Jews. But the time is coming—it has, in fact, come—when what you're called will not matter and where you go to worship will not matter.

"'It's who you are and the way you live that count before God. Your worship must engage your spirit in the pursuit of truth. That's the kind of people the Father is out looking for: those who are simply and honestly themselves before him in their worship. God is sheer being itself—Spirit. Those who worship him must do it out of their very being, their spirits, their true selves, in adoration.'

"The woman said, 'I don't know about that. I do know that the Messiah is coming. When he arrives, we'll get the whole story.'

"'I am he,' said Jesus. 'You don't have to wait any longer or look any further.'"

That's quite a trip to the well. The woman, not knowing this day will change the course of her life, is just going to get some water, an everyday, mundane chore. And then she meets Jesus. Jesus deals with her sin. He gives us principles we can use in discipleship, especially for confronting sin.

So, what do we learn from Jesus and this adulterous woman? Let's look at two main principles we can glean from this passage. First, we see that Jesus went out of His way to love her unconditionally. The passage actually says that Jesus "had to go through Samaria." In the original language, literally the term used is "must needs." Jesus was very intentional about meeting this woman.

Jews and Samaritans were forbidden by Jewish law to interact. Nor was it the practice of men to speak with women in public. Jesus did both. This startled the woman (and His disciples upon their return from the city). I believe this communicated that He valued her and that unlike others; He didn't believe that her sin defined her. He saw her as being made in His Father's image, but fallen.

This was a supreme act of unconditional love from Jesus. Jesus knew her past, but that did not deter His love. When we confront sin in our friends' lives, it requires intentional and unconditional love just like Jesus expressed.

Second, though Jesus knew her sin, He addressed the deeper issue. She was thirsty for living water, for abundant life. The woman's lifestyle of adultery and promiscuity was not the main issue, though Jesus didn't avoid it. He knew her behavior was an attempt to fulfill a deeper, legitimate need for real life. Her attempt to fill it with sex and relationships was at the root of her sin. Sin is an effort to meet a legitimate need by illegitimate means. Jesus knew her need and He was the only one who could fill it.

Too often in confronting sin habits in the lives of our friends and disciples we simply look at the behavior. We seek to change the behavior, but ignore the deeper need and false beliefs that drive the behavior. Without addressing the need, more than likely, the sinful behavior will continue and our friends will get discouraged and begin to feel that victory over the particular sin is hopeless.

The rest of the story about the woman at the well is about her victory and changed life. I've often heard her referred to as the first evangelist. After her encounter with Jesus, she ran back to her city leaving her water pot at the well, and told the rest of the village that she thought the Messiah had come. These were the same people who scorned and persecuted her, perhaps including her five previous husbands. They believed her and after hearing from Jesus for two days, many became followers of Him. Her story of repentance and a changed life was used for God's glory.

There is more to confronting sin than these two principles, but I maintain that these are the most important. Remember, unconditional love does not seek its own self interests (1 Corinthians 13). Check your motives. With love and gentleness, get to the deeper issue, the deeper need. It is often the case that your friend or disciple is hurting much more than you realize. Love empathizes. Hurt with your friend. Stick with her through the repentance and healing. Hold her accountable. Give your time and patience. Celebrate the victory with her. Unconditional love does all of these things.

And yes, love always brings risk. There is a chance she will not repent. And that hurts. But consider Jesus. How many times has my unrepentant heart hurt Him who so unconditionally loves me? Thanks be to God for His grace that He lavishes upon us. He has already taken the biggest risk of all by loving each one of us.

Of course, nothing I've said will help you get over your fear of the confrontation. Confrontation is not easy. And nothing I've said will tell you what to say when you're faced with confronting a dear friend or disciple. My advice is to pray and go forth in the power of the Holy Spirit. Pour out your angst to Jesus. Beseech Him for wisdom and words and courage. Ask Him for a quite and gentle spirit. Pray that your friend will repent. Just pray.

I'm still not sure how to proceed with my friend. Her sin, I think, will require some professional counseling that is way beyond me. But my heart hurts as I see her struggle. I will choose to go out of my way to love her unconditionally. I will intentionally communicate love to her. I will listen closely to her hoping to discern the deeper issue. And I will pray desperately for her and for me. I pray for her eventual victory. And I pray it all will be for God's own glory. After all, that is what it's all about.

A BENDING OF THE WILL

Submission: What Americans Hate About The Gospel

One of the most unattractive character qualities in someone who claims to follow Christ is rebellion toward authority.

I know, I know. In our American society, having authority issues is often a quality to be emulated, not avoided. Just for fun, let's list all of our favorite Rock songs that tout respect for leaders, submission, and honoring our parents: _____ , that should be enough space. Well, as believers, we should be different.

Our mandate in the campus ministry is to raise up a generation of students who will stand against the culture and honor God and His commands. We say it all the time: "The college students of today are the leaders of tomorrow." But our disciples will never be ready to lead and give authority until they have first learned to submit and sit under authority.

Rebellion isn't always overt. If someone has trouble submitting to authority it may manifest in any number of ways: as pride, lack of teachability, unwillingness to be a team player, or a judgmental spirit. This phrase comes to mind: "This self-will, characterized by an attitude of active rebellion or passive indifference, is evidence of what the Bible calls sin."

But when someone refuses to submit to earthly authority, the root issue is the most deadly of all. At the heart level, they are demonstrating an unwillingness to submit to the authority of God. We need to learn to trust that God has put every authority in place as part of His sovereign plan for the world. When we obey our earthly authorities, we are demonstrating our faith in God's character, and displaying the glory of His authority over the whole earth.

The following are suggestions of ways we can cultivate hearts of submission in those we disciple.

SUBMISSION IS NOT A FOUR-LETTER WORD, IT'S TEN ACTUALLY

One of the reasons submission is not a positive virtue within our culture is that it smacks of inequality, which if you haven't noticed is not highly valued in America.

Therefore, as you teach this virtue or correct this sin, underscore that submission is actually based on equality. Submission, choosing to order my will under another, is only a virtue if it is footed on equality. Following someone or submitting to their leadership because you think they are better than you is not really submission; it's a low self esteem. If they are superior, submission is not a virtue, but common sense. However, choosing to submit to someone that you see as an equal, or even less qualified than you, truly is a virtue for you are submitting out of respect for God's establishment of leadership, not their qualifications.

The foundation for our submission is found within the Trinity: "Each of you should look not only to your own interests, but also to the interests of others. Your attitude should be the same as that of Christ Jesus: Who, being in very nature God, did not consider equality with God something to be grasped, but made himself nothing, taking the very nature of a servant, being made in human likeness" (Philippians 2:4-7).

Few would question whether the persons of the Trinity are equal. The passage clearly states that though Jesus is God, He didn't regard His position or title something that needed to be grasped or clung to. He willingly relinquished it submitting His will to the Father. Again, Jesus' submission is seen as virtue in light of equal standing within the Trinity.

EXPLAIN WHY GOD VALUES SUBMISSION

"Slaves, submit yourselves to your masters with all respect, not only to those who are good and considerate, but also to those who are harsh. For it is commendable if a man bears up under the pain of unjust suffering because he is conscious of God" (1 Peter 2:18-19).

The value of submission is that there is no earthly reason why we should do it. If a person is wrong, a lousy leader, or lacks the capacity to lead, why should we listen to them? Humanly speaking we follow and listen to someone based on competency. But submission is not worldly wisdom. It reflects a belief that God has sovereignly put our leaders in their appointed place, and that we trust Him to place us in leadership when He so desires. We don't need to seize control.

Submission also seeks the opportunity afforded to worship God: response to our leadership becomes a venue to show our respect for

God's ultimate leadership. And according to the above passage, the worse the leadership, the greater the opportunity we have to express our worship and reverence for God.

The other reason why submission is so highly valued by God, and should be by us, is that the heart of submission is humility. Humility seeks to *do* what is right, not *be* right. Humility is an accurate appraisal of our own failings and weaknesses. And humility is always other-seeking, vested of personal interest. The main reason we don't like to submit is that it may not be in our personal interest to do so. The humble heart waits for God to bless and to lift up, and doesn't seize or commandeer the process.

UNEARTHING AMERICAN VALUES

If we characterized the American mindset, we would conclude that humility and submission are downright un-American. They are. And bound together with humility and submission is another cultural vice, interdependence. Autonomy is of the highest magnitude in the America psyche.

John Wesley wrote to the church in America before the Revolutionary War suggesting that if the issue for war was oppression than why does America still have slaves? "I wonder," said Wesley, "if the real issue is autonomy, not oppression. Americans just don't want to be led by anyone." And the same is true today. This is one reason why we have 21,000 denominations in America. Rather than submit, we cry oppression, stage a revolution, and come out from under the authority to become our own authority.

It should be obvious by now, why submission is such a difficult subject. It is deeply entrenched in ideas and values contrary to our culture. Submission digs at the roots of some fairly significant cultural baggage, which is one of the best reasons for addressing the subject.

SUBMISSION A PASSIVE FORM OF LEADERSHIP

A last perspective that I have found useful in helping my disciples see the beauty in submission (for to most it seems quite unattractive) is to explain that submission is really a form of leadership. In the 1960s, how did Martin Luther King bring about social reform? It was through sit-ins, boycotts and non-violent marches. Instead of using violence, coercion and manipulation, he employed passive tactics of leadership.

When we submit and support our leaders, it creates a pull of gravity in the seat of leadership causing the leader to want to lead. One of the ways we lead, as followers, is to submit. It is a passive tactic, the one employed by the follower.

TAKE THEM TO THE WORD AND SHOW THEM HOW GOD FEELS ABOUT REBELLION

The place to go now is God's Word to provide support and instruction. Let's first look at how God sees rebellion. Because our culture says the sin of rebellion is no big deal, it's tempting to blow it off, in ourselves and in others, and move on. But the Bible speaks differently. In 1 Samuel 15:22, the Lord says, "Rebellion is as the sin of divination." Rebellion and divination are equally serious because they both illegitimately usurp God's ordained leadership structure and seek to go around it.

When we attempt to place ourselves above or outside God's ordained authority, we are following the example of Satan. Isaiah records that Satan said in his heart, "I will ascend to heaven; I will raise my throne above the stars of God...I will make myself like the Most High" (Isaiah 14:13-14). To punish Satan, God expelled him from heaven in disgrace, and consumed him in fire, sending him to a fitting end (Ezekiel 28:16-19).

These examples may seem extreme, but I place them here because they show the seriousness of rebellion—this is not exaggeration or forgetting to say grace before dinner.

TAKE THEM TO THE WORD AND SHOW THEM HOW GOD FEELS ABOUT SUBMISSION

In contrast to Satan is God's son, Jesus. In Philippians 2, the apostle Paul writes that even though Jesus was actually God, He "did not consider equality with God something to be grasped, but made himself nothing, taking the very nature of a servant....He humbled himself and became obedient..." God honored Jesus' humility and submission by exalting Him "to the highest place."

The passage also states that "our attitude should be the same as that of Christ Jesus." If Jesus submitted Himself to authority, certainly we as creatures can do the same.

HELP YOUR DISCIPLES RECOGNIZE THE AUTHORITIES GOD HAS DESIGNATED IN VARIOUS AREAS OF THEIR LIVES

The major areas to think through are:

THOSE WHO SUBMIT	THOSE WHO ARE IN AUTHORITY
Citizens	Government officials and laws (Romans 13:1-7; 1 Timothy 2:1-3; Titus 3:1-2; 1 Peter 2:13-17)
Church members	Church leadership and policies (Acts 16:45; 1 Timothy 5:17-19; Hebrews 13:17; 1 Peter 5:1-6)
Children	Parents and rules of the home (Ephesians 6:1-3; Colossians 3:20)
Wives	Husbands (Ephesians 5:22-24; Colossians 3:18; Titus 2:3-5; 1 Peter 3:1-6)
Workers/servants	Bosses and policies at work (Ephesians 6:5-8; Colossians 3:22-24; Titus 2:9-10; 1 Peter 2:18-24)
All believers	God and the Bible and its commands (Psalm 119; Matthew 28:18-20; John 14:15-24; Hebrews 12:7-11; James 4:5-10)

Help them think through how they can pray for their authorities, proactively honor them, cultivate hearts of thankful submission toward them, and more joyfully obey them. Come alongside them in prayer for difficult struggles.

TAKE THEM TO THE WORD AND SHOW THEM HOW TO RE-SPECTFULLY DISAGREE WITH THOSE IN AUTHORITY

There are times when those in authority over us are in the wrong.

However, this still does not give us the right to rebel. The Bible gives several examples of God's servants who respectfully stood up to their erring authorities. Acting against Egyptian law, Moses' parents did not kill him when he was born, but hid him for three months (Exodus 2; Hebrews 11:23). Esther approached King Xerxes uninvited (a capital crime) in order to keep him from wiping out her people (book of Esther). Shadrach, Meshach, and Abednego refused to worship false gods, and Daniel prayed openly to the Lord (Daniel 3 and 6). Peter and the apostles refused to stop preaching the gospel (Acts 5).

Let it be clear that these examples were of rulers who were giving orders that directly opposed God's laws. Most of us are tempted to rebel for things like having personality differences or a disagreement over ministry philosophy with our local leader, or being inconvenienced by a policy handed down to us. While usually there are venues for us to voice our disagreement or displeasure, the principle is that we should always do this with a heart attitude of humility and respect. And if our authority does not change his or her mind, we must willingly continue to submit.

There are two beautiful biblical examples of men who withstood unjust authority without disagreement: David, whose authority (Saul) tried to unlawfully kill him, and Jesus, whose earthly authority (the Roman government) did kill him. David even openly repented when he was tempted twice to mock or harm Saul (1 Samuel 24 and 26), and took great pains to honor Saul publicly (2 Samuel 1 and 9).

REMIND THEM OF THE BENEFITS OF BEING UNDER AUTHORITY

While some authorities might be unpleasant or even incompetent, remember it is God who has placed them in our lives. God designed the world's authority structure to protect us, as well as to provide for us. Being submissive to authority can bring a great sense of peace and rest to our lives. (It allows us a break from trying to run the world!) At the very least, God is using each of our positions of submission, even the painful ones, to conform us to the image of His Son.

We need to constantly guard our heart against the temptation to feel prideful or resentful toward our authority. In my life, I have often been tempted to think I could do a better job than those in authority over me. Then when I reach that level of authority myself, I soon realize the position was much harder than I thought! The more authority I have been granted in my life, the more grateful I have become for the authorities, past and present, God has placed in my life.

The work of bearing authority is difficult, and one day leaders will give an account to God for how they cared for those entrusted to them

(Hebrews 13:16-17). We should do all we can to make our authority's burden lighter, not heavier.

JUSTIFYING REBELLION

As you are in the scripture I think it's important to mention that a major obstacle to submission within the church is that every issue of rebellion can be framed in such a way as to seem like it is a compromise of the gospel. This provides a theological justification for not submitting. Few issues are ever about compromising the gospel, though we can honestly come to believe that they are. Unless your leadership is telling you to worship Satan, it's usually safe to assume that the gospel isn't in jeopardy.

HELP THEM TO RECOGNIZE DISRESPECT

We live in a culture saturated with disrespect, so much so that we don't recognize it when we see it, or worse, do it. Your disciples may honestly be unaware of being disrespectful of leadership. Be diligent to gently point out to them when they have stepped over the line. If their heart is good, and you confront graciously, they will respect you for setting boundaries.

EXAMINE YOUR OWN HEART, AND THEN MODEL A LIFE OF SUB-MISSION AND HONOR TOWARD AUTHORITY YOURSELF

We need to start with ourselves and model godly submission to authority, if we want to see changes in our disciples. The older I get, the more I become increasingly aware of my own carelessness toward authority at best, and rebelliousness toward authority at worst. Although outwardly I may not look or seem rebellious, I know that deep down I struggle with not wanting to give control of my life over to someone else.

Here are some areas I have personally struggled with over the years:

> Grumbling about, or simply not following, Cru policies I don't like, whether handed down from the local, regional, or national level.

> Bad-mouthing or telling jokes about a governor or President whose political agenda I disagree with.

Not believing the best about Cru leadership, or talking about them behind their backs.

Not obeying traffic laws, such as the speed limit.

Trying to make end runs around placement decisions to try to get them changed.

Ask the Lord to reveal to you specific sins of rebellion in your own life. Confess your sin to Him, and to those you have sinned against, if necessary. Ask the Lord to show you how you can grow in this area.

MOST IMPORTANTLY, PRAY FOR YOUR DISCIPLES

Ultimately, rebellion is a heart issue, and can only be changed from the inside out. Pray for your disciples to be constantly filled with the Holy Spirit, who will lead them into lives of humble submission and joy.

Ministry &

Application

SYNTHETIC EVANGELISM

What's Old And New In Evangelism Discipleship

There is probably no topic more foundational to our discipleship as a ministry than evangelism. I'm not sure anyone is entirely worthy of the task to write a complete treatise on evangelism. As a long time regional director, my observations are not based on personal insight or ministry but that of many others: their trials and failures, innovation and stagnancy, good, bad and ugly. This is the most valuable perspective I can offer.

In an innovative and evangelistic ministry like Cru, you would assume that we would be on the cutting edge of evangelism strategies and philosophy. We are not, and for good reason. Most campus directors grow to despise the latest fads, not wanting to restructure their entire ministry only to find that the flavor of the month has changed—"Hey! Everyone in the emergent church is now doing scented worship evangelism. Peach flavor, I think." Staff have a mission to accomplish and cannot afford, even momentarily, sideways energy that might turn out to be a fruitless rabbit trail. So, in campus evangelism, we have a somewhat lethargic rate of adaptation. In many ways, this has worked for us, but change has been accruing nonetheless. How can it not?

The great thinker Georg Hegel's philosophy of history was simple: thesis, antithesis, and synthesis. Someone introduces a revolutionary viewpoint, someone else propagates a reactionary one, and eventually a happy median is found—evangelism should be initiative, it should be relational, maybe it should be both. The truth of this template can be found in most issues.

As I look at evangelism, on campus I think we are moving toward synthesis, where people are taking the best of the old and the most effective of the new and creating thoughtful models for campus evangelism. The synthesis looks different on variegated campuses but what follows is a general picture of that synthesis, and as a result a blueprint for discipling others in evangelism.

THE EVANGELISM MODEL

The evangelism model has begun to permeate the thinking of our campus staff and there is much within this model that could be integrated into our personal discipleship. But the major adaptation that has been made and has had the greatest impact on discipleship is what Keith Davy has termed the *modes* of evangelism.

According to the Bible, there are three major modes by which people come to Christ: the body mode which speaks to people coming to Christ through the corporate witness of the believing community; the natural mode which describes relational evangelism; and the ministry mode which describes initiative evangelism outside of existing relationships.

Before we had this ministry model we were pushed into an either/or bind as it related to relational and initiative evangelism. The model has freed us up to teach our disciples the biblical necessity, and role of each one, and to encourage them to engage at some level in all three.

This is a dramatic shift in how we disciple people in doing evangelism. It has shown us the need to train our disciples in how to do each mode. Here are some of the shifts and integration I have observed taking place in evangelism discipleship (teaching your disciple to do evangelism) under these three modes.

1. BODY WITNESS

> "When the body of Christ is gathered together and functioning, as it should, it has the potential of being a powerful witness to unbelievers who are exposed to it. The proper functioning body is not defined by the activity or setting. Rather it is a body that is building itself up in Christ through speaking the truth in love (Ephesians 4:15-16). We have (or should have) in our communities what an unbeliever truly desires—love and truth. Whether the gathering is a formal activity or an informal setting, both elements of love and truth can have a profound influence on unbelievers." (from the Evangelism Model)

Fall Retreats

I spoke recently at a fall retreat for a school in the Midwest. The first night I asked the obligatory question "Are there any non-Christians in the audience?" Obligatory, because the response I always get is a couple. I was told, in this case, that anywhere from 15 to 20 percent of those at the retreat were non-Christians.

Throughout the weekend I heard reports of decisions (unfortunately none of them tied to my speaking) being made at proportions ridiculously high: somewhere close to half of the non-Christians. You just don't see this many people trust Christ in a day on campus, but if you're at a fall retreat, a really good one, the question is, "How could you not see results such as this?" The worship, the *outstanding* biblical messages, the relationships, and the godly character of the believers are absolutely compelling.

But this is an article on discipleship not evangelism, so here is the point. Those students had been taught to think about evangelism in the three relational modes, and they were well aware of what they were doing in bringing their non-Christian friends to the retreat. Advertising and invitations went out far beyond the boundaries of their Cru membership. In fact more people came to the retreat than were attending their weekly meeting.

This was a product of good discipleship on body evangelism.

Weekly Meetings

On another campus I visited, the weekly meeting was devoted to an evangelistic topic. Nothing new there. But here's something that was different. Each new person who came got a $5 coupon to Starbucks (about enough to buy a Starbuck's cookie). They were told to use it that night to go out with the person who had brought them and discuss the topic. This tactic helped disciple the students in the ways of body evangelism.

Small groups

At another university, the small group ministry had shifted to cell groups. But the significant shift I witnessed did not revolve around the concept of the cell. It was a change in the way students thought about evangelism. There was an excitement, or at the very least a desire, to invite their friends to the Bible study. Regardless of what type of small group system is employed on a campus, the value—because of the power of the body—of students being able to invite other students to a local small group, or social, within their dorm is an important one. Our initiative efforts are just not successful enough to be able to throw away small groups as a point of entry for non-Christians.

Personal Discipleship

One staff person I know has her disciples write down on a calendar, where and when they will be applying the three different modes of evangelism. For example, one week, she may challenge her disciples to invite their friends to fall retreat. Another week they may follow up some surveys. This is intentional discipleship based on the modes of evangelism. This is different. This is synthesizing the best of what's new in evangelism and integrating it to the level of one-on-one discipleship.

2. NATURAL WITNESS

As believers live their daily lives, they naturally inter-
sect the lives of countless unbelievers. These natural
relationships can be intimate and long-term (such
as family and long-term friends) or casual and brief
(schoolmates, acquaintances, even people they will
only meet once). The key in witness is not the duration of relationship or depth of intimacy. Rather, it is
the context as a natural relationship. That context will
shape the opportunity to witness. (from the *Evangelism
Model*)

If God is at work in the unbeliever's life and the believer
is a usable witness, then God can work through these
natural connections in powerful ways.

This is a helpful description of natural evangelism, and I applaud the use of the word "schoolmates" as I haven't heard it for 30 years. Natural evangelism is perhaps the most effective mode for students, or anyone, to do evangelism, which is why our ministry has recently given it emphasis. But emphasis does not equal training and the bleak reality is we have not taught our disciples how to effectively carry this out—at least not to the point where large percentages of students are seeing at least one of their friends trust Christ. For you would assume, if they were actively sharing with their friends, at least one person they know would want to follow Christ.

And so I have asked myself the question, "Self, what tools do we have available to train our disciples to be more effective evangelists with their friends?"

CoJourners
One answer is found in the new *CoJourners* material which includes a small group equipping pack (seven or eight minute training segments) and a daily *CoJourners* devotional. *CoJourners* is designed to train students to effectively witness to their friends. The challenge of new

ministry tools is that unless we were discipled in the use of them, we simply don't have the time to master a new method. The other problem with new tools is that it can be difficult to determine where they fit into our overall strategy of evangelism and discipleship. So make this mental note: *CoJourners* goes in the file folder for training for natural/relational evangelism. Whether you use the equipping pack in your small groups or give your disciple the daily devotional, *CoJourners* is going to be a significant part of training your disciples in natural evangelism.

E-mail

In a recent campus visit, I met a student who was sharing with me something meaningful to her, but I have selfishly forgotten what it was. I do remember this: at some point in the conversation she mentioned that she had e-mailed an article from everystudent.com to her friends and family, with the addendum, "E-mail me back and tell me what you think." People have probably known about everystudent.com for years, but I made a mental note that this was significant in discipling students how to share Christ with their friends. It is relational evangelism at the lowest possible level of effort, risk, and required training. What do you have to know to do this? It is a simple and effective way, not only to send spiritual content, but also broach the topic of Christianity for discussion.

If I were leading a small group, I would make as an application some week that everyone find an article they wouldn't be embarrassed to send to their friends, and have them do just that with an attached note like this woman's. I'd have the group praying all week for the people they were sending the article to, and have everyone share the following week what happened. Of course, in my mind I do all kinds of imaginary ministry. And in my mind they are always wonderfully effective. Imaginary ministry is the key to being a Regional Director.

Testimony

Synthesis involves mixing the old with the new—something old, something new, something borrowed, something blue. And something we have always done well is taught people how to share their testimony. In the original ministry context, testimonies were used most often in large group meetings. But a testimony has its natural application in relational evangelism, sharing the gospel from the impregnable position of "this is my story, so I can say anything I want without incurring your judgment—so shut up and listen." It certainly is a more natural way to talk about Christ within the context of a relationship. What we need to do is invest more time to help our disciples become proficient in doing this in the context of a conversation. Giving people a worksheet is not enough. Role playing conversations I would say is a bare minimum.

Demonstrate how to bridge and alter their testimony from different conversational points. Our disciples must become adept at sharing their story sprouting from an existing conversation.

One-Verse Evangelism
If there was a missing link in the process of relational evangelism it would have to be the ability to communicate the gospel message without having to go through a booklet (not that there is anything wrong with doing so). There are a variety of ideas for how this can or should be done. The approach that fits well with our ministry is what has been labeled one-verse evangelism—training on how to share the gospel message from one verse: a verse we are more than familiar with, Romans 6:23:

> "For the wages of sin is death, but the gift of God is eternal
> life in Christ Jesus our Lord."

Besides training our disciples to share *Knowing God Personally* and their testimony, I feel this is an invaluable ministry tool with which to equip them. Without use of a booklet, and with only a pen and paper, they need to be able to communicate the gospel message clearly and comfortably. This is easy to teach in a discipleship appointment or small group. The key is to let them do it several times on their own until they've mastered it. I've attached a basic training sheet on one-verse evangelism.

Being Insiders
Finally, in the category of best of the old is discipling students to remain insiders on their campus. Twenty years ago almost every upper classman wrestled with the decision to remain living on campus in order to keep or acquire relational networks for the gospel (we also walked 10 miles to school each day). Today, students wrestle with which off campus monastery or convent to join. I strongly feel if we are serious about reaching the campus with the gospel, pulling out our best trained and most committed students from the campus community is not an acceptable option. You can't forbid it, but you can disciple people away from it, helping them to see the importance of maintaining a web of non-Christian relationships.

3. MINISTRY WITNESS

> "There are many people (in most settings, the majori-
> ty of people) who are neither near enough to a body of
> believers to be impacted by body witness, nor in rela-

tionship or contact with any healthy believer to be im-
pacted by their natural witness. The only way these individuals can be reached is through the ministry mode
of evangelism." (from the *Evangelism Model*)

What we have always done well as a ministry is to teach our disciples
to share the gospel, using a book like *Knowing God Personally*. Ideas
come and go about how to tweak the effectiveness of ministry evangelism, but it should be said that we do an awful lot right—Heck, at least
we do it.

This tried and true method of evangelism is only enhanced in teaching your disciples about the different relational modes. In the past,
false dichotomies have been erected, pitting relational against ministry
evangelism. It's always hard to argue with a holistic philosophy. We
teach the biblical foundation for each mode, give each their due credit,
but continue to plow through to the irrefutable logic that many people
on campus simply do not have a close relationship with a non-Christian. Thus we must engage in initiative evangelism. When you teach all
three, it is more difficult to object to any one kind.

What seems to be new is the current conversation about how the gospel should be presented to a postmodern audience. The *Knowing GOd
Personally* booklet, for all of its flaws, is a transferable method that is
simple to use and we can all sleep better at night knowing our disciples
have at least mastered one tool that accurately explains the gospel. The
third millennium did not mark the expiration date on any of the four
principles.

Backstory
But someone, mainly Keith Davy, has done some of the synthesis on
postmodern thinking and how the *Knowing God Personally* might be
presented more effectively to the current audience. The result is the
Backstory booklet. The gospel is given greater context by the addition
of three more panels or points beginning with the relationship of God
and man in Genesis. The gospel follows this relational theme ultimately
leading to Jesus and how He has reconciled us.

Here is how the gospel flows:

Intimacy
God created man for intimacy with God and with each
other (Genesis passages).

Betrayal
Life was forfeited and intimacy marred. Sin now affects
us all.

Anticipation
God gave hope in the promise of a coming Savior.

Pursuit
God's sends us His Son, Jesus.

Sacrifice
In an act of love, Jesus died for us

Invitation
Forgiveness is a free gift we are invited to receive, by accepting Jesus' invitation.

Reunion
Those responding to the invitation have eternal life, a relationship with God forever.

Context is knowledge power, and relationship is emotional power. *Backstory* provides more of both. If this tool can be mastered, it is a useful adaptation of *Knowing God Personally* to today's audience. On the lowest level of implementation, if your disciple were simply to give the booklet to someone, that individual would probably comprehend the gospel message better than if he had received a copy of *Knowing God Personally*. I think that's fair to say.

In discipleship, I would introduce *Backstory* once a person has mastered sharing *Knowing God Personally*. This is still standard training throughout Cru (summer projects, etc). I would not just give it to them, but I would explain it in the context I just described and then walk them through the seven steps so they can see how they hang together. It is important for your disciple to understand the difference between the two booklets, and why *Backstory* follows the direction it does. If the context for new tools is not explained, they add confusion to ministry, rather than aid.

EveryStudent.com
I begin with this irrefutable fact. More than 6,000 students indicated decisions to trust Christ on the everystudent.com website, comprising a large portion of the total number of decisions for Christ reported by the campus ministry last year. If something is working well, you need to find a way to incorporate it into your evangelism discipleship.

The synthesis of media, in my mind, has been effectively accomplished at James Madison University. They do three important things. First, they disciple their students in how the site works and walk them through the content. They actually bring up on screen the website in their weekly meeting. They don't just say, "Hey, check out this site." This is not discipleship. We must teach people how to use these tools, and to do so, we must invest the time to become proficient ourselves.

Second, they let the students write their own ads. Anyone can write an ad (used guitar for sale—see did it!), everyone would kind of like to, and anyone can make it look half-way decent with a computer and a font other than Times Roman. Spending virtually no money, students would print out their ads and put them up in their dorms: new ones all of the time. The site has recorded hundreds and hundreds of hits from JMU students alone.

Third, if you are going to invest the money in running an ad in the school paper, make it worth your while. At Easter or Christmas you can run an ad, unapologetically full of gospel content. The season provides a temporary ban on religious bigotry—go wild. Conservatively, a thousand students will read through the gospel message in an attempt to ward off on-campus boredom. That ain't bad. You may never see who trusts Christ, but it's an issue of stewardship. Everyone should hear the gospel at some point in their four years on campus. And, if the Holy Spirit is on the job, we can safely assume that some students will come to know Christ through the ad. So what if they never show up in statistics or a weekly meeting. I mean that, really, so what?

Hopefully that rather broad brush of the current synthesis of evangelism strategies and philosophy will help inform, in some practical ways, how to teach and train your disciples to do evangelism.

CHAPTER SIXTEEN

SPIRIT FILLED TEACHING

We Can't Afford Not To Get This Right

Let's begin with an honest evaluation. For a ministry committed to teaching the Spirit-filled life, we've done a pretty lousy job of explaining it. As a young Christian, I sat through seminars of people making chocolate milk, illustrating the influence of the Spirit, and always left wondering what the heck I was being asked to do. Worse, *I* made chocolate milk in student seminars not knowing what the heck I was saying.

We are all agreed that there is nothing more foundational to the Christian life than reliance upon the indwelling power of the Holy Spirit. For it is the other half of the gospel message: Christ died for our sins but was resurrected and desires to live His resurrected life through us. He accomplishes this by proxy: the indwelling third person of the Trinity, the Holy Spirit.

I thought it most productive, in helping us disciple others in the ministry of the Holy Spirit, to give greater background and context to our understanding of the Holy Spirit's ministry, for a better understanding of these concepts will elevate the level of our teaching.

THE OLD TESTAMENT CONTEXT

One of the great books of our time on the ministry of the Holy Spirit is Gordon Fee's *Paul, the Spirit, and the People of God*. In one of his chapters, Fee provides the Old Testament context for the anticipated fulfillment of God's promise to send His Spirit. I think without this context the full impact of the notion that God's presence indwells us will always evade us. Here is a brief summary of that history:

Out of Egypt

It's about 1446 B.C. and as the Israelites venture out of Egypt to find the land God has promised to them, they stop at Mount Sinai where God's presence dwells. This fact was impressed upon the people by rumblings, smoke, and fire that came from the mountain. At Mount Sinai, God tells Moses, the Israelites' leader, His presence will leave the mountain and He will go with them to the Promised Land. God reveals to Moses that a portable temple known as the Tabernacle, or the Tent of Meeting, will house His presence on the journey. Chapter upon painful chapter describes the exact instructions for making this Tabernacle.

What distinguishes this wandering nation from all nations of the world is that the presence of God goes with them everywhere. They will be known as the "People of His Presence." Equally symbolic, as they camp along the journey, the Tabernacle is always erected in the midst of the tribes and clans of Israel—God's presence is in their midst. When they first erect the Tabernacle, they know immediately that God's presence is in their midst. In Exodus 40:34-35, we read:

> "Then the cloud covered the Tent of Meeting, and the glory
> of the LORD filled the tabernacle. Moses could not enter the
> Tent of Meeting because the cloud had settled upon it, and
> the glory of the LORD filled the tabernacle."

Was it always that smoky in the Tabernacle? No, this happened only at the inaugural erection of the Tabernacle. God gave them a visual aid that His presence was truly among them. It was quite a thing to conceive that the God of the universe *tabernacled* or *dwelled* among men.

The Temple

Remember that the Tabernacle was like a portable Temple. It was constructed like an enormous tent—God under the big top. God's place of dwelling among the Israelites would remain in this portable housing for about 450 years until King David's son, Solomon, built the actual Temple—a more permanent structure.

It's now about 980 B.C. God tells Solomon to build the Temple in Jerusalem as the permanent dwelling place for the Lord's presence among His people. Solomon builds it, and on Inauguration Day, or the day of dedication for the Temple, the same amazing phenomenon happens again. Once again, there is no doubt that God's presence has filled the Temple.

> "When Solomon finished praying, fire came down from
> heaven and consumed the burnt offering and the sacrifices,
> and the glory of the LORD filled the temple. The priests

> could not enter the temple of the LORD because the glory of
> the LORD filled it. When all the Israelites saw the fire com-
> ing down and the glory of the LORD above the temple, they
> knelt on the pavement with their faces to the ground, and
> they worshiped and gave thanks to the LORD, saying, 'He is
> good; his love endures forever.'" *2 Chronicles 7:1-3*

The Temple was the hub of Israel. It was the symbol of God's presence dwelling among them. Everyone traveled to the Temple several times of year, because this is where the presence of God dwelled.

Here's where the story could get confusing. Several hundred years later (about 600 B.C.), due to continued disobedience to God, the Israelites are exiled from their land by the invading Babylonians. Jerusalem is ransacked and Solomon's Temple is demolished.

In their exile, preachers, called prophets, tell the Israelites that they will once again be restored to their land and that they will again enjoy the presence of God in their midst. Sure enough, 70 years later, through God's miraculous provision, the Israelites are enabled to return to their homeland, Israel. Their first order of business is to rebuild the Temple, the symbol of God's presence.

The Rebuilt Temple

So, they rebuild the Temple (now about 520 B.C.), but with little resources. It's a pretty scrawny looking Temple. It looks more like a movie theatre than a house of worship. Still, they dedicate their new Temple just as Solomon did. But, low and behold ... nothing. No sparks. No smoke. Nothing.

This disappointment, along with more messages from the prophets, inspired a national expectation that there was another Temple yet to come. A future Temple, more glorious than even Solomon had con-structed would eventually be built. When the Messiah came, He would be the one to rebuild the Temple and God's Spirit would be poured out in an abundance that they had never experienced or could imagine (Haggai 2).

The Coming of Christ

We now fast forward to 32 A.D. Israel is once more dominated by a for-eign power, the Roman Empire. Jesus, the Messiah, had come. He was crucified and resurrected. Many probably wondered if he had been the Messiah, why was there no new Temple? Why were the Israelites not liberated? Why was God's Spirit not poured out in overflowing measure like the prophets had foretold? But then we read in the second chapter of Acts:

"When the day of Pentecost came, they were all together in one place. Suddenly a sound like the blowing of a violent wind came from heaven and filled the whole house where they were sitting. They saw what seemed to be tongues of fire that separated and came to rest on each of them. All of them were filled with the Holy Spirit and began to speak in other tongues as the Spirit enabled them." *Acts 2:1-4*

Throughout the rest of Acts there is a new dynamic. We read "and the Spirit told them to go here," and "the Spirit led them there," and the disciples were "filled with the Spirit," and "spoke in the Spirit." People were being healed, the disciples preached powerful messages, and people believed in Christ. It was apparent that God's presence was once again in the midst of His people. His protection, wisdom, direction, and power were all back, and in ways more dramatic than ever experienced in the history of God's people.

Now, if you're a Jewish Christian—like the disciples—you'd be ecstatic. The anticipation of the powerful coming of the Holy Spirit throughout the Old Testament is a hallmark of the Messiah's reign. You would finally be able to tell your neighbors, "Hah! Told you so! Jesus is the Messiah." But you would also have one big question: Where in the world is the new glorious Temple the Messiah was going to build to house His Presence?

Then, it dawns on you—you are the new temple. God's presence dwells within you. His Holy Spirit is inside of you! .And, well, you freak out. How could you ever sin again with His Holy presence within you?

Now, I know that was a terribly long story. But, you simply must appreciate this amazing truth: God dwells in you. And, if we need to drudge up 1,500 years of Jewish history to appreciate it, it is well worth it.

Go through these passages with your disciples so they can grasp this ungraspable truth. It also makes it clear why Paul, in dealing with sexual morality, sees as the greatest scandal that we would bring such impurity into the new house of the Lord.

INFLUENCE CONTEXT

History provides a helpful context, but it doesn't answer the most pressing question, "How does the Holy Spirit actually exert control over our lives?" It's kind of like finding yourself married without the clear understanding of how two separate wills are suppose to function as one—how do we both control the checkbook? Scripture gives us an instructional analogy I've found useful in helping others understand the dynamics of living a life under the influence of the Spirit.

In Ephesians 5:18, it says, "Do not get drunk on wine, which leads to debauchery, instead be filled with the Spirit."

This is a commonly quoted verse in connection with the Spirit-filled life. But, one is compelled to ask, "What does getting drunk on wine have to do with being filled with the Spirit?" The link between drinking and being filled with the Holy Spirit seems to be the concept of control or influence. On this account they are similar. Contrasted, however, drinking alcohol is a counterfeit to the reality found in the Spirit.

Because the way and manner by which the Holy Spirit influences us is somewhat mysterious, or at least not easily measurable, the parallel of drinking might offer us a backdoor into a better understanding of how the Holy Spirit exerts His control within our lives.

What It Looks Like to Be Filled With the Spirit
Interestingly, this is not the first place that drinking and the Holy Spirit occupy the same passage of Scripture. Acts 2 contains the story of the Holy Spirit's first descent upon the church. As onlookers witnessed the effects of the Spirit upon the believers in the crowd, they become convinced that the Christians were actually drunk. Peter stands up and explains, "These men are not drunk, as you suppose" (Acts 2:15).

So what is it about being filled with the Spirit that would cause people to suspect that a large keg party was underway? One manifestation would be the open display of love. As alcohol removes inhibitions, those intoxicated are much freer with their emotions and affections. Likewise, a hallmark of the Holy Spirit's work in our lives is a greater capacity to love, demonstrated in words or actions.

Next, people turn to alcohol for comfort in difficult times. In contrast, the Holy Spirit is referred to in Scripture as the great Comforter. Life is hard and the Holy Spirit promises comfort and the ability to live above life's circumstances.

There is also great boldness exhibited by those who have been drinking. They are liable to say anything to anyone for any reason. Similarly, after the Holy Spirit comes upon the disciples, we next see them boldly proclaiming the good news about Jesus Christ.

There are other comparisons we could make, but you get the picture. While alcohol is a good example of an unhealthy influence affecting our wills and behavior, similar effects can be noted in states of rage, lust, or greed. Yet in all of these examples, we get a better picture of what it means to have a foreign influence affect our thoughts, feelings, and behavior, while not eclipsing our individual personality.

The Contrast
While, in some ways, this helps us to better understand the influence or empowerment by the Holy Spirit, realize that alcohol is a cheap

counterfeit (or expensive counterfeit depending on the brand). What people are really thirsting for is the presence of God. Alcohol-induced states only create the temporary illusion of a reality that only the Spirit can produce in our lives. In fact, alcohol's control tends to be coercive, and usually means a loss of our own will and control. In Matthew 20:25, Jesus says, "You know that the rulers of the Gentiles lord it over them ... not so with you." Jesus is telling the disciples that their leadership and influence should be of loving encouragement, not coercion and domination. Such is the Spirit's influence.

How Can We Be More Under the Influence of the Holy Spirit?

As we have looked at alcohol as an example, we may further note that there are differing degrees of intoxication. Likewise, there are differing degrees by which a person can be controlled or influenced by the Holy Spirit. While sin hinders the influence of the Spirit, there are clearly things we can do to improve our sensitivity to the Spirit's leading, making His presence more acute. Frequent prayer throughout the day, for example, avails us much more to the Spirit's direction than if our day is prayerless. We'll consider here five things that contribute to greater influence by the Spirit.

Complete Submission to the Will of God

How does one become more drunk? They consume more alcohol. In the case of the Holy Spirit, we have all of Him that we will ever have. What determines how much influence the Spirit has over us is how much of us we let Him consume, or how much of our lives are we willing to allow Him to control? The question we must consider is: Do we desire to live for His will above our own in every area of life (dating, vocation, relationships, etc.)?

This decision to submit to the Lord is both progressive and critical. It is progressive in the sense that we are always becoming aware of new areas into which we have never brought God or submitted to Him. It is critical, meaning a point in time, in the sense that there are critical junctures in our Christian lives where we tell God from our hearts, "I will do anything, or go anywhere you want. My life is yours."

Confession

Sin is choosing to live our own way in order to satisfy our needs, wants, and desires, rather than living God's way. When we sin, we seize control of our lives from the Holy Spirit. We turn them over to our sinful desires. When we've sinned, we need to confess it to God. Confession literally means to *agree with God*. We agree that we have sinned without rationalizing or justifying our actions. We agree that Christ's death has paid the price for our sin, and thus, we are forgiven. We repent and that means turning back to God and agreeing to do things His way.

How do we maintain the Spirit's maximum influence on our lives? We keep short accounts of sin. As soon as the Spirit brings awareness of sin to our minds, we confess it immediately.

Reliance

Have you ever watched a cigarette smoker? Every time he senses a need in his life, he lights up. If he feels lonely, he lights up. If he feels scared or nervous, he lights up. If he needs confidence, he lights up. I find myself doing the same thing with food, music and coffee. Did you ever eat something when you weren't hungry? You realize later you were relying on food to fill your loneliness. Throughout each day, we sense the need for empowerment. Whether we're eaters, coffee drinkers, or smokers, all of us have this reflex. You feel a need for _____ (fill in the blank). God wants us to reflexively turn to Him throughout the day and ask for comfort, empowerment, wisdom, and direction from Him.

This constant reliance on the Spirit keeps us intimately connected to the Lord throughout the day. It allows our thirst to be met by His living water.

Cultivating Our Hearts Toward God

In Ephesians 5:19-20, Paul talks about singing spiritual songs and hymns and having a thankful heart. The important lesson here as it relates to maximizing the Holy Spirit's influence over us is that we can foster an environment in our hearts that facilitates the control of the Holy Spirit. Just as going to the mall might foster materialism's control, so certain activities such as thanksgiving, praise, singing and prayer enhance the Spirit's influence. As we sing spiritual songs, and cloak our hearts with thanksgiving throughout the day, we find ourselves much more in tune with the Holy Spirit's direction, leading and presence.

Community

It is in community with other Christians we experience a dynamic of the Spirit-filled life we can never experience alone because we encounter the Spirit who indwells the lives of others. We are empowered to live the Christian life as we receive encouragement and teaching from others. We find fresh life when we are able to share our sins and struggles. We are blessed as we pray together and minister to one another. The Christian life was never meant to be lived independent of the Spirit-empowered ministry of the larger body of Christ.

A Paradigm of Influence

For Spirit-led Christians it's not always helpful to think of the Holy Spirit's influence as either on or off, but rather how much we are allowing, cultivating, or hindering the Spirit's influence. We think instead of how we can maximize the Spirit's influence.

However, there are those who are not aware of the Spirit's ministry in their lives; they may not even know that He indwells them. They live their Christian life independent of the Spirit's power or have made decisions to walk away from His reign in their lives. This is the ministry context of the booklet called *Satisfied, which* introduces Christians to the ministry of the Holy Spirit. But before we look at *Satisfied*, it might be helpful to have a theological context for the booklet.

THEOLOGICAL CONTEXT

As we think about the Holy Spirit's ministry in our life, it's helpful to realize that different theological traditions and denominations hold viewpoints along a spectrum. On one end of the spectrum are those who focus on a Holy Spirit event, meaning there is a time and lordship decision, separate from conversion, when people yield their lives to the control of the Spirit, after which begins a process of walking in step with the Spirit. The focus here is on a Holy Spirit/ Lordship decision.

Those in this camp often speak of three types of people: non-Christians, Christians who are indwelt but not empowered by the Spirit, and Spirit-empowered Christians.

On the other end of the spectrum are those who believe that our growth in the Spirit is a seamless and gradual process that begins the moment we trust Christ. The focus here is on the process.

This camp holds that there are only two types of people: Christians and non-Christians, with Christians being at various places in their maturity and yielding to the Spirit.

With this as a theological context, a review of the *Satisfied* booklet reveals that it walks a fine line between both. For those who have never heard of the Holy Spirit, never understood that the Christian life is one yielded to God's authority, or thought that the Christian life was simply lived out in one's own strength, there is an opportunity to make a decision to yield to the Spirit's control—a Holy Spirit decision.

Yet for Christians familiar with the Holy Spirit, the main application of the booklet is to walk in the Spirit, which involves the daily process of reliance, yielding, confession of sin (spiritual breathing), and trusting God to empower us—the things we do daily to walk, or keep in step with the Spirit.

Great credit should be given for the effort it took to navigate through this theological minefield, seeking to address both needs and both audiences. However, in addressing both the *process* as well as a point-in-time *decision*, the booklet can be confusing.

Perhaps this context will help you focus your presentation to your audience: do they need to pray to be filled (did they not know of the Spirit's ministry), or do they simply need to know how to better walk in step with the Spirit—yielding control, confessing sin, moment-by-moment reliance?

SATISFIED CONTEXT

Rather than look at tips on how to share the *Satisfied* booklet, let's follow its theological flow, which should equip you to more effectively share it. It is the concepts you are sharing not just a booklet.

Introduction
(John 7:37-3). Jesus affirms the Old Testament promise that God would send His Spirit to satisfy our spiritual thirst. The sending of God's Spirit to enable His people to live Holy lives is a major theme in the Old Testament. This verse allows you to go back to those promises should you choose to.

The Gift
(John 14:16-17). God has given the Spirit to us as a gift: His abiding and empowering presence in our lives. His presence allows us to experience: the love of God, assurance of being in the family of God, and a new and abundant life. In emphasizing that the Spirit is a gift you may want to point out that it is exactly like our salvation. We do not earn it, but trust God to provide what we cannot do for ourselves—live a holy life.

The Danger
(Galatians 3:3; 5:17; 3:1-3). You may not be experiencing the empowerment of the Spirit because of:

One
Self effort and lack of reliance.

Two
You have not yielded control of your life to Him (self centeredness).

The scripture is clear that it is possible to have the Spirit within you yet not walk in step with His direction and empowerment. That is the focus here as well as the reasons why a person may not be doing so.

The Journey

One
(Galatians 5:16, 25; Galatians 5:22-23). The answer is to walk in the Spirit: the ongoing process of being empowered and directed by the Spirit.

This does not address the way or manner by which we are empowered, only clarifies that walking in the Spirit is God's method for us to live out a holy life.

Empowerment
So how are we empowered? This step attempts to zoom in on how the dynamic of empowerment works.

One
Reliance: I choose to seek His empowerment rather than accomplish through self-effort. "God will you please lead me in this?"

Two
Submit: I need to be willing to submit and follow His direction (yielding).

Three
Faith. We choose to believe that God will direct, empower, give wisdom, whatever. And after asking, trust that He is leading, empowering, etc.

Four
Confess: when we become aware that we have taken control through sin, we confess and yield our will back to God

The difficulty here is that each of these plays an important role in walking in step with God's Spirit. You would be well served to give examples of each and to spend a whole other week talking about each. This is where we need to focus and elevate our teaching of the Spirit filled life.

Turning Point
If one has never lived this way, or never knew of the Spirit's ministry, there is an opportunity to yield one's life right then and there to His control. However, communicate that from this point on it is a daily

process of yielding and reliance to walk in step with the Spirit.

LIFE CONTEXT

Because of the sheer volume of concepts being tossed around (yielding, faith, empowerment, etc.), it would be helpful to provide the context of how the Spirit functions in your life: How do you yield control? When do you confess your sins? How do you rely on God for empowerment? Walk through your day or week and drench the discussion with examples and don't stop until you see the fog lift from their eyes. Here's an example:

I was sharing my faith with Bob. I asked God to give me the right words to say. I trusted Him to lead the conversation and when it took turns different from what I thought, I allowed God to lead. After the appointment, I began to think that I had said the wrong things. But then I said to myself, "No, I asked God to give me wisdom so I choose to believe (by faith) that I said everything I needed to."

CHAPTER SEVENTEEN

WHERE'S JETHRO?

Why Leadership Matters Whether We Want It To Or Not

There have been many books written on spiritual leadership, each with a major omission: leadership. Most books offer an appropriate focus on the spiritual life and disciplines of a ministry leader. But some asked the question, "Are there other leadership qualities that need to be developed that don't directly relate to topics like prayer or preaching?" The answer seemed to be a resounding "yes," but with qualifications.

First, the "yes." Let's begin with a question we can answer personally. Is it possible for you to be a godly man or woman, full of prayer and faith, and be lousy in your personal finances? I think most of us would say "yes." Then, here's another question. Is it possible for you to be a godly man or woman and yet be miserable at public speaking? Again, most of us would say "yes," as we have all had to endure poor public speaking on at least one Sunday morning. Let's assume you happened to be lousy at both—broke and babbling. Do you think checking out books on basic skills of public speaking and financial management might be a good idea? Probably so.

There you have your answer. Leadership, like finances, requires a cluster of skills and abilities. Yet, like public speaking, it is an area that can be personally developed. And as a church will be blessed through a leader who exhibits excellence in personal finances (and potentially ruined by incompetence), so will a church whose leaders have developed some basic skills of leadership.

Now, the qualification: In response to prayer, faith, and faithfulness God can choose to bless a person or ministry in spite of incompetence in any area. He's God and He can do that. He's God and sometimes he does do that. But Christian maturity requires the development of stewardship and character, meaning that as we grow in maturity, we seek diligence in areas of weakness. As with children, we encourage them to develop in areas rather than bailing them out and enabling them to continue in incompetence. God can and does bail us out, but desires that we seek to grow in competence.

So God *can* compensate because He is God—caveat granted—but He is also our Father and desires us to develop in our weaknesses as well as partner with those who are gifted where we are not.

Here's a thought: What if every Christian in the world became better at finances and giving? Well, there might not be a world hunger problem; there's more than enough Christian wealth to eradicate it. What would happen if every Christian involved in ministry became a proficient leader? Leadership, and the development of leadership skills, is worthy of allocating precious discipleship time.

We are not interested in grooming Christian CEOs to take over Microsoft and other Fortune 500 companies, but it might be nice if those who gave leadership to our ministries knew how to plan, strategize and solve a problem when one falls across the road.

NEHEMIAH

Let's look at one biblical example that clarifies the distinction between spiritual and leadership. Take a moment to read through these passages from Nehemiah.

> "I also said to him, 'If it pleases the king, may I have letters to the governors of Trans-Euphrates, so that they will provide me safe-conduct until I arrive in Judah? And may I have a letter to Asaph, keeper of the king's forest, so he will give me timber to make beams for the gates of the citadel by the temple and for the city wall and for the residence I will occupy?'" *Nehemiah 2:7-8*

> "By night I went out through the Valley Gate toward the Jackal Well and the Dung Gate, examining the walls of Jerusalem, which had been broken down, and its gates, which had been destroyed by fire." *Nehemiah 2:13*

> "Therefore I stationed some of the people behind the lowest points of the wall at the exposed places, posting them by families, with their swords, spears and bows." *Nehemiah 4:13*

> "From that day on, half of my men did the work, while the

other half were equipped with spears, shields, bows and
armor. The officers posted themselves behind all the people
of Judah who were building the wall. Those who carried
materials did their work with one hand and held a weapon
in the other, and each of the builders wore his sword at his
side as he worked. But the man who sounded the trumpet
stayed with me". *Nehemiah 4:16-18*

"Moreover, from the twentieth year of King Artaxerxes,
when I was appointed to be their governor in the land of
Judah, until his thirty-second year—twelve years—neither
I nor my brothers ate the food allotted to the governor".
Nehemiah 5:14

Let's survey some of the decisions made by Nehemiah. Before arriving in Jerusalem, Nehemiah sought the raw materials needed for the
rebuilding of Jerusalem. Upon arriving he does a night inspection of
the damage. To upgrade the local work ethic, he has each person labor
on a section of the Jerusalem wall that protects their home. When
threats of violence come from without, he devises a plan by which Israel
can remain battle-ready and yet not abandon the building project When
famine strikes and accusations are made of royal usury, he refuses to
eat the food rightly allotted to his position.

Besides being a godly man of prayer and faith, Nehemiah is a wise
leader: he plans, prepares, motivates, and innovates solutions in the
midst of adversity. He might be excellent at running Microsoft. God
chose a man of faith and prayer to steward this project, but he also had
the leadership skills necessary to pull off this Herculean task. Now what
if God still wanted to use Nehemiah to lead, but he lacked the necessary
skills. Again, God could compensate through intervention, but in all
probability God would place someone alongside him who had leadership skills to help him execute the plans. This appears to be a pattern
in Scripture. Consider the example Moses and Jethro from Exodus
18:14-24:

"When his father-in-law saw all that Moses was doing for
the people, he said, 'What is this you are doing for the people? Why do you alone sit as judge, while all these people
stand around you from morning till evening?'

"Moses answered him, 'Because the people come to me to
seek God's will. Whenever they have a dispute, it is brought
to me, and I decide between the parties and inform them of
God's decrees and laws.'

"Moses' father-in-law replied, 'What you are doing is not good. You and these people who come to you will only wear yourselves out. The work is too heavy for you; you cannot handle it alone. Listen now to me and I will give you some advice, and may God be with you. You must be the people's representative before God and bring their disputes to him. Teach them the decrees and laws, and show them the way to live and the duties they are to perform. But select capable men from all the people—men who fear God, trustworthy men who hate dishonest gain—and appoint them as officials over thousands, hundreds, fifties and tens. Have them serve as judges for the people at all times, but have them bring every difficult case to you; the simple cases they can decide themselves. That will make your load lighter, because they will share it with you. If you do this and God so commands, you will be able to stand the strain, and all these people will go home satisfied.'

"Moses listened to his father-in-law and did everything he said."

Legal problems in Israel have turned Moses into a workaholic, and Jethro shares with him a simple principle of leadership he apparently never considered: delegation. Employing solid leadership principles can be the difference between leading a successful Bible study or a failing one. It can be the difference between the capacity to lead two people or the capacity to lead two hundred. And in the case of Moses, the difference between thriving in ministry or burning out. So where do we get a Jethro, someone to teach us basic principles of leadership so that we in turn can be a Jethro to our disciples?

JETHRO PRINCIPLES

Fortunately some motivated and wonderful Cru staff (perhaps named Jethro) read through the vast library of material on leadership, looking to glean principles common to leaders and useful for situations of leadership. Here is a distilled summary of that research.

QUALITIES OF A LEADER

If you were to interview a thousand of the world's best leaders, you would note that the following four personal character traits would surface again and again. The four traits follow the acronym DICE, which fails as a mnemonic device, as dice has nothing what so ever to do with leadership.

Dynamic determination

This is the determination to get a job done, no matter what it takes. Determination is seen in one's passion: the heart-felt belief that what you are pursuing is worth expending your best hours, talents and resources to achieve. Passion comes from the heart and will ultimately be more determinative in the ability to lead than position or personality.

For example, each year millions of people start diets and fail. Yet, there are always some who can break the pull of gravity and arrive at their destination. They have what others don't—an uncommon drive. Successful leaders have this uncommon drive.

Intellectual flexibility

Leaders possess the intellectual tools to conceptualize, assimilate and synthesize ideas and information. This skill is more than basic IQ. It is a learned process of relating the parts to the whole, learning to see the big picture. Leaders use information to spot trends and correlations, which gives them insight into where and how to lead. Great leaders aren't always brilliant, but they are bright.

Character

Character is the earned right to be trusted, believed and followed. Ben Franklin defined character as "the ability to carry out a worthy decision long after the emotion of making that decision has passed." Character, for the believer, is always related to Christ-likeness. But as recent scandals will attest, moral character and integrity are qualities leaders must demonstrate or it can spell ruin, or worse, impeachment.

Emotional well-being

Emotional well-being includes a strong, healthy, secure self-concept. If leaders do not have a strong sense of self-worth, they will be threatened by the ideas and suggestions of those around them, and they will be driven by their own neediness and insecurity rather than the necessity to make wise decisions. Some of the most powerful people in the world have failed in their leadership because of insecurity and unstable emotional states.

RELATIONSHIPS WITH OTHERS

Successful leadership hinges on quality interpersonal relationships. Here are several indicators of healthy relational dynamics between leaders and those they lead:

- Involves others appropriately
- Treats others with respect
- Allows others to make decisions
- Creates an atmosphere of trust
- Gets others to own the work
- Relates well with peers, supervisors and with those they supervise

ROLES OF A LEADER

Leaders perform a zillion different functions, which is why they usually have assistants. But distill these functions, and you would find four distinct roles that must be performed proficiently to lead well.

Direction Setter
The leader must perform the role of setting direction, in essence saying, "This is where we are headed." A leader functions as the rudder of the ship. If you are under good leadership, you have a clear sense of where you are headed, what you are seeking to accomplish, and why.

Spokesperson
A leader must also communicate the company vision to those outside the organization. Picture a presidential press conference. If a brilliant president speaks unintelligibly to the world, we will loose confidence in our leader. Leaders can exercise this role through a variety

of mediums—in person, on film, or in print, but they must articulate direction.

Coach
A coach builds a team. A coach maximizes the potential of each player and molds these individuals into a team so they will maximize their chances of winning. Great leaders bring together the gifts and talents of various individuals to accomplish more than any individual could achieve.

Change Agent
A leader pursues useful and adaptive change in light of the future. A leader is always a change agent. Leaders shape the future, while others manage the present. To them, the gap between the way things are and the way things ought to be calls for action.

The failure in any one of these areas can lead to the performing a fifth role: that of Slurpie maker at the local 7-Eleven.

RESPONSIBILITIES OF A LEADER

Under each of the roles that leaders must function are responsibilities that enable them to execute these roles. There are four major responsibilities that, if done well, will enable the leader to be a wise direction setter, effective coach, compelling spokesperson, and efficient change agent.

Vision casting
How do I effectively motivate a team of people to go in the direction that I have set? It's fairly easy if you are a born vision caster, though most people are not. Vision casting paints a picture of a future reality so desirable that those you lead are compelled to want to go there. Some of the most memorable speeches of political and social leaders are those where vision casting was accomplished with excellence, and everyone felt stirred to head for the stated destination.

Strategy Formulation
"How can we do this?" Strategy formulation is the ability to transform dreams into a plan of action. Feasibility is a major

motivator in leading people. They have to feel that they are heading to a destination, and it's possible to get there. Strategy formulation charts the best course to get to the vision.

Aligning

Aligning is people working together, sharing a vision, owning the responsibility, and cooperating in order to fulfill the vision. Aligning is another way of saying that you have the ability to get people on board with you. What brings people on board can be a variety of things already mentioned, but often there is a relational trust component that relates to character. The leader captures their imagination (vision), mind (strategy), and hearts.

Motivating

Motivating is about tapping into people's core values so that they want to work together to fulfill the mission. A leader finds ways to connect the vision to what personally motivates the individuals involved. John Kotter in *A Force for Change* writes:

> "Being able to generate highly energized behavior is as centrally important here as are direction setting and alignment. In a sense, direction setting identifies an appropriate path for movement, effective alignment gets people moving down that path, and a successful motivational effort assures that those people will have the energy to overcome obstacles in their way."

THANKS FOR THE BRAIN DUMP

Jethro just pulled up his dump truck onto your front lawn and unloaded the secrets of successful leadership. So what do you do with this mound of dirt?

Well, this is about discipleship, so you could just take this sheet, copy it, and move the mound onto your disciple's lawn. But if you would like to more thoughtfully process this and disseminate it, here's what I would suggest.

First, you must internalize these concepts. It's actually an easy process. Go through the list and think of a leader who demonstrates the role or responsibility well or horribly and write a name next to it. Then try to diagram the different roles and responsibilities out on a piece of paper in some coherent sort of way, even if it is simply listing the information. What you are trying to do is create new file folders in your head for processing the topic of leadership.

Once you have done this, you will begin to notice when public leaders are either doing these things well, or failing miserably. You begin to make connections between book knowledge and reality. If you want to speed up the process, read a biography or watch a movie on a great leader and look for these skills. For example, you might get a documentary on Martin Luther King, Jr. and note the vision he paints in his speeches as well as his strategies for bringing about social justice. If you're a student, think about your teachers: how well do they set direction? Do they align and motivate you to learn? Do they paint a picture of why it would be desirable to learn the information? A great teacher is a great leader. Making these connections is the process of learning.

Next, you will begin to notice you are performing these roles or responsibilities. You will begin to wonder how well you have aligned people, and if you have clearly set direction. You are now personalizing the information, and you will never look at how you lead the same way for you now have file folders and mile markers by which to assess your effectiveness.

DISCIPLESHIP

Now you can think about how to help your disciple lead. In basic follow up, this shouldn't be a concern. But as your disciples take on ministry responsibilities and leadership, it will then be incumbent upon you to become Jethro to them, passing on leadership wisdom that will enable them to be more effective.

To help your disciples process these things, bring them through the same process you just went through. Expose them to the new material and ideas—grow their brain and help them to create new file folders. Then help them to make connections between the material and the real world. Perhaps as a small group you could watch a biography or movie about a person who led well and discuss these leadership concepts. The movie Coach Carter is a perfect film to dissect leadership skills. Ask them questions to help them digest the material: "Can you think of a leader who was a good spokesperson?" Ask questions that personalize the information: "What role would you gravitate toward, and which one would you need to work on?"

Having done that, all that remains is to reinforce the ideas periodically by providing feedback using the common terminology that you taught them: "How well have you aligned people to this? What could you do to align them?"

That's all you need to do. You are not running a leadership school, but simply recognizing the value of teaching your disciples some basic leadership skills, just like you might impart skills on time management. Expose them to the concepts, help them make connections to leaders in the real world, and begin to make personal connections.

SOMETHING YOU ACCOMPLISHED WITHOUT REALIZING IT

By simply exposing your disciples to these principles of leadership you will be shaping their unconscious value system. For example, why do people not plan or prepare for a meeting they are to lead? A value of informality or spontaneity, or a value of simply wanting the Spirit to lead. There's nothing wrong with any of these values, it is how much we value them and the lack of other values that is the problem. For example, professionalism, competence, preparedness, diligence, and articulation are also values. They are values that are more aligned with leadership, and interestingly they are also values that the Scriptures highlight in relation to how we are to teach the God's Word.

When we focus on leadership, and excellence in leadership, we are raising the value of the latter list of diligence, competence, etc. Our disciples begin to see the importance of competence as opposed to spontaneity, which is important because God's Word does not exhort us to be spontaneous in our leadership and teaching, but serious, diligent, and prepared. When you emphasize principles of competent leadership, you will rearrange your disciple's values and that over time will alter the competence.

WHAT ABOUT THE SPIRITUAL?

Couldn't this go too far overboard to the point where I'm asking my disciples how well their Bible study is aligned, rather then how much they are praying for them? Sure, so don't do that. You know the primacy of the spiritual and that these are simply useful tools, like becoming a better public speaker, or manager of finances. You know that these are no substitute for the power of the Spirit. It is hard to imagine that you would communicate them in a way that would eclipse the centrality of soul and Spirit in the work of the ministry.

But biblically, I think we can see that Jethro's role, a role model leadership development, can greatly aid the work of the ministry.

CHAPTER EIGHTEEN

UNDER CHALLENGED

Why No One Responds To Your Invitations

As legend has it, Apple Computers was started in the 70s by two guys in a garage—Steve Woz and Steve Jobs. Woz was the technical genius, Jobs was the visionary. Jobs had a vision of literally changing the world with what he considered "insanely great" computers. He had a passion for the Macintosh.

In fact there's a story told about how Jobs got the president of Pepsi Corporation to leave his prestigious, secure, and well-paying job to come work for his upstart company. He gave the president his pitch told, and told him of the need. But the Pepsi executive wasn't willing to leave behind his future of power, prestige and money. Not willing to accept a "no," Jobs looked at him and said, "Do you want to spend the rest of your life selling sugared water, or do you want a chance to change the world?" With that question ringing in his ears, John Sculley left Pepsi, and came to work for Apple.

One responsibility of a discipler is to be a fork in the road for young followers of Christ. That fork is a "biblical challenge." It is a well-exe-cuted, carefully worded, non-manipulative, visionary, confrontation with the truth, like the one given by Steve Jobs.

The difference between an invitation and a challenge is a small but significant one. An invitation says, "Come if you want," "Come if you can" or "Come if you have nothing better to do." The problem is that disciples don't want to do many things that would benefit their spiritual growth; they are as initially reluctant as John Sculley. The other prob-lem is that they can't: at least in their minds they simply don't have the time. The reality is, of course, they can, but it would require the reorder-ing of their priorities.

A challenge, therefore, goes beyond invitation. It contains a compelling vision of why this course is the right one, why passivity or neutrality on the issue is unacceptable, and compels a commitment. Reread the challenge of Steve Jobs to John Sculley and you'll see all of these elements, you will also note that he said "no" to a simple invitation.

Why we choose to invite instead of challenge is quite simple. A strong challenge can strain a relationship, puts us in an uncomfortable authoritative role, and risks that our disciple will take a step back rather than forward. On the positive side, that sounds a whole lot like the way Jesus dealt with His disciples.

The bottom line need to challenge disciples is that they will not respond to an invitation to do many things that will be to their spiritual benefit (I certainly didn't). In campus ministry, there are a small handful of opportunities for growth that will often require such a challenge.

THE CHALLENGE TO SMALL GROUPS

It would be nice if all disciples saw their need to be involved in community and upon conversion committed to join a Bible study and bring refreshments to the Weekly Meeting. But this side of the Second Coming that ain't gonna happen, so to invite them to a Bible study is like inviting them to join a book club—"Sure sounds like fun. How about if I meet you there?" Why should they bother, they have no idea what this thing will be like, and they have a spiritual counselor who makes a house call once a week.

What they need is to be challenged. The first aspect of a challenge is a compelling spiritual passage. The passage should demonstrate the need to take steps of obedience in order to grow. I have often used the Parable of the Sower. Parables with questions work better than the bluntness of a single verse, "What this verse says is you should go to my Bible Study."

Next, communicate why you think they need to be involved in a small group. This would include the spiritual benefits to them as well the biblical reasons why this needs to be a priority. Take time to go through some verses. Share your own story of how being in a small group changed your life. Paint a passionate picture. Honestly, if they don't get plugged into a community of believers, things do not bode well for their spiritual future. Our faith was designed to be lived out in community and you break that design principle at your own peril.

Challenges should not be open ended or vague, but must contain a specific commitment: this group will meet for seven weeks and will last for ninety minutes. When you give time parameters, the ones you challenge have the opportunity to count the cost and the limited duration makes it feel less like their opting into Social Security. It also shows what your expectations are: a challenge for seven weeks means you expect them to attend your small group for seven weeks. So include the itemized receipt to let them know the exact costs.

Challenges always end by asking for a decision—"So, who's with me!" This is the hard part because you become the fork in the road: they must say yes or no. You have taken away the option of neutrality by drawing a line just in front of their toes and asking them to either step over it or away from it. The gamble is that they will step back, the alternative is to perpetually invite them to something they will never know the benefit of until they actually get involved.

Finally, put your challenges on paper. Paper makes everything more real, which is why people have business cards even when they don't have a business. It makes the challenge more tangible and carries the appearance that you're not simply making this stuff up—it must be real, it's on paper. It also provides you with something to refer back to should they not follow through on their commitment.

CHALLENGES TO LEADERSHIP

> "Since an overseer is entrusted with God's work, he must be blameless—not overbearing, not quick-tempered, not given to drunkenness, not violent, not pursuing dishonest gain. Rather he must be hospitable, one who loves what is good, who is self-controlled, upright, holy and disciplined".
> *Titus 1:7-8*

The challenge to leadership contains the basic ingredients as the Bible study challenge but with a few additions. First, stress the spiritual requirements, as exemplified by Paul's Pastoral Epistles. The issues faced by Titus "pursuing dishonest gain" might not be something to specify but be very clear what those requirements are: "The role of leadership requires that you are having a daily quiet time, involved in a small group, taking out the garbage, wearing deodorant, etc." Even if they decline the leadership role they should feel honored that they were asked. It's hard to find a place where Jesus bent the requirements of discipleship to accommodate hesitance—"OK, you don't have to sell everything, but at least get rid of the major appliances."

Communicate the commitment and expectations: "We will meet once a month without exception." Because so much happens at conferences, it is crucial that you include in the requirements for leadership, attendance at major conferences. Perhaps an allowance for one truancy a year, but any more than that will compromise your leadership structure.

And throughout any challenge, communicate the heart behind the request or requirement: "The church would look quite differently if Jesus was never able to gather the twelve together in the same time and place" or "People will be sharing their heart, joys, and even sin, so you could imagine how it might feel in that environment if some weeks you showed up and others you didn't."

CHALLENGES TO CONFERENCES

Does going to a conference make someone a better Christian, or not going mean they are not walking with God? Obviously not, but it is one of the few places on the planet where one experiences true biblical community and where community is created. Community to a Christian is as water to a plant: it is that important. Therefore sewing your disciple into a community of committed Christians is perhaps the greatest way you will ever serve them. A challenge is the way this service is executed, because until you've been to a conference it will always sound like the waste of a perfectly good weekend. Your spiritual child needs to eat green beans and simply offering them on the menu is not going to get the job done.

A challenge to a conference focuses on two things: the benefits of going and addressing the obstacles to not being able to come. First, go through the many benefits of being at the conference using God-inspired overstatement where possible: "It's like putting your spiritual life on steroids." Next, ask the question: "What would be some of the potential barriers for you attending this conference?" Write them down as they speak and address each one. If it's money, offer a scholarship; if it's an upcoming test, go with them to the dumpster and help them rummage for the discarded answer key (It's just a joke).

If all of this has been to no avail, I would be quite pointed: "I'll be honest with you. I really feel that this is the next step for you spiritually. You've hit a ceiling to how much you can grow on your own. Would you be willing to pray about it and honestly tell God you are willing to do whatever He shows you?" There is a point when you can press too far, especially for someone new to the ministry. But if you have been involved in a discipleship relationship for a year or more, and they still remain on the periphery of community, you must take a further step and become not only a fork in the road but a fork, spoon and knife.

SUMMER PROJECTS

Perhaps your persuasive skills and empowerment by the Spirit far exceed mine, but to challenge someone to give an entire summer of their lives is difficult. I've found it better to challenge them to a retreat and have them learn about summer projects through a promotion at the retreat before I ever address the issue. It can also be helpful to inform them of a summer project that aligns with a known area of interest: perhaps an inner city project, or hiking in Yellowstone. I generally sit down to challenge someone to a summer project if I have leverage for doing so: if a person has articulated a desire to do full-time ministry, or holds a leadership role in the ministry.

If they have been considering full-time ministry, it is only logical that they give it a try for a summer. They will never have the opportunity again, unless they're fired from a job, to devote an entire summer to ministry. It is wise stewardship on their part to invest a summer before investing their lives. If they can't carve out a summer for ministry, it's unlikely they will have the tenacity to leave their life and career trajectory at some future point to abruptly enter the ministry. People take progressive steps of faith and obedience, not leaps, though our minds like to rationalize to the contrary.

I also challenge students to a summer project if they have significant leadership in the ministry. I come to them as a co-laborer asking them to consider the additional training they would receive. The reality is, which I am choosing to communicate, is that they are critical to the ministry and an increase in their training would be an enormous boost to the ministry.

STAFF AND FULL-TIME MINISTRY

"Then he said to his disciples, 'The harvest is plentiful but the workers are few. Ask the Lord of the harvest, therefore, to send out workers into his harvest field.'" *Matthew 9:37-38*

Pastors serving Christ under communism, church planters in South America, evangelists in Asia, missionaries to the Muslim world. Trace back the spiritual journey of today's most influential Christian leaders and you'll find that most of them came from a campus ministry. They were involved in a campus movement just like the one you're in (perhaps from your campus), which led them to a vocational choice of full-time ministry.

Which leads to an important question: Where will the next generation of Christian workers, pastors, and missionaries come from? From the college ministries of Cru and other Christian groups in the United States and around the world. From these campuses will come the generation of laborers who will help see the Great Commission fulfilled.

For this reason our role in raising up Christian workers is arguably the most influential in all of Christian ministry. Many Cru staff desiring to serve internationally have remained on U.S. campuses knowing that every year they remain they will multiply themselves many times over in laborers for the spiritual harvest.

Consider Roger Hershey, the former campus director of Miami of Ohio. On his wall is a map with more than 500 pins placed in locations all over the world. These pins represent the students that have been involved in his campus ministry and now serve as pastors and missionaries around the globe. In raising up these laborers, Roger's ministry and influence now extends to the hundreds of ministries begun by his disciples and hundreds of thousands reached with the gospel, making Roger's impact for Christ beyond calculation. Can you think of another church or ministry that sees this degree of influence for expanding the kingdom of God?

This is just the spiritual reality: the most committed and best trained students reside in our campus movements. If God is going to call people into the harvest, we should expect that it will be from among our ministries. It certainly has been historically.

For this reason, Cru as a ministry does its fair share of recruiting because even the "called" need a little push out the door (I know of what I speak). But in so doing your disciples can feel like they are perpetually being recruited to ministry or Cru staff. On the positive side, if your disciple has gone to enough events they've already heard a challenge to full-time ministry. This takes some of the pressure off of you—they've heard, and the Holy Spirit is at work.

But you are their spiritual parent and how and when you challenge them (provided you believe they are qualified), will be a significant event.

In light of people's sensitivity to pressure, and the recruiting environment of Cru, I seek to have one, and only one, conversation on the matter—unless they bring it up at another time—and I am very sensitive as to when that conversation should take place.

> A student I discipled once told me, "I feel like I am always being challenged to join staff."
>
> I asked, "When have I ever mentioned joining staff to you?"
>
> He had to say, "You haven't."

In our Cru environment, I have deemed that one strong challenge is more powerful than many challenges, and my challenge is usually to join the staff of Cru (unless it has become clear in our relationship that they have a calling elsewhere). The reason is disciples only need to be challenged when obedience requires a nudge, and without such a nudge obedience seems unlikely. Other vocational ministry options, including seminary or a pastorate, particularly because they do not require raising support, do not require a nudge. On the other hand, a willingness to join staff with Cru and raise support, will also make them available to God for any possible missionary post or organization to which they might be led.

Some of what I share with a disciple is written above. If God is at work in their life, little of what I say will be new, but what I focus on, are the sticking points: their reasoning and obstacles.

I pray as they speak asking God to show me if there is any layer of rationalizing in their thinking process. The bottom line is that those feeling they should enter the ministry will usually not deny the fact, but will struggle with postponing the event: I need to work for a few years, pay off debt, live at home and be a witness to my parents for a year, get my masters, get married, go to seminary, etc. Sometimes the reasons are legitimate, many times they are not.

It is only when you've been in ministry for many a few years, that you realize you've met few people who didn't need to so *something* first, which makes you more discerning to what appears on the surface to be legitimate reservations. As they speak you begin to hear Luke 9 rattle around in your mind:

> "He said to another man, 'Follow me.' But the man replied,
> 'Lord, first let me go and bury my father.' Jesus said to him,
> 'Let the dead bury their own dead, but you go and proclaim
> the kingdom of God.' Still another said, 'I will follow you,
> Lord; but first let me go back and say good-by to my family.'
> Jesus replied, 'No one who puts his hand to the plow and
> looks back is fit for service in the kingdom of God.'"
> *Luke 9:59-62*

God will give you wisdom on how to gently uncover some of the sticking points, but it is not your responsibility to convince them. It is your responsibility, with wisdom from the Spirit, to unveil hidden fears and motives as to where and why they might be delaying obedience; to tell them what you honestly think of their plan, to challenge thoughts and assumptions that are clearly not true or biblical, and to call them to pray about certain issues with a willingness to do whatever God reveals to them. To be the best detective, you too must be open to whatever God is saying even if it means they should not go into ministry.

Obstacles are more fun to discuss. They are not rationalizations, but legitimate barriers to which God will provide solutions if your disciples seek to do God's will and He is calling them into ministry. These obstacles include: parental approval, debt, or perhaps even sin issues.

Some of the answers and encouragements to these obstacles can be found at CruPress.com in resources like *InTransition* or *The Finishers* by Roger Hershey.

SUMMARY

As a parent, I've experienced many times when my children simply will not choose to do what's best for them. The beauty of being a parent is I possess the leverage of discipline to accomplish their greater good. As a discipler we do not. What we have is a challenge, which moves up the proximity of truth and takes away the position of neutrality. It is the wise use and application of a biblical challenge that really makes the difference between a good and great discipler.

This is a sample of a challenge sheet.

Mark 4 "Parable of Sower"
- Why is wealth deceitful?
- How have you felt the busyness of life?
- What does it mean to bear fruit?
- Which soil are you? Which would you like to be?

Purpose of a Leadership Group
- Learn how to effectively lead a small group (Mark 3:14)
- Grow in spiritual leadership (1 Timothy 3:1)
- Learn how to better disciple others (2 Timothy 2:2)
- Build biblical community (Philippians 2:3-4)
- Encouragement and spiritual accountability (James 5:16)

Benefits of a Leadership Group
- Personal character development and leadership development (Galatians 5:22-23)
- Training in ministry (Colossians 4:17)
- Deep Christian friendships (1 Thessalonians 2:7-10)
- Opportunity to trust God in greater ways (Hebrews 11:6)
- Cultivate a deeper walk with Christ (Psalm 42:1)

Qualifications
- Heart that is actively seeking to know Christ more intimately
- A desire to be taught and learn from others
- Consistent personal evangelism
- Development of a Bible Study that you would lead
- Commitment to at least one conference per semester
- Weekly time commitment for semester: 6.5 hrs.
- Leadership meeting (2.0 hrs.) Weekly meeting (1.5 hrs.)
- Leading Bible study (2.0 hrs.) Discipleship time (1.0 hrs.)

Challenge
- Do you want to be in a leadership group?
- Read Ecclesiastes 5:4-5, Deuteronomy. 23:21-23
- Are you willing to commit yourself faithfully to these qualifications?

IN WISDOM AND STATURE

Other Subjects Up For Discussion

> "And Jesus grew in wisdom and stature, and in favor with
> God and men". *Luke 2:52*

Here's what strikes me about this passage: Jesus grew spiritually but that was not the only way Jesus matured as He grew into adulthood.

This has taken a long time for me to grasp. I used to operate on the assumption that if I continued to pray, read the Bible, and take steps of faith, I would naturally become a mature godly man. It has not happened that way. No matter how well I know my Bible, I still don't know how to cook, I'm always late, I oversleep and I have no idea what's going on in my checkbook.

(Please note that it is not that the Bible does not discuss these things either directly or by implication. The problem is not knowing how to search the scriptures with a grid to see principles of life wisdom.)

By extension I assumed the same about those I disciple: If I gave them enough spiritual content I would, on the other side of the process, churn a godly widget out of the discipleship factory. I don't assume that any more; I have too many dysfunctional spiritual children running around.

This raises the question, what else could we or should we teach those we disciple besides the typical theological lessons and content that might contribute to them growing into godly men or women, or to put it another way, growing "in wisdom and stature and favor with God and men." I will stay away from the question "what else should we teach?" and opt for the easier "What else could we teach?" allowing me to suggest anything I want with plausible deniability—"I never said you should teach that." But guaranteed, somewhere within here are probably some "shoulds," like this first topic.

EMOTIONAL AND SOCIAL DEVELOPMENT

One critical area of development that I had never considered was emotional and social maturity. Consider this question: Could you be knowledgeable of the Bible, have a heart for God, and yet be socially immature? Second question: Would not your lack of social development (let's say you had the behavior of a 10-year-old) affect your spirituality? And how would that affect the degree of community you were able to both contribute to and receive? Do you see the point?

Besides God's Spirit and His Word, community is unequivocally the most essential ingredient of spiritual development. But what happens if people are relationally stunted or can't make significant emotional connections with others? Now you have a context for understanding the book *Changes that Heal* by Dr. Henry Cloud. In the book, Cloud discusses four issues of emotional and social maturity that are important growth components of maturation. For the most part they have foundations in the scriptures, if you had known where to look or had been thinking in the category of "emotional maturity." But of course most people do not. You'll also find ideas in the book based on observation. There is always wisdom to be gained from someone who sat for years with a clipboard observing the behavior of sociopaths. And the book of Proverbs gives a solid biblical foundation for wisdom acquired from observation.

So, if you are at least reasonably satisfied with that rationale, here are the four issues that Cloud sites that need development if a person is going to move on to relational adulthood.

Bonding

"Bonding is the ability to establish an emotional attachment to another person," says Cloud. "It is the ability to relate to another on the deepest level." Bonding needs to take place on both a personal level and a professional level. We all need concentric circles of people with which we have relationships that go below the surface. Are you doing things to build attachments and understanding? How committed are you to others? Can you build attachments but also maintain healthy limits? The answers to these questions give clues to a person's ability to bond. There are a lot of gifted people who have consistent morning devotions who have not developed the ability to bond and connect with others.

Boundaries

Henry Cloud makes the following statement: "Boundaries, in a broad sense, are lines or things that mark a limit, bound, or border. In another sense boundaries are the realization of our own person apart from others. This sense of separation forms the basis of personal identity. It says what we are and what we are not, what we will choose and what we will not choose, what we will endure and what we will not, what we feel and what we will not feel, what we like and what we do not like, and what we want and what we do not want." Boundaries define us. Do you have the ability to say "no" to others? Do you take personal responsibility for the poor choices and actions of others? Do you manage your time and money boundaries well or do you spend more than you have? These are boundary issues.

Sorting Out Good and Bad
This developmental task is the ability to tolerate and deal with the simultaneous existence of good and bad in this world, in others, and in ourselves. In other words, emotional immaturity causes us to continually define and label people and things as either "all good" or "all bad." Can you articulate both your strengths and weaknesses? Can you see the good and the bad of organizations? The good and bad of your parents? Can you manage the gap between the ideal and the real? These are issues that relate to managing the split between good and bad.

Think about the genre of some of the Proverbs. Have you ever noticed how one thing is stated and then, almost immediately, the exact opposite is said? The Proverbs, even in form, are structured to develop wisdom. Wisdom is not always black and white, sometimes it is found in antithesis: holding two opposite truths in dynamic tension like the strings on a tennis racket. The point is, while not overt, the concept can be found in scripture. But even if it couldn't, it would still be a true observation that the emotionally infantile put a black or white hat on everything, and therefore valuable wisdom on emotional growth.

Adulthood
"Becoming an adult is the process of moving out of a 'one-up/one-down' relationship and into a peer relationship to other adults," Dr. Cloud says. Becoming an adult is assuming the authority position of life, which is an important part of the image of God. Can you be peers where it is appropriate? Are you able to submit to those you see as under you? What is your ability to take criticism as reality and not as a comment as to whether you are good or bad?

In all four of these areas (bonding, boundaries, sorting out good/bad, adulthood), you may want to refer to Dr. Cloud's book and look at the skill sections under each task. It may give you some ideas on what you might want to share with a disciple. Reading the Cloud library doesn't make a person competent to counsel; even when I can identify an issue, I'm not really sure what I need to do to change it. But my awareness helps me seek sanctification and discernment from the Spirit as to how I might progress, and causes me to embrace opportunities to grow rather than avoid them. So, as a mentor, simply making your disciple aware of an issue, and pointing them toward a resource like a book, is a valuable and sufficient service.

POLITICS

Here is where you want to answer the question of whether Jesus is a Republican or Democrat and encourage them to "Rock the vote." Well, almost.

The events in the Bible take place within the context of a dominant political motif. Many issues of church history have risen and fallen on differing views of how the kingdom of God interacts with the body politic. We might not be a nation without, whether right or wrong, some politically weighted Puritan preaching. And then there's this whole church and state wall of separation issue. All that to say, in the course of a long-term discipleship relationship, it's probably not a bad idea to discuss political issues. Not convert. Discuss.

Personally I never thought about politics until my first campus director discussed it with me. In my interactions with him, I learned what moral issues eclipsed the political arena, and why people felt strongly about those issues. I developed a better understanding of the relationship of church and state in this country and how that issue was being played out on our campus. I became informed on what my rights were as a Christian and to recognize when they were being violated, as well as a godly way to protest. I learned how to become more informed on issues and candidates, and from his example, I have felt a sense of duty to this day to cast my vote on Election Day. I am grateful he chose to tread into these waters with me, and grateful for how he did it.

The role this country plays in spreading the gospel to the world, and the role that politics plays on the issue of religious freedom, speak loudly to the peril of avoiding the topic. However, there are cautions to be observed.

Because parties and politics can be a stumbling block for the gospel, this is an issue for much later on in the discipleship process, and even then you need to be wise, as your opinions can end up being broadcast along the ministry back-channel frequencies. You can be informative without being partisan. You can address an issue without getting deeply into your own personal beliefs. If your ministry were to be seen as politically partisan, for some this would be a hindrance and such a thought should make you fearfully careful of who, when, and how you talk about politics.

If you find it difficult to discuss these issues without planting seeds of animosity, bitterness, or malice, you should take it off the table for discussion. On the other hand, issues that divide can provide a wonderful stage to demonstrate charity and grace, not witnessed in the world. How you speak about those with whom you disagree is the one thing your disciple will commit to memory.

ART, MUSIC, AND CULTURE

Non-Christians tend to take music and art at face value, but both deeply manifest the soul, ideas, and beliefs of man and society. Consider Michelangelo's great sculpture David: he is depicted by Michelangelo as uncircumcised, looking off into distance (the future?), bold, powerful (oversized hands), confident, and enormous in stature. Michelangelo is making a statement about the new autonomy of man birthed in the Renaissance, no longer in need of God.

And then there is the work of Jackson Pollock: random paint thrown on a canvass, creating art After all, doesn't this represent the randomness of who we are? A product of brute random forces.

Music, movies, art, and literature are an enormous part of our culture, and shape the beliefs of the world around us. At some point our disciples must turn a Christian eye of discernment to these issues, especially as they consume iPods full it.

We need to give our disciples a template, or introduction to these issues so they begin to develop the muscles of discernment in regards to popular and artistic culture (which really are separate cultures but have been recently layered together by Photoshop).

A Bible study structured around the discussion of a movie is a good way to begin awakening students to the philosophical roots of pop culture. Francis Schaeffer's book *How Shall We Then Live* is a more in-depth look at the history of thought expressed through art. On issues of popular culture I would also suggest getting them an issue of *Relevant* magazine, which deal with the music, movies, and stars of popular culture but from a Christian framework.

LIFE MANAGEMENT

For years Cru has made time management a standard part of our discipleship, realizing that few college students do it well, and if we didn't teach something on the topic no one would ever show up on time to our Bible studies. Time management is a life skill, and to be a poor manager of time jeopardizes the full impact we could have for the kingdom of God. Our life, every minute of it, is a stewardship.

Money and how to manage it is also a critical life skill. I usually teach this as students are ready to graduate so they will remember to support me, or the ministry. Actually, the real reason is that money is a hypothetical concept until students graduate and so I make discipleship in this area a part of a package of equipping them for graduation.

How people control their money, time, and eating is evidence of their self-control, and the exercise of control in these areas usually has a positive influence on spiritual growth. So, any life issue that requires stewardship and self-control is a worthy topic for discipleship. Perhaps a whole semester could be dedicated to the topic: How to Use a Credit Card!

It should also be noted that some of the greatest barriers to going into the ministry, or reasons for leaving, relate to a failure in handling basic life skills, such as How to Use a Credit Card!

Increasingly students are lacking a host of basic skills that keep them living like children, though they may be maturing in Christ. A simple, "Dude, you need to learn how to tie a tie," may be sufficient, but I see nothing wrong with discussing life skills for a week or two with an advanced small group, perhaps beginning in Daniel 1, where Daniel is distinguished for his social proficiency. To address the issue without devoting copious time, get them a copy of *Things You Should Know by Now* by Jason Boyett or something similar addressing skills of adulthood. Just go to relevantbooks.com

ACADEMIC DISCIPLINES

"Just picture an outboard motor on a boat and you get a pretty good picture of how the bacterial flagellum functions, only the flagellum is far more incredible. The flagellum's propeller is long and whip-like, made out of a protein called *flagellin*. This is attached to a drive shaft by hook protein, which acts as a universal joint, allowing the propeller and drive shaft to rotate freely. Several types of protein act as bushing material (like washer/donut) to allow the drive shaft to penetrate the bacterial wall (like the side of a boat) and attach to a rotary motor. ... Not only that but the propeller can stop spinning within a quarter turn and instantly start spinning the other direction at 10,000 rpms.

The flagellum's molecular motor requires 50 proteins, all working in synchrony, to function. Like a partially constructed mousetrap, the flagellum would be worthless and perish unless all 50 proteins were fully developed."

This is from Michael Behe's book *Darwin's Black Box*. The irrefutable point is that cells contain complexity that could not have evolved incrementally. Who knew? Or here is something interesting from astronomy. Stephen Hawking states, "If the rate of expansion, one second after the big bang had been smaller by even one part in a hundred thousand million, million, the universe would have recollapsed before it ever reached its present size." Add to that this conversational gem: if the gravitational force were altered by 0.00000000000000000000000000 0000000000001 percent, neither Earth nor our Sun would exist—and you would not be here reading this.

Science is often seen as antithetical to faith, but recently science that affirms the presence of intelligent design in the universe is getting more attention. In a country where any product or experience is only valid if a Ph.D. says so, this is of great spiritual encouragement for students. It also protects and arms them with information to handle the spiritually adverse climate of the campus.

To this end it can be helpful to give your disciples something to read that contains some synthesis of faith and science. In most cases you don't have to be a lab rat to understand what they are talking about. In an academic environment, you should expose your students to some academic information that points in the direction of God, as most of what they hear points in the other direction.

Another important reason for discussing academic issues, is the need to teach your disciple how to integrate their faith with their field of study. To keep academics quarantined from issues of faith produces an unhealthy duality.

THEOLOGY AND READING

In one sense all that we learn about God in discipleship comes under the category of theology. But beyond the basics that equip believers, are deeper waters and streams branching off into a variety of disciplines. What I've found is that most Christians read and study more deeply if they can connect to the right topic. Find out what they want to read. Once they're hooked, it will invariably lead to more reading, which will lead to great progress in their faith.

For example, every now and then you find a student who actually likes systematic theology, meaning studying subjects such as sin, angels, Satan, etc. Such interest is rare, so after you have performed a battery of psychological tests, you might pass along a book on basic theology.

Some students like literature so getting them a book such as *Blue Like Jazz* by Don Miller can give them a taste for this type of writing. Or, there are always students who can't get enough apologetics, so so I give them something by Timothy Keller, Ravi Zacharias or C.S. Lewis. Then there are the men's and women's books and studies (anthropology) which surface a felt need in many young Christians. And, while not a discipline of theology, finding a good biography can also get them reading. For example there are a dozen biographies of Christian athletes that are ideal material for any disciple into sports.

Evangelism, worship, music, social issues, art, even Christian rock stars: odds are good you can make some match between your disciple's interests and excellent Christian books. Peruse one of those Christian Mustard Seed bookstores and, heck, show that your love has no bounds and get them a "Jesus Loves You" eraser while you're there.

RELATIONSHIPS

What interested me most about the guy who led me to Christ was seeing how he related to his wife and kids. Any time our disciples observe us in different relational dynamics they are deeply influenced, or as the apostle Paul puts it:

"We loved you so much that we were delighted to share with you not only the gospel of God but our lives as well, because you had become so dear to us" (1 Thessalonians 2:8).

Be intentional and thoughtful as to what relational contexts you can bring your disciple into.

LEADERSHIP

There is a whole field of study dedicated to helping people lead well. In light of both the importance of our mission, reaching lost people with the gospel, and the complexity of it, Cru has mined this field of study for principles that can increase one's capacity to lead. For example here are four critical responsibilities that leaders must grow in their ability to perform:

- Vision casting: communicating a picture of the future that motivates people to act
- Strategy formulation: coming up with intelligent, reality-sensitive ways to accomplish the vision
- Aligning: the ability to bring all people and resources together to carry out your strategies and accomplish your vision
- Motivating: tapping into a group's core values so that they want to work together to fulfill the mission

The full list and explanation of these principles can be found on any of the 2.3 billion Cru websites floating around in cyberspace, or in the chapter on leadership. Teaching your disciple principles of leadership may not seem that spiritual, but it provides them tools that can be applied to leading in a spiritual setting. The reality is that many churches and ministries have failed because they were managed (led) poorly.

CHAPTER TWENTY

WORLD POVERTY

Global Missions, And A Brief History Of The World

There is a starving world and yet every day I scrape mounds of food off my plate and into a bloated garbage bag. The problem isn't a lack of compassion and certainly not a lack of food. It is an issue of feasibility: I have no simple way to ship my plate of food overseas and no clue of where I would send it—"Third World Poor Box 3700." This has also been the struggle of world missions: the need for a feasible plan or strategy to bring the gospel to every nation. The campus ministry and its missions strategy really does provides a compelling solution, but that does us little good if we ourselves don't fully understand it, and the majority of us don't.

My chief concern is to help our disciples become world Christians. World Christians are followers of Christ who have taken personal ownership of the Great Commission and who share Christ's heart to see all nations receive the gospel. The most compelling element in creating vision for world evangelization is the feasibility to pull it off. When our disciples understand that this is possible, then they are more likely to engage in the mission. What follows is a brief history of campus missions, where we are today, and where may soon be headed. While history is only interesting to a select few, you really do need to know this and if it helps start you in a history mood here are a few random dates to memorize: 1923, 1847, 536, 1941, 1742, 1812, 1963, and please don't forget 1492.

THE HISTORY OF CAMPUS MISSIONS

The history of campus missions began at universities in places such as Wittenberg, Zurich, and Geneva. At these places, the first missionaries received their training, motivation, and marching orders. These movements gave rise to the Reformation. The impetus of the university system in America was the pedagogy of missionaries and pastors. (The curriculum to ridicule them being a later development. But for the sake of time and space we will fast forward to the last century or so.)

In 1886 the first Christian conference for college students was held in Mount Hermon, Massachusetts. On Friday evening, the last day of the conference, 250 students were given a challenge by Robert Wilder to consider taking the gospel to the world as foreign missionaries. One by one, coming forward to except the challenge, were 100 students from schools such as Yale, Harvard, Dartmouth, and Cornell. As a symbol of their commitment, each student signed a pledge, which read:

"We the undersigned, declare ourselves willing and desirous, God permitting, to go to the unevangelized portions of the world."

Seeing God's hand at work, Wilder spent the next year feverishly traveling to more than 150 campuses giving the same challenge, and seeing an additional 2,100 students sign the pledge. For more than 50 years, missionaries would pour out from the Student Volunteer Movement to the far corners of the earth—a total of 20,500 missionaries, the greatest missionary foray in the history of the church.

In 1948 the Student Volunteer Movement splintered. Most of the movement began to focus its attention on social issues. But those still with a heart for evangelism, joined with a newly formed college ministry and held their first missions conference in Urbana, Illinois. That group was InterVarsity.

In his book *Revive Us Again*, author Joel Carpenter notes that after World War II the call to fulfill the Great Commission once again ran into a slump in this country. It was at the point of its lowest ebb that this first InterVarsity conference was held. Of the 526 in attendance, 300 made decisions to go into full-time Christian ministry. InterVarsity was soon joined by Cru and other campus ministries and a new missionary enterprise springing from the campus and flowing out to the world was once again underway.

The Strategy Behind Campus Missions

As best as I can tell, no one sat down and thought up the strategy of fulfilling the Great Commission by reaching the college campus. Campus ministry is more the result of the observation that God has chosen to use college students as His vehicle to accelerate the evangelism of the world. Reaching the college campus is His strategy to help fulfill the Great Commission.

When you think about why God might have chosen to have spiritual revival and world missions emanate from the university, you begin to realize what a profound strategy it is. Consider the following questions.

When is a person most spiritually open to the gospel?

Before a person leaves college, his worldview and trajectory in life will be set, and it is not easily altered. There is a unique window of time when a young man or woman breaks from their parents and their beliefs, and decides for themselves what they will believe and what they will live and die for. This window of time is the college years.

How can we most easily communicate the gospel to other countries?

English is spoken on almost every college campus throughout the world. It is the common language—the *lingua franca*. This is not true of the many villages, towns, and cities where people are less educated. You can walk onto almost any university in the world and get involved in a spiritual conversation in English without having to go through years of learning the language.

Who will most effect change within a foreign country?

All of the key leaders (political, social, military) in any foreign country ultimately come from universities. The most strategic way to reach a nation with the gospel is by reaching its next generation of leaders, and the greatest collection of them will always be at the campuses.

How can we best access countries where Christianity is not legal?

The answer is a student visa. There are many Islamic states, for example, which won't allow missionaries to enter their country. However, if you enter the country with a student visa, go to their university, and spend your U.S. dollars to take a class, you are relatively free to do anything you like and remain in the country. Thus reaching foreign universities in not only easy due to the speaking of English, in some cases it's the only way to access a country with the gospel.

Where will the next generation of spiritual leaders come from in this country?

The majority of church leaders today were influenced or led into ministry through involvement with a campus ministry. It is in the context of a campus ministry that students learn to share their faith, disciple others, and lead spiritually. It is this introduction into ministry that brings to light for many their calling into the pastorate or some form of Christian leadership. Think about this for a moment. How many people from your home church have gone into ministry? Each year anywhere from a handful to several dozen leave the local campus ministry to be Christian leaders in their church or full-time pastors and missionaries.

How will we get more laborers to fulfill the Great Commission?

College students have their summers relatively free. Over the course of the summer, college students can go on missionary trips, get into any country with a student visa, and plant a ministry. College students have turned out to be an unforeseen (part-time) missionary labor force. There will be no other time in their lives where they will have three or four months free unless that time is preceded by the words, "You're fired!"

The Refinement of the Strategy

The history of missions is one of zeal not acumen, hindsight instead of foresight. Missionaries are typically doers: they blaze a trail and then note after the fact what worked and what didn't. Which, in hindsight, is probably best for the greatest challenge to missions is to go, and too much strategizing on the front end can lead to the planting of new missions agency in the states rather than new ministries overseas.

The campus ministry is no different and our current strategies are a product of several decades of adaptation, refinement, and probably some major screw-ups forever buried in a file drawer in Lake Hart with surviving members in Federal relocation programs. Many years ago we sent summer missions teams wherever there was be an open door, or wherever anyone had a "heart" to go. But if these missionary initiatives were to bear lasting fruit, they needed more focus. This came in three areas.

First, there was the birth of the partnership strategy. Each region of the U.S. would take responsibility to pioneer ministry in three to five countries—no overlaps or overlooked nations. Agreements were drawn up to ensure that the task was completed and the labor force didn't dry up—campus staff and students would continue to come for summer missions. When needed, multiple U.S. campuses would share the task of honoring these agreements. The shotgun missionary approach of the previous decades was becoming a little more like a guided missiles.

Second, there needed to be a refinement of the partnership process. This was broken into five stages sequencing U.S. involvement in developing the countries campus ministry. Here are those five stages:

> ### Stage One: Summer Project
> In about eight weeks, visiting teams of Christian students are able to create relationships, share the gospel, and disciple young believers on international campuses where the gospel has never traveled. They leave behind the seed of what will become a growing ministry on that campus.

> ### Stage Two: STINT
> How does this planted mustard seed become a growing movement? Short-term International (STINT) missionaries were sent to invest one or two years cultivating

what was sown over the summer. They also provide leadership, teaching, and further evangelism so that by the time they leave, a healthy maturing ministry is in place.

Stage Three: International Campus Staff
Like the ministries planted by the apostle Paul, these movements still lack maturity, need leadership continuity, and require someone to make gospel inroads on campuses elsewhere. Filling this "Timothy" role are missionaries who will dig in and invest three to five years, or longer, in the culture.

Stage Four: National Leadership
In this cycle of ministry, the leadership on the campus and in the country is properly passed on to nationals: to those original converts now mature enough to lead the ministry in their own country.

Stage Five: Partnering Nations
At this final stage new life emerges in two areas. The nation, young in its faith, becomes a participant in missions, sending their own students to minister in other nations. Concurrently, U.S. students are now free to partner with new campuses in other countries. This is the process.

Not all countries and not all campuses are equally strategic in getting to the entire world, which is why we don't have campus staff at Hoboken Culinary college, though I would volunteer if it became available—mmm donuts. So the third area of focus was to identify 200 of the most highly leveraged campuses in the world and plans were made to pioneer ministries at these locations. As of a couple of years ago, all 200 had an established ministry.

These strategic refinements in our campus missions strategy were significant enough to warrant a name and dedicated staff to aid in their development. This ministry focus within the Campus Ministry is now called "Global Missions".

THE NEW FRONTIERS

Well that brings us just about current. So where do we go from here? The following are the newest Global Missions initiatives and they all revolve around one principle, partnership.

Nations partnering with nations
As the leadership of these countries mature, we are entering a new phase in world missions, the final phase of multinational partnerships: nations partnering with nations to reach still other nations. This is where the missionary enterprise will grow exponentially.

Take, for example, a recent missions project held in Turkey. In the past, these projects were typically led by U.S. staff and students who travel to a partnership country to share the gospel. This was not the case here. This project comprised of staff and students from nine countries partnering together to reach Turkey.

And Europe is not the only place seeing this happen: Mexican students will be going to Chile; Thai students are going to Cambodia; Poland to Russia; Albania to Turkey; Egypt to the Middle East. We are witnessing a growing network of nations partnering with nations.

Partnering with churches to plant churches
The campus ministry continues to pioneer in cities throughout the world and as the ministry grows and students graduate (which they tend to do), there is often no local church able to support and sustain these young believers. The situation, viewed from another angle, is not a problem, but an opportunity. Here is the critical mass of new Christians that could form the core of a church planting effort in that city and nation—a church planters dream.

This was always the long-term vision of Cru to reach every nation with the gospel using the college campus as the stepping stone. *No Boundaries* is a new strategy to take the vision beyond the college campus by forming partnerships with local churches, helping them to mobilize their labor, and linking our international campus ministry with their congregation, all with the goal of planting churches in that city.

Global Partners
Global Partners is a growing network of business and professional leaders whose hearts are surrendered to Christ, and desire to leverage their access, platform, finances, and expertise to open up doors for the gospel around the world.

Globalization is the new economic realty. The world tethered ever tighter through the strands of technology, telecommunications, free markets, finance, and business.

This gives American business leaders a powerful platform to access countries around the world. The Global Partners strategy attempts to seize this opportunity, connecting godly business leaders with ministry venues, paving the way for evangelism and missions opportunities internationally.

MISSIOLOGY

Hopefully that provides a working knowledge of campus missions, which is a very strategic and very large slice of the mission's pie. But it is not the whole pie. There is a world of church missions focused on the Great Commission but with a mandate to plant churches within every people group on earth. In helping your disciple become a world Christian, you will find it useful to be familiar with the books and publications dedicated to church missions. They are a treasure trove of resources and information highly applicable to campus missions.

I highly recommend the book *Perspectives*. It contains the current thinking on world missions, the latest strategies, historical errors, motivation for missions, writings of the great missionaries, biblical teaching on missions, current statistics: it has everything. There are a ton of articles to pass on to your disciples to help them develop into world Christians. The book is a compendium of the class reading for a course of the same name—Perspectives. This course is taught at churches around the country and if it is available near you, consider taking your disciples with you.

This course and book come from the U.S. Center for World Missions, a great missionary organization. They also publish a monthly magazine called *Frontiers* that will help you keep in touch with what is happening in church missions around the world. Between the *Perspectives* book and the magazine you will have invaluable resources to share with your disciple.

While the focus of the U.S Center for World Missions is on church planting, there is so much commonality that it transfers well into campus missions. You'll also find that some of the new ideas in church missions are already being implemented in some form in campus missions.

CAMPUS, COVERAGE AND CITIES

The organization of Cru is the umbrella name for dozens of ministries other than campus. So where do all of these fit in? In fulfilling the Great Commission, Cru has a three-fold approach to reaching a country with the gospel. As mentioned, there is the campus mission strategy reaching the country through targeting the college audience. In addition to this is what is called the City strategy, which targets the major cities through a variety of means: business and athletic ministries, community outreaches, providing school teachers, assisting church plants, and whatever other creative means might be employed.

If you reach the epicenters of the campus and city, you have done much to reach the population of a country. But you still haven't fully saturated it with the gospel. That's why we have a coverage strategy. A good example of how this works, and by far the most effective, is the use of the "JESUS" film. Film teams scour the countryside looking to show the film in towns and remote villages. The team members who show the "JESUS" film partner with multiple churches and denominations to follow up and plant churches from the evangelistic fruit. More than six billion people have been exposed to the gospel through the "JESUS" film (this includes multiple viewings by people).

Briefs &

SECTION FIVE

Letters

CHAPTER TWENTY ONE

THIRTY YEAR'S WAR

On Theological Debates

A cursory reading of the New Testament alerts us to the theological debates and differences that are a part of ministry, and a part of discipleship. I have presided over my fair share of ministry divisions and unfortunately ministry splits, and am convinced that how we deal with these differences and conflicts is every bit as important as the outcome. While wrestling with theological issues is unavoidable, wrestling with people over them can often be averted by maintaining three simple values: be knowledgeable, be honest, and be charitable.

KNOWLEDGEABLE

In dealing with theological differences, as a non-denominational ministry we have a greater challenge (because we don't defend one position) as well as greater freedom (because we don't have to defend one position). What we need to strive for is a greater understanding of the different positions on issues most likely to surface divisively. For example, let's take the issue of free will and predestination. Wherever there's a crack in the sidewalk, you'll often find this weed growing out of it. Being knowledgeable means that I can lay out the two opposing viewpoints and give at least one verse that strongly supports their position. I want to express to my disciple that neither side is crazy. I want them to honestly understand why a person would hold this perspective. More important than the issue itself, I am helping my disciples respect these people by showing them that their belief is biblically justifiable.

After laying out the adjacent views, in this case a Calvinist and Arminian perspective, I now explain that there are those who hold a mediating position between the two. Here it would be some form of compatibalism. Whatever the issue, there are always two opposite convictions, with alternative positions held along a spectrum. One of the points of this exercise is to move my disciple away from polarities to the broader, but grayer road on which most people traffic.

Having accomplished this, it is important to state that within every major theological dispute there are viewpoints which go outside of acceptable parameters. For example, there are those who hold the view of an "openness of God" perspective in the free will/ predestination debate. This teaches that God may not fully know the future. There are some in the charismatic camp that believe people cannot be certain they have the Holy Spirit if they do not speak in tongues. You will need to drive in certain tent pegs and explain where the debate crosses over a line and leaves the camp of orthodoxy. There are acceptable evangelical positions along a spectrum, and you need to define that spectrum. In a non-denominational movement you are a good steward if you can accurately map out the major geography of the debate, but also define where the map ends and where dragons and sea serpents dwell. To do this you must be knowledgeable.

HONEST

Now, even though I may have a viewpoint on the issue, the next thing I try to do is to be as honest with the biblical data as possible. For example, on the issue of eternal security, I might say that if Hebrews was the only book in the New Testament, I could be persuaded to believe that loosing my salvation was a viable option. (It's best to acknowledge the difficulty of certain passages.) I would then state, "when combined with the entire council of scripture I don't think these verses could be teaching this, and what makes more sense would be...." (In essence I'm teaching the need for a systematic theology not just a biblical one). Or on the issue of charismatic gifts, I might say that to whatever view one holds, it would be difficult to justify from Scripture a cessation of the gifts. I may deem them to have ceased but it would be based on observation and other factors more than a biblical argument. You may disagree, but this is my honest appraisal of the biblical data and that is what I share with my disciple.

Again, as important as the theological issue, I am teaching character: that truth and being truthful is more important than someone thinking I'm right. This will shape their biblical scholarship making honesty in interpretation the highest value, instead of looking for verses to justify a position.

CHARITABLE

Many theological convictions contain an underpinning of values. Let's go back to the issue of Calvinism and Arminianism. Calvinists concerned for God's glory see the limits of human freedom, defined by Arminians as detracting from the sovereignty of God. Those who hold to some position of free will are often concerned that in removing free will, God could seem responsible for evil and His governance could appear dictatorial and not benevolent. The point being, both are concerned with God's glory and see the other perspective as limiting that glory. There is a common value of God's glory—He is amazing—and with that comes a desire to defend against theological positions that impinge upon that glory.

I'm not saying that theological positions are relative. Some are true and others are false. Some are more accurate than others, and we should choose a perspective that has the most and best biblical support. But there are relative components to why we align with certain perspectives based on our experience of God and what we value about Him. When analyzed, Spirit-filled Christians often share a value of God's glory, which they think their position best defends. I have found it helpful to bring out this shared value in creating a foundation for unity in the body, and keeping my own mind from casting the judgment, "Idiots."

HERE'S WHAT I THINK

Last, I think your disciple has a right to know what you think on the issue. And having created the context, you should explain your perspective. They will actually be more inclined to embrace your perspective having gone through the process because they see you as knowledgeable, gracious, and concerned for what is true. You have educated them on the issue, given them guidance, demonstrated character, and avoided sowing seeds of discord. Congratulations.

CHAPTER TWENTY TWO

YOU ALWAYS SAY THAT

On Conflict Resolution
(Adapted from the *Compass*)

If I could snap my fingers and impart one skill to people, it would be the ability to address and resolve conflict. When someone is upset with someone else, their first move is to go and talk trash about them to someone else. There is a tendency to gossip, complain, and malign them. That, of course, is an ungodly response and though it might be gratifying to our flesh, it does nothing to restore the relationship.

We tend to avoid going to the other person we're upset with because we don't know what to say. I'd like to show you a five-step guide to follow when you need to have a hard conversation with someone. Who knows, if you and they follow these rules, you could start an epidemic of healthy conflict resolution.

Typically when someone's mad at someone else, the anger builds until it reaches a personal boiling point. Then the person unloads: "You always do that. I can't believe you're such a jerk. It's no wonder nobody likes you. How could you be so stupid?"

Well, that was nice. The good news is you finally decided to address what's bothering you, sort of. But all the other person caught was this garbled mass of accusations and emotion. Unfortunately, he has no idea what you're talking about, and is totally on the defensive. Good work. Here's a better idea.

FACTS

Start by letting him know what the heck you are talking about. But do so dispassionately. Pop quiz: Is the following a statement of fact? "When

I called you last night, you were so incredibly rude. I stayed up late waiting for you to call, but did you care? No! I swear you are the most inconsiderate person who ever lived. I hope you choke to death on your own blood."

Uh, no. That's a bit of fact loaded with interpretation, opinion, accusation, and lunatic ranting. Try this instead:

"Hey Oscar, do you have a few minutes? There's something I need to talk to you about. Last night I was expecting to hear from you. By 11 o'clock I hadn't received a call from you, so I decided to try your cell. When you answered, the conversation was brief, and you hung up before I got to ask you my question."

Catch all that? No interpretation, just the cold hard facts with no attempt to spin them or read into them. We're off to a much better start.

THOUGHTS

Having established the facts that all should be able to agree on, you are free to move to step two, in which you state clearly your interpretation of the facts. Avoid saying things such as, "And on the basis of the aforementioned facts, I think you rot." Instead, try something like this:

"Oscar, I thought we agreed to connect at 9 p.m. since I had to finish the paper and you were the only one in the group who had that citation that you agreed to look up. Since the paper is 40 percent of our grade, I thought it was irresponsible for you to not give me the information I needed when I finally called you."

See, you're being honest, the facts are out there, and now so is your basic interpretation and complaint. Keep going.

FEELINGS

This is where you should let the other person know how you feel. Be careful though. If you begin your sentence by saying, "I feel that ... " you are almost never describing a feeling. I know that sounds screwy, but it's true. "I feel like you are a jerk." "I feel like choking you with my own hands." "I feel that the world would be a better place if you were eaten by a pack of wild dogs." None of those describe feelings. They may reveal feelings indirectly, but they are really statements of thought. Try again.

"I need to tell you I was really angry when you hung up. I had been growing more frustrated as the night went on because I knew it meant I'd be up late finishing this paper. And I was disappointed that you didn't own up to your obligation when I called."

DESIRE

In this step, make it clear what you wish were true. Or in the language of the Middle East peace process, "Lay a roadmap for the future." Since we are trying to be civil and win hearts, not inflame rage, try not to say, "I swear if we get stuck in the same group again I'm going to chain you to the desk in the library and superglue your eyes open."

Instead, try, "It's really important to me to get a good grade in this class so I can get into my major. I'd also like our group to stay together for the next project. You've got some good ideas and I think we really benefit having you take part."

ACTIONS

The final step is when you offer specific actions for the future. What are you asking the person to do? What are you pledging to do? Avoid statements such as: "So in the future, why don't you grow up and do your stinkin' homework? I'm sick and tired of you sucking the life out of me and leeching off my work."

Instead, try: "I'd really appreciate it if you could get the bibliography done by Friday like we decided. If you can't, let me know so the group can reassign that job and give you a different assignment."

Facts. Thoughts. Feelings. Desires. Actions.

CHAPTER TWENTY THREE

THE WHOLE TRUTH

On Christian Counseling

In discipleship we can hit difficult problems and issues far beyond our capacity to handle. When this occurs a wise course of action can be to refer our disciple to a local Christian counselor that you trust or has been recommended by your church. But a haunting question for many of us is, what goes on in these counseling sessions? For some it's a curiosity, for others it's a desire to pick up some pointers, and for others it's a suspicion that some form of voodoo is being employed. So we decided to part the curtain and ask a few questions of a trusted Christian counselor and see what light she might be able to shed on our questions or what trade secrets she might divulge.

Where do you start when someone comes into your office?
I have them fill out an intake form, which is an assessment tool allowing me to understand their issues, history, background, and spiritual maturity. It also helps me to know what kind of Christian community they are currently involved in.

What is the first question you ask someone?
What brought you to this point where you felt you needed a counselor? Unlike campus discipleship, we immediately get to the issue. They are coming to work through a specific problem.

What makes Christian counseling, Christian counseling?
Many things, but the major one would be the agreement that Scripture is the standard of truth for diagnosing the problem and for restoration. We are all spiritual beings and the answer to all spiritual problems is ultimately Jesus Christ.

Can secular theories be applied with a Christian emphasis?
I would say it is helpful, but people would answer differently. Some theories would be more adaptable than others.

What are you trying to discern as you listen to the person?
As a counselor you try to discern what is the errant thought, motive, or behavior, and from there, you try to get to the root of it. And this leads to the question of how best to apply truth to the problem.

How do you locate the source of the problem?
The first couple of sessions are really dedicated to uncovering the history of what has brought the person to this point. This history is what aids in locating the issue. As the person talks, I'm writing things down including a note of what steps I should take with the person in our next session.

What would be some ways you help people experience grace or apply truth?
A variety of things: first, of course, would be looking at scripture. Then I might give them an article or chapter from a book that deals with their problem. Getting them into a support group might also be a way to help them to experience truth and grace. I also might have them take some action steps, like writing a letter to extend forgiveness. All of these are tools or tactics helping them to metabolize the truth and experience God's grace. I've actually had the person write out their list of sins and write 1 John 1:9 across the list and tear it up, just like we do in basic follow up.

What happens in between sessions?
I'm a big believer in homework. I never give a whole book to read but chapters from books that might be helpful. A helpful resource is June Hunt's *Counseling Through the Bible*. She covers every possible topic and provides a definition of the problem, root cause, as well as solutions and scripture. As they read the material, I ask them to write down their thoughts and reflections. This will also help me in my detective work.

Let's say it's abuse. Where do you go with this?
Like many issues involving shame, the key thing is to get the issue out into to the light, hopefully getting to the point where this person can articulate what exactly happened to them. This is probably the first time they've ever done this. My hope is that this issue will become a part of their testimony of Christ's work in their life. I also seek to get them into a recovery group where they can connect and share with others who have had a similar experience. Finally, I desire them to get

to the point where they can forgive the person(s) who sinned against them.

How do you deal with the need for ongoing forgiveness?
Continuing in unforgiveness, after you have forgiven someone is like any other issue of the flesh: it needs to be daily yielded to God as we put Him back on the throne.

What about medication?
Before I would encourage that direction I would refer them to another counselor. I think medication can be helpful in certain circumstances but I am slow to move to that as the answer.

What if you are not seeing change over many weeks?
I would refer them to someone else. Proverbs 24:6 says, "For waging war you need guidance, and for victory many advisers." I am limited in my abilities and someone else may be able to help them in a way that I cannot. In about nine session I've really shared all that I have to offer.

Is a person ever too badly gone to help?
I believe that there is hope for everybody in Christ

When do you assess that there might be a demonic element?
Well I think we are all under attack. Satan wants to defeat us all. I'm very comfortable suggesting that they work through a book that deals more in-depth with issues of demonic harassment. If I don't bring up the issue, who will?

Do you ever teach people simple coping mechanisms?
Yes, we need to be able to function in the midst of our issues and certain things can help us to cope or keep ourselves under control as we work to get to the root of a problem.

What are the ultimate destinations you seek to bring a person?
I want to see them vitally connected in a loving community, and to experience God's forgiveness and extend to others. I want them to have assurance of their salvation and to be able to handle the Scriptures. I want them to see this as a part of their testimony of Christ's work in their life and to move past this impasse in their spiritual growth. In some cases I would also look for a change of behavior.

There are dozens more questions we could have or should have asked but hopefully this is of some help. It seems to me that Christian counseling is specific discipleship focused on working through one particular issue that has become a major obstacle to growth: a clogged artery that is not allowing the free flow of grace and truth.

The skilled counselor does a lot of listening and detective work over a handful of sessions to locate the root of the problem which lie beneath the felt emotions and mental duress.

The essence of counseling seems to be an encounter with truth: sharing the truth about yourself and problem, getting to the truth about what's causing the problem, applying God's truth to the problem, and learning how to experience this truth. The counselor seems to be gifted in truth telling, and their objectivity and position allow them to traffic in areas where others have not been allowed to tread. Like radiation treatment for cancer, the special focus given to an issue or problem seems to radically increase the dosage of truth exposing everything hidden to the light of God's truth.

CHAPTER TWENTY FOUR

WINDOW OF THE WORD

On Journaling

When I was little, I was fascinated with the concept of cooking. My mother didn't enjoy it, but my father loved nothing better than to experiment in the kitchen with new recipes and flavor combinations. The mixing of things together with the addition of heat and stirring could result in the most marvelous tastes. He would often let me help him, pouring in some of this, stirring some of that. He was very cautious when it came to heat; he constantly reminded me that I needed to keep my eye on whatever I was stirring and to be especially mindful of covered pots that were supposed to boil.

As I helped him make spaghetti sauce one day, I became distracted by a book I was reading and didn't pay attention to the sauce as it sat covered on the stove. Suddenly, I was being pelted by blobs of red sauce as the lid danced around the pot, spewing its contents as the steam periodically lifted the lid. Not thinking, I took the lid off, and the spaghetti sauce began bubbling over everywhere, making a mess on the stove and burning me in the process. A painful, but well-remembered object lesson.

As I've gotten older, I've realized that so many of the things we encounter in daily life that are small inconveniences or uncomfortable experiences are actually greater life lessons that I need to heed. Not to sound too much like Forrest Gump, but life is a lot like that pot of boiling spaghetti sauce. We are constantly mixing things into and adding activities to our lives, becoming busier as time goes on. And the stress of deadlines and expectations and disappointments and responsibilities becomes the heat that brings the contents of our lives to a boil. This often causes us to say and do things in the height of emotion that we would never say or do in our saner moments. We need something in our lives that will allow us to monitor the heat more closely so that we can diffuse problems before they boil over uncontrollably and we begin to spew words that are more hurtful than hot spaghetti sauce.

I have found that journaling, writing down my thoughts and ideas, can act as a significant release to the pressure that builds up day after day. Author Isabel Colgate once wrote, "It is not a bad idea to get in the habit of writing down one's thoughts. It saves one having to bother anyone else with them." Journaling is much like sitting back and looking through a window at what is happening in your life, and then writing down what you see and what you think and feel about it. It is a process of taking the thoughts and feelings from inside and giving them a voice on paper, a silent yet tangible expression of who and what you are. The beauty of journaling is that it can act as a release to things that build up inside, freeing passion and pain, gratitude and grief, delight and disappointment in a way that won't infringe on anyone else's feelings.

I have been journaling consistently for more than twenty years, and in that time I have dealt with crises, joys, sorrows, fears, excitement, anticipation, worry and a multitude of other emotions, circumstances and decisions in the pages of my journals. It all began, innocuously enough, as a challenge in a Bible study, to journal fourteen days in a row without missing a day. The idea was to read a portion of Scripture, rephrase it, and write briefly what it meant to me and my walk with the Lord. It took me several tries to get the fourteen days in a row—I'd forget a day and have to start all over again. Oh, the frustration of rules, the tyranny of the musts and have to's! There was no way I wasn't going to do it when everyone else in the group was succeeding. It became, I am almost ashamed to admit, a game to see how many days in a row I could go without missing.

The game, however, turned serious and personally beneficial when I began to look at the passage in light of my present experiences, what I was feeling, and questions I was pondering. I found myself writing more and more, recording not only my perspectives on Scripture but also attitudes I was dealing with, prayers I was needing to bring before the Lord, people in my life that required more of me than I had to give.

Writing became a process of actively dealing with the situation at hand. Getting it down on paper in black and white helped me focus on what was truth, what was emotion, and what was merely perception on my part. I was moving ahead in the development of a workable solution, an opportunity to advance in my thinking and processing of whatever I happened to be going through at the time. It helped diffuse the intensity of my feelings so I wasn't as prone to take my frustrations out on others.

How does this work? Journaling can be personalized to who you are and how much time you have. Author Joan Didion wrote, "I write entirely to find out what I'm thinking, what I'm looking at, what I see and what it means; what I want and what I fear." This has become my time with the Lord, my quiet time, and I begin with writing out my heart to the Lord. It ends up being the most honest, vulnerable and transparent praying that I do because I hold nothing back. The things that burden my mind and my heart are the things I pour out on paper, directing it toward the God who knows all that I am, everything that I think, each and every thing that I do.

The most difficult part is beginning—applying pen to paper. But as I come before the Lord, desiring to connect with Him heart to heart, I find my voice and the words come.

And it often looks different every day. At times it begins with simple narrative, what is happening in my life, how I feel about it. I can write opinions about anything and everything, right or wrong, because feelings are barometers of how I'm dealing with life. I can rant and rave about a person I'm struggling with or a problem that confounds me or a situation that causes me despair. Writing things down and getting them out of my head and down on paper keeps me from saying things (usually) that are inappropriate or hurtful to others.

Sometimes I write words of praise and thanksgiving because I'm simply grateful. These will become your prayers, as you allow yourself to be real before God, no holds barred. He knows us completely anyway—being honest and transparent is freeing to the soul.

I then read a passage of Scripture. My preference is to read through the Bible, cover to cover and then I take a few moments to summarize it in my journal. What is the author saying? What are my questions on the passage? Then I take another few moments to comment on how this passage impacts my own life, the possible applications, and things I may never have seen or understood before. It is amazing how the Holy Spirit will illuminate passages for me that seemed at one time confusing. Even if I still have questions, I write them down to research later.

You may only write a few lines, or you may write pages—time and the Spirit of God will help you set your parameters. And as the days go on and you look back at what you've written, you'll learn even more about yourself than when you were writing it the first time. You can see growth, answered prayer, and your life in perspective.

It has been said that it takes six weeks to develop a habit. What began as a game for me, developed into a habit which amazingly transformed into quality time with my Friend. It began as a matter of discipline; there were some days that were rich with insight and others were as dry as fallen autumn leaves—no life, just duty. And there are still times today when my time with the Lord is dry, but I have the freedom to write that down and express my wandering mind or my wilderness soul, and I know He is not bothered by that. But as I take the time to write what is truly on my heart, I am convinced that there is Someone who knows me better than anyone else, and it feels really wonderful to be fully known.

Challenge yourself to fourteen days of journaling and spending time in God's Word. It doesn't have to take hours; anyone can set aside fifteen minutes for something they value. Find a time in your day that works best for you on a consistent basis, a time you plan into your schedule so you know it won't be overlooked by busyness or deleted by hurry. Anyone can do something for fourteen days, and who knows—you may find that it is the highlight of your day.

CHAPTER TWENTY FIVE

PAINT BY NUMBERS

On God's Will

Your disciples will spend the rest of their Christian lives as detectives, always hunting for clues and sifting through available data in search of what can seem like an elusive fugitive: God's will. For as soon as we momentarily apprehend it, time moves on and so does God's plan for our lives, and we are once again back in the hunt. You, therefore, are charged with a great responsibility; you must teach your disciple to become good detectives of God's will. Here is what I would include in the introductory class.

First, there are different ways we identify or discern God's leading in our lives. I will not attempt to be exhaustive or to deal with the possible nuances of each method, but a biblical case could be made for discerning God's will through any of these seven means:

- Discerned through wisdom: your accumulated knowledge of how God works in the Bible, the world, and your life
- Discerned through circumstances: Open doors, closed door, or an alignment of circumstances can point you to God's direction
- Discerned through the counsel of others: Christians who have a mature understanding of you and/or the Lord can provide guidance as to what God may be saying to you
- Discerned through the mind: The Holy Spirit is not truncated from your mind and therefore distinct impressions, dreams, thoughts, and images can be informed by God to give direction

- Discerned through emotions: Your feelings can also be influenced by the Spirit, and so likes and desires as well as strong negative feelings can provide clues to God's leading
- Discerned through the brain or reasoning: Logic and reasoning can be valuable tools in discerning God's leading. A pro/con list is an example
- Discerned through the Scripture: Most importantly biblical principles inform our discernment of God's will

This creates a pallet of colors, which if mixed properly by the hands of a mature Christian can yield a beautiful portrait of what God is doing and how He is leading. In the hands of an immature Christian who will have a tendency to use simply one color (say emotions) you can get an unrecognizable mess. We will spend the rest of our lives growing in our ability to mix these paints, ever increasing in our ability to discern God's hand in our lives.

After teaching your disciples the various colors, the first lesson of application is to not use only one color. Instead, what they are to look for is several of these methods to align with one another: what they are thinking and feeling is also the same as what a more mature Christian has suggested or what they've been learning in their quiet time.

Satan likes to play with paints as well and can paint a pretty decent forgery, which is why they would be ill advised to make a major life decision simply because a few circumstances seem to line up.

Second lesson: As a young Christian, stay with the primary colors like God's Word, the counsel of mature Christians, or reasoning. The reason being, they have had little time to cultivate their relationship in the Lord so they possess zero wisdom paint and their emotions and thoughts are not yet saturated in the God's Word. So for now, they should try to stick with blue, red or green.

Third Lesson: Emotions are powerful. and try as you might it will be difficult to keep your disciple from dabbling with this color—it's pretty. So I try to help them to use it better. I teach them that our emotions are a mixed bag and they need to learn how to isolate competing feelings. I once had a disciple tell me he was not interested in going into ministry. Then I asked him, that if he had no relatives and was independently wealthy what would he do with his life? The answer was ministry. His feelings were reliable, but he just had several of them competing with each other: he wanted his family to be proud of him, he didn't want to raise support, but he did want to spend his life in ministry. What I didn't do was forbid him from the practice of using his emotions, but I helped him grow in his knowledge of how to better use the color.

Lesson four: Circumstances do not mean signs. Assuming the Holy Spirit is at work in your life, it is wise to look at the fabric of circumstances He has woven over time as a clue to where He may be leading. A decision to study abroad based on a grilled cheese sandwich that strangely had a burn mark shaped like Italy is not responsible detective work or responsible living. God does not encourage this type of reasoning to discern His will either. Help them discern their circumstances not hunt for miraculous signs.

Finally, the most important lesson of all is found in Romans:

> "Therefore, I urge you, brothers, in view of God's mercy, to offer your bodies as living sacrifices, holy and pleasing to God—this is your spiritual act of worship. Do not conform any longer to the pattern of this world, but be transformed by the renewing of your mind. Then you will be able to test and approve what God's will is..."
> *Romans 12:1-2*

Discerning God's will is predicated on complete submission and willingness to do His will, whatever He may require. When I was dating the woman who is now my wife, I remember coming to a traffic light and saying if the light turns green in the next 15 seconds I'll ask her to marry me. (In my immaturity I was looking for a sign.) But when the light didn't turn green, I thought, "That was stupid, and it means absolutely nothing." On other occasions when the light did turn green I thought, "See, I knew it. I should marry her" The point is I was only open to one verdict and when that is the case we will always fudge the numbers; we will interpret all signs as pointing in the direction we desire. We cannot begin to use any of the colors on the pallet until we completely resign to God's bidding, otherwise we're simply painting a self-portrait.

A FINAL NOTE

Teaching our disciples how to paint is messy. We can make things easier on ourselves by limiting the colors, teaching only that God leads through His Word and a pro/con list. But they will never fully mature and appreciate God's dynamic leading of His people if we do not encourage experimentation, teaching them from their errors. I know many mature Christians who seek only a pro/con list for their major decisions, because a discipler somewhere in their past told them this was the only paint permissible. I'm sure it kept them from making some really stupid decisions, but their understanding and appreciation of God's leading has unfortunately remained black and white.

CHAPTER TWENTY SIX

HEADING NORTH

On Using The Compass

Cru has always provided follow-up material for the first five disciple-ship lessons. Recently we were finally able to release *The Compass*. *The Compass* is a discipleship tool that provides content and direction for the next 40-plus personal discipleship lessons. Here is a brief overview to help you and your disciples maximize the content.

Like most trips, this one is more fun when traveling with a companion. And like all adventures into new places, you get more out of them if you can travel with someone who has been there before. It's likely you were led to Christ by someone who had already "crossed over from death to life." By God's grace they were willing to come back and get you, and walk over that bridge again with you. The same is true if you have had the priv-ilege of being discipled. Even a stud like Paul needed a Barnabas to guide him until he was ready to lead himself. Life in Christ is not meant to be experienced alone.

Now it's your turn to guide others as they begin, or continue, to walk with Jesus. In this small window of infinite consequence, you can set the trajectory for another student's entire life.

The Compass is designed to assist you, the discipler, in becoming a wise and helpful guide to another younger believer. Each lesson is written directly to you, the discipler, not to your disciple. There are no lessons to hand out, no blanks to fill in. Rather, *The Compass* contains information for you to read, internalize, prepare, and present to your disciple. The lessons aren't designed to make lame discipleship easy, but to make great discipleship possible. Glance over the material for ten minutes before a meeting and your disciples will know it, and you'll feel like a loser. (I know that of which I speak.) If, on the other hand, you take the time to rigorously interact with what you learn here, and combine it with your own passions and experience, you'll change their lives and they'll love you forever.

We recommend you go through a four-step process as you get ready for each appointment. Step one is to read the lesson. You can read it aloud, read it quietly, or laminate it and read it in the shower for all I care. Just read it taking notice of the main sections.

This Week's Excursion
This is a brief description of where you are headed this week. It highlights the biblical objective or main idea that you want your disciple to grasp. It reminds you of the forest in case you can only see the trees.

Conversation on the Journey
Here you will find the heart of the lesson. We'll tell you what's on our hearts about a particular topic. Or maybe we'll be sharing with you the tightest way we know to communicate a key idea. Some of these will seem like a private Bible study lesson; others may explain a diagram you can sketch out on the back of a grease-stained napkin. As the heading implies, it should inform you of what to talk about as you lead your disciple down this leg of the trip.

Next Steps
According to the Westminster Larger Catechism, sanctification is a work of God's grace whereby the Holy Spirit puts into our hearts all saving graces and so stirs up, increases, and strengthens those graces, so that we die unto sin and rise unto newness of life. In this section, we give ways you can challenge the thoughts and actions of your disciples so as to stir up those graces.

Side Trails
Sometimes on a trip you might decide to spend an extra day or two to explore areas you hadn't anticipated. As you are discipling believers, the same will be true. Here we will mention an extra resource or two that you can either read yourself, or recommend to your disciple to study in greater depth.

Step two, is to *internalize* the content. Chew on it, think about it, and look up the scriptures. Build up the concordance in your head by thinking about what other passages from God's Word speak to the same issue. If there is a passage you like better, use it as your main text for the lesson. Scribble on the sheet, use diagrams, and let your mind wander to come up with an illustration from your life that can drive the point home. Quiz yourself to see if you can remember the main points we outlined. Do a "Google" search on a key term and see where that takes you. Bust out a commentary and see if you can prove we are really heretics bent on corrupting a new generation of college students. For step two you've got to think. Think, think, think.

Step three is *prepare* for the time. How are you going to present this to your disciples? Here's a hint. You don't need to tell them about this tool. Let them think you are a genius, a spiritual giant who knows all, and by whose mere grace has condescended to share with them from your everlasting fount of knowledge. If you've done a good job of step two it should be easy to make a couple of cheat sheets for yourself and stick them in strategic places in your Bible.

Our motive in suggesting this isn't to encourage deception, but to facilitate learning. People don't learn well from handouts where they only need to fill in the blank. It's the Ferris Bueller phenomena:

Read Acts 17:10: "As soon as it was night, the brothers sent Paul and Silas away to Berea."

Question
Where were Paul and Silas sent away to?

_____
_____
_____
_____
_____
_____

Anyone, anyone?

It's such an awful way to teach. Don't do it. Instead, plan to have a conversation. Know what you want to talk about and be prepared to explain the passages from the Bible, but don't pass out sheets, and don't ask questions that would bore a 6 year-old boy. Use Post-it notes.

Finally, *present* the material. If you have been diligent with steps 1-3, all you really need to do is show up and love your disciples. If their heart just got broken, you probably should postpone the lesson for a week, otherwise you should be all set to take them on the next stage of the great journey.

Read. Internalize. Prepare. Present.

Oh, yeah, one last thing. Before you get started, listen to Roger Hershey's talks included on *The Compass*. Roger is a fantastic discipler, and a great trainer of disciplers. Listening to those four talks will provide you with the best overall understanding of discipleship. If I were you, I wouldn't venture out until I had listened to his talks.

CHAPTER TWENTY SEVEN

LOST IN TRANSLATION

On Bible Versions

I went to a Christian bookstore to make a simple purchase: I needed to buy a Bible for someone I was taking through basic follow-up. Could anything be simpler, more right with the universe, than to purchase a Bible from a religious bookstore? Apparently not. I should have been clued in when I saw an entire aisle of the store cordoned off for the task of selling Bibles. They sold every conceivable color, shape, size and design—including a camouflage cover should my disciple be having a quiet time while hunting wild game. And then there is the question of translation. I'll leave it up to you to decide if a camouflage version or a translation containing Esther's dieting tips is best for your disciples, but perhaps a general background on Bible translation will help you decide on what is the best translation for them.

The books of the Old Testament were primarily written in Hebrew while the books of the New Testament were originally written in Greek. This is why both languages, at least at an elementary level, are taught in seminaries and Bible schools. We do not have any of the original man-uscripts of the Bible books. If we did they would be significantly more valuable than a Babe Ruth rookie card so perhaps it's worth rummaging around your attic to see if you can find one. What we do have is thou-sands of early manuscript copies—sometimes fragments, sometimes full books dating as far back as the second century.

The first step in Bible translation involves piecing together from the many manuscripts what exactly the originals said. You can imagine in a pre-printing world that manuscripts had various misspellings, omis-sions, and errors. It's usually clear what the originals were communi-cating, but what happens when two different manuscripts have variant readings of a verse or word? That's where Bible translators earn their expense account and fancy cars. They have to make decisions on the basis of the age of the manuscript (older versions get preference) and number of manuscript copies to decide which variant is most likely the original. Occasionally, if all this labor still comes up indecisive, they will put the variant reading in the margin of the Bible so that we know what it was.

With that as a background I think we can better address the question of which version to select. The next step in the process is translating the Bible into another language, in our case English, from its original Greek or Hebrew. This exercise is fraught with challenges as some words, phrases, idioms, or ideas can be difficult to translate into another language.

Translators have to move in one of three directions. One is to maintain a "literal" translation of the Greek or Hebrew. Why wouldn't they always do that? Think of the Spanish phrase mesa verde. Translated literally it means "table green" as opposed to the "green table." Maintaining the original sentence structure can actually make reading it in English more difficult. On the positive side you know you are reading exactly what it said in the original language. Perhaps the most favorite of the literal translations is the English Standard Version (ESV). This is a great translation. The New King James Bible would also fall into the category of literal translations.

The second direction translators take is to retain the accuracy of the original manuscripts but find close English equivalency. Let me give you one example and you'll see what I mean. The literal reading of Genesis 31:35 is, "The manner of women is upon me" (ESV). The English equivalent would be, "I'm having my period" (NIV). You haven't lost any of the meaning of the original. In fact you may actually understand it because the translators have found an English equivalent of the thought. An example of this type of translation and perhaps one that is most useful to a young Bible reader is the New International Version (NIV). This version is both accurate to the original as well as very readable. We read and hear the Scriptures with the thought clarity of the original audience. It's a bridge between the two languages and worlds.

Dude, like the third translation approach is an attempt to take the original and put it in today's vernacular. You can loose a little of the meaning when a phrase such as "light on the path" is translated as "flashlight on the path," but what you get in return is a text that reads like today's English—awesome. There's nothing wrong with these translations, but they do make some editorial leaps that can obscure the depth of meaning. "Light" for example makes me think of all kinds of spiritual concepts: "flashlight" makes me think of Sears or Target. It is probably good to have an NIV or ESV around so you can quickly look at a reading closer to the original text. The Living Bible is perhaps the most popular translation of this type.

Hopefully this will make your trip to the Bible aisle less intimidating. I personally recommend either the ESV or NIV, and for a very young Christian, I would usually purchase them an NIV.

CHAPTER TWENTY EIGHT

WHO'S IN CHURCH?

On Being A Parachurch Organization

Let's say I was a child in Albania and came to Christ and was discipled through the relief organization World Vision, a compassion-focused parachurch structure whose mission is to mobilize the church to help the poor and hungry around the world. It would seem to me that if I was discipled within this context, surrounded by those with the gift of compassion who feed the poor, I would develop a one-sided view of the full missionary endeavor of the church.

The same is true of any parachurch structure which has as its mandate the accomplishment of a specific ministry or task Christ gave to His church. Cru with its evangelistic mandate is no exception. Like the analogy of World Vision, our perspective of the church and the Christian life could become skewed if all we ever experience in the body of Christ is our local Cru chapter.

All who minister within Cru ultimately feel this tension. What is strategic for an evangelism mission might not always be so for the local church: reaching leaders, freshmen, and athletes, as opposed to the homeless, makes sense if your goal is a missionary one (you must find the best carriers of the gospel message). But such outreaches to the poor and homeless by the local church are an essential part of the broader Christian witness within the community.

Though there are several alternatives to dealing with this tension, I believe only one of them is correct.

One alternative, which I have viewed on numerous occasions, is to watch the Cru movement evolve into a church to correct the chemical imbalance. But the church already exists and God has called Cru to a special mission to help the church fulfill its evangelistic objectives. When we deviate from our mission, we step out of God's calling to us as an organization. We never fully achieve the full-orbed mission of the church on campus and we never accomplish our mandate to take the gospel to every student.

Another option is to obliterate the parachurch altogether and let local churches own the ministry currently being accomplished by the parachurch. But the parachurch structure is indeed part of the overall church structure and always has been. Did Paul's missionary endeavor and network flow out of the ministry of a local church? It really functioned as a separate structure with a focused mission, answerable to Paul's leadership. Another way to look at it would be to ask this question: Could a local church accomplish the mission focus, administration, and partnership required to meet the global needs of the poor as World Vision has? The answer is obvious. From seminaries to monasteries there have always been voluntary associations within the body of Christ who provide the necessary focus, administration, resources and broader cooperation necessary to execute the constituent components of the church's mission.

The best alternative is to make sure your disciples are involved and attending a local church. Here they are exposed to a broader range of biblical teaching and ministry, such as outreaches to the aged, poor, sick and widows. While many functions essential to the church do take place on campus, they are always mitigated in some way by our mission, which is why church attendance has always been a high value as an organization. Bill Bright never intended Cru to be a church.

Furthermore, when we embrace and encourage involvement in a local church, we can point to such ministries of the church and be unapologetic in our strategies to evangelize the campus. Otherwise we will always seem cold and heartless in the strategic nature of our outreach.

So let's fulfill our mandate and make sure every student on campus has a chance to hear the gospel. But let's also encourage our disciples to attend and get involved in a local church. Otherwise they may think the mission of Cru is the only responsibility given to the church, with the only gifting required being that of evangelism.

CHAPTER TWENTY NINE

HOPE YOU GUESS MY NAME

On Spiritual Battle

In the true story that lay behind the movie *The Exorcist*, several Jesuit priests (6 in all) were sought in St. Louis to perform an exorcism of a young boy who, incidentally, is still alive today. The exorcism apparently lasted 20 days, the events being preserved in the diary of Father Bowdern, one of the exorcists. The church does not allow priests to speak of the events of an exorcism, but Bowdern's diary was published in the appendix of Thomas Allen's recent book *Possessed*. The following are excerpts:

> March 14: A stool flew across the room and landed with a loud crash, but no one was injured. The mattress of the bed shook, as on many occasions. The shaking continued for two hours.

> March 16: Three large bars were observed to be scratched on the boy's stomach. The marks were sharply painful and raised above the skin similar to an engraving. The most distinctive marking was the word "HELL" imprinted on his chest. They would appear as we read through the exorcism.

> March 17: The new phase of the case emphasized diabolical spitting. He spit at Father Bowdern and tore his shirt. He spit directly in the faces of his father, mother, and uncle. He fell exhausted after the ordeal.

> April 7: During the praying, at least 20 scratches or brands

appeared on the boy's body, usually at the mention of "Jesus." The first mark was clearly the number 4; several times four strokes or claw marks of various lengths appeared on his belly and legs. There was considerable profanity and crudeness concerning sexual relations with priests and nuns.

The case was witnessed, signed, and verified by 46 Jesuit Priests. The true life Exorcist account ended when the boy uttered "dominus," which is Latin for "Lord" or "Christ."

I'm really not trying to creep you out only to underscore a single point: Satan is real and the struggle of discipleship will always have a component of spiritual battle.

The apostle Paul says this in Ephesians 6: 11-12:

> "Put on the full armor of God so that you can take your
> stand against the devil's schemes. For our struggle is not
> against flesh and blood, but against the rulers, against the
> authorities."

Let me explain the context and importance of this verse. Throughout the book of Ephesians, Paul has addressed many issues of holiness and godliness. At the end of the letter he revisits every issue previously discussed (a summary) only through a different lens: the righteousness he's talked about is now referred to as a breastplate, truthfulness is seen as a belt, faith a shield, and the Spirit a sword.

His point is that we are in a war, and that righteousness, truthfulness, faith, etc. are more than wonderful virtues; they serve as protection in this war. And to be ensnared in immorality, lies, unbelief, etc., is worse than just sin, it provides the enemy a stronghold in our lives by which he can wreak havoc. Paul is not only concerned that his disciples will be living in an ungodly manner, but that their ungodliness will provide an opening for spiritual attack. Sin's consequences go beyond the moral realm.

A good shepherd always keeps an eye out for the spiritual war that surrounds their disciple, "in order that Satan might not outwit us. For we are not unaware of his schemes." (2Cor. 2:11).

Being aware is being a good detective: open to clues and information that the Holy Spirit draws to our attention so we can pray specifically about these areas or issues, and address them where possible.

I was meeting Danny for a follow-up appointment and he told me to go into his room and wait for him, and that he would join me shortly. As I entered his room I happen to see a pornographic magazine sticking out from under his bed. I didn't know him well enough yet to address the issue, but I know that God wanted me to see that magazine (but of course not look at it), so that I could pray specifically about what turned out to be a spiritual stronghold in his life.

Another time I was walking down the dorm hallway to a discipleship appointment and the walls were reverberating from the base beat of music coming from one of the rooms. As it turned out it was the room of the guy I was meeting. All students listen to loud music, but I was compelled to believe that this was not an accident—that God wanted me to know this, or rather hear this. And, by faith (faith that my hearing this was not accidental) I began to pray specifically for this student, that music would cease to exercise a controlling influence in his life.

When we are prayerful and alert going into discipleship times we will often find God giving us windows into hidden areas that we would otherwise be oblivious to, for God doesn't want us to be unaware of Satan's schemes to ensnare our disciples.

> "The weapons we fight with are not the weapons of the world. On the contrary, they have divine power to demolish strongholds." *2 Corinthians 10:4*

Amongst the weapons we wield are faith, the word of God, and prayer. Using the truth of scripture we can pray for the protection and deliverance of our disciple and against Satan's strategies and strongholds in their life. In prayerfully following up clues, sometimes you will notice changes in their lives, other times you may not. Our job is to be alert and faithful to follow through with whatever we think God may be showing us.

While it's possible to read more into things than is actually there, I see no danger in erring on the prayerful side, and I'm convinced that if we were able to pull back the curtain and peer into the spiritual world, we would not find that there was less going on than we thought, only more.

CHAPTER THIRTY

EVERYBODY'S DIFFERENT

On Personality Tests

Have you ever noticed that everyone is not the same? I'm not talking about the way people look but the way they act and the reasons they do the things they do. (Half our conflict seems to come from misunderstanding those reasons and actions. The other half probably comes from the fact that we think the way they do things is wrong.)

As an introvert (25 percent of the population), I have been reassured by others, usually extroverts (75 percent of the population), that my introversion will be cured in heaven and I will become as they are. I have not come across introversion in any biblical list of sins nor have I noticed extroversion being referred to as the natural result of being filled with the Spirit. Instead, thankfully, we find a world that is neither peopled entirely of extroverts nor of introverts but is a unique mix that brings the fullest glory to God as we live together and express His handiwork.

Some people could spend hours pouring over personality tests, loving every minute of analyzing the subtle nuances of themselves and their friends. Others find the process constricting and limiting, typecasting of the worst kind. Personality tests can be one tool for understanding the unique way God has wired the people you are discipling. Knowing who they are can help you tailor the discipleship process to partner with God's unique design for each person.

What follows is a layperson's take on Myers-Briggs, a common personality type indicator named after its developers.

There are a few things to keep in mind with any personality type tests. They are human efforts to categorize and create order, drawing conclusions about the ways people tend to behave from a systematic structure. A personality type can never be used as an excuse for sinful behavior. When we express a right behavior, it may look different depending on our personality, but our personality can never serve as an excuse for unholy actions or attitudes. Our nature is marred by sin. The outspoken boldness of the Apostle Peter's personality was positively reflected as he proclaimed the gospel but also got him into trouble when he impetuously used his sword to defend Jesus.

It is also good to keep in mind as you explore various personality tests that most have at their foundation a presupposition that does not allow for the transforming power of God's Spirit. We are not unchangeable. As you disciple others you may need to evaluate if your ministry tends to focus on and value certain types of students over others. Will the quiet and faithful, yet highly influential introverted evangelist be overlooked and overshadowed by the gregarious, loves-to-be-up-front, extroverted social leader who motivates others to come to weekly meetings and Bible studies? Will the quiet evangelist find this a place to be mentored without having to change her personality?

So, with our disclaimers out of the way, let's do an overview of the Myers-Briggs components of personality. This is only one way to look at personality types, and should not be used as a comprehensive test for anyone.

Just as one discovers potential gene combinations using a punnett square, the eight personality type elements produce sixteen four–element combinations. Each individual element is affected by the other. The types are broken down into four preference opposites: E (Extroverted) or I (Introverted), S (Sensing) or N (Intuitive), T (Thinking) or F (Feeling), J (Judging) or P (Perceiving).

E OR I (EXTROVERT VERSUS INTROVERT): WHERE DO I RECEIVE OR FOCUS MY ENERGY?

Not necessarily a marker for friendliness or shyness, E and I refer primarily to a person's preference for the external or the internal world. In terms of interaction with people, an E tends to get energy from outside ideas or being with people while an I tends to be restored by time alone. E's relate primarily externally whereas I's tend to process and relate internally. E's generally have a greater number of relationships than will an I, although an I's few relationships will usually be deep ones.

S OR N (SENSING VERSUS INTUITIVE) HOW DO I GATHER & USE INFORMATION?

For the S, information taken in through the senses (seeing, touching etc.) and past experience describes and dictates reality whereas for the

N, intuitive reactions and future possibilities are more likely to shape their interpretation of circumstances. Often an N will come to a conclusion through analyzing concepts and without the systematic processing of facts that an S will be able to describe. S's make up 75 percent of the population, while N's compose only 25 percent.

T OR F (THINKING VERSUS FEELING) WHICH HOLDS MORE WEIGHT IN MY DECISIONS?

For 50 percent of the population (T), decision making rests on logical, objective principles, whereas, for the other half (F), a more personal, subjective approach is preferred. When name-calling T's tend to be labeled as "cold-hearted" and F's as "too emotional" or "illogical".

J OR P (JUDGING VERSUS PERCEIVING) HOW MUCH DO I NEED CLOSURE?

J's are readily identifiable by their need to plan out what's happening. They work best with specific deadlines. P's are all about the possibilities of life. They are often characterized by an open approach to life. They revel in the process. J's prefer closure and will work hard to achieve that. They are usually uncomfortable until decisions are made. P's enjoy the process and may be much less concerned about time and deadlines.

Have your four preferences leapt off the page at you? Already you may be able to figure out the preferences of those you disciple. Can you see any areas of potential misunderstanding? Knowing personality tendencies may also help you focus your discipleship. Evaluate if you are asking them as a disciple to follow Christ in a manner that matches the way God made them, or are you simply recreating another "you."

Ask an extrovert to look for numerous evangelism opportunities in large social settings and she will probably be excited and motivated. But, put an introvert in the same social situation repeatedly and she will tire quickly if that is her primary setting for evangelism.

For a J whose need for closure may provoke anxiousness when decisions are yet to be made, teaching them how to rest in God's peace and sovereignty may be beneficial. But even when a P whose go-with-the-flow, open-ended approach doesn't seem to exhibit anxiousness, you can't assume they are trusting in God. Perhaps planning ahead and making decisions where they would prefer to let things happen may be an outworking of trusting God in a particular situation.

How would you advise students making decision about a conference or career path? Consider the ways in which he processes information (S or N), or whether objective logical reasons (T) are more important to them than the circumstances and people surrounding a particular situation (F).

There are numerous ways to tailor your discipleship to God's design. Even the early believers weren't cookie cutter images of one another. Where would we be without the faith of Mary, the strong steadfastness of Paul, or the devoted encouragement of Barnabas? Each one uniquely lived out a life of obedience and love for the Lord. How will you help those you disciple live out their design?

CHAPTER THIRTY ONE

SEVEN KINDS OF SMART

On Reaching Multiple Intelligences

I am on a discipleship journey of growing in learning, teaching, and asking the right questions. As I was studying for my master's degree in education, I was drawn to the challenge of finding ways to reach every kind of student in my curriculum plan. You know everyone is wired differently, but you may not be aware of the theory of multiple intelligences developed by Howard Gardner, professor of education at Harvard University.

The intelligences (seven kinds of smart), briefly described, are:

Linguistic The intelligence of words.
Logical-mathematical The intelligence of numbers and reasoning.
Spatial The intelligence of pictures and images.
Musical The intelligence of tone, rhythm, and timbre.
Bodily-Kinesthetic The intelligence of the whole body and the hands.
Interpersonal The intelligence of social interactions.
Intrapersonal The intelligence of self-knowledge.

It's unlikely you will be able to prepare a Bible study or discipleship time that involves all of these learning styles. You could ask your disciples to read a verse while doing push-ups and playing the trombone, but that might be a bit impractical. To help prepare, I ask some of the following questions to bring in different learning styles wherever possible.

Linguistic How can I use the spoken or written word?

Logical-Mathematical How can I bring in numbers, calculations, logic, classifications, or critical thinking? I think about movement building principles, freshmen strategies and multiplication.

Spatial How can I use visual aids, visualization, color, art, metaphor, or visual organizers?

Musical How can I bring in music or environmental sounds, or set key points in a rhythm or melody? I consider playing music in the background for reflection time, as well as rap key principles.

Bodily-Kinesthetic How can I involve the whole body, or hands-on experiences? Ideas to consider are role plays, prayer walking, games, or Walk Thru the Bible key words with hand motions.

Interpersonal How can I engage students in peer or cross-age sharing, cooperative learning or large-group simulation?

Intrapersonal How can I evoke personal feelings or memories, or give choices to students?

Here is a practical example of some ideas that come to mind when I think about helping my students grasp the idea of an eternal perspective.

Linguistic Study 2 Corinthians 4 and 5. Do word studies on key words in the passages.

Logical-Mathematical Have your disciples process together about areas of their lives that would have to change if they lived with an eternal perspective. You could do this in the format of a PrEFACE or a personal strategic plan.

Spatial Talk about eternity and have them come up with an artistic illustration or a metaphor to explain the concept. For example, you could use the dot/line metaphor where the line is eternity and the dot is an 80-year life. I remember a pastor explaining "forever" by talking about a stone a hundred miles high, deep and wide. If a bird pecked away at that stone until it was a pile of sand, there would not be one less day, hour, or minute to spend in eternity.

Musical Listen to worship music or sing a few hymns that focus on heaven. Any Passion CD or hymnbook would do.

Bodily-Kinesthetic Take the group to a cemetery and

have them walk around making observations about the emotions and thoughts that surface. Point out that the dashes between the two dates on a tombstone represent the sum total of these people's lives. Discuss the implications.

Interpersonal Go to a retirement home and have them ask questions of believers and non-believers about their lives, regrets, values, and if appropriate, on dying.

Intrapersonal Journal a few lines about the things we put our trust and hope in, and hold on to in this world that do not have eternal value. Write out a prayer in response to this lesson.

CHAPTER THIRTY TWO

STUFFING MY SOUL

On Fasting

There was Peter's threefold denial, Jesus' temptation in the wilderness, and my battle with a ham sandwich on day six of my forty-day fast: these are the great crisis moments in recorded church history. Thankfully, Jesus escaped the temptation, while I faltered having been lured to the brink of perdition by that sumptuous pig. Though I failed in my forty-day fast, the good news is that I never sinned, because eating a ham sandwich doesn't transgress any moral laws at least in this corner of the universe. To me, this is the beauty of fasting.

While they were worshiping the Lord and fasting, the Holy Spirit said, "Set apart for me Barnabas and Saul for the work to which I have called them" (Acts 13:2).

Fasting is a practice deeply grounded in God's Word and one that I have tried to pass on to my disciples. Finding a biblical precedent for fasting is easy, while finding a passage that explains its purpose is not. Like the tassels on the High Priest's garments, I'm sure they serve a God-ordained function. I'm just a little vague on what that could possibly be. What I have learned about fasting has primarily come from doing it and noting its spiritual value. These are the things that I share with my disciples—the reasons I encourage them to fast.

First, fasting seems to create habits or triggers of reliance in my life. My hunger, which normally arose every 5 or 6 hours, becomes acute every 5 or 6 minutes when I am fasting, and hunger is my trigger to turn to God for strength, or at least I use it as such during my fast. Of course a tragedy in my life accomplishes the same thing, but fasting creates this necessary environment for reliance without the nasty side effects of inoperable brain cancer or the loss of a loved one. While I'm fasting, all day long I call out to God, for strength, endurance, self-control, empowerment, and wisdom, which in fact, should be normative for a Christian, but it is not for me which is why I fast.

Second, is what I would call "practice choices." When I fast, my flesh, in a very persuasive way, demands to be fed, and throughout the day I continually have to tell it, "No, you can't eat, so stop your whining." It is the same fleshly dynamic of sin and temptation, particularly lust. The only difference is that if I stumble during my fast and give in to the terrorist demands of my flesh, I have not compromised myself morally. Through fasting, self-control is cultivated, and I habitualize saying "no" to my flesh. It's like a full day of practice in preparation for game day.

Food is life and my umbilical cord is definitely tied to the kitchen. When I fast I am snipping the umbilical cord, which causes me to go to God for greater life in order to compensate for the life I am now denied. Many things impart life to us. Some of them, like relationships and Playstation, are God-ordained sources. Other sources are not necessarily sinful but deriving too much life from them, rather than God, does damage to our souls. The godly man or woman aware of this dynamic is willing to pull the umbilical cord where and when it needs to be pulled. Fasting is a spiritual discipline that makes such suicidal choices (which paradoxically leads to deriving greater life from God) a regular part of my life. Say "no" to food for a week and turning off the TV for a few days is a piece of cake (mmm... cake).

When I fast I am weak, and when I am weak I am humble. Fasting gives me a firm grip on my smallness and lack of omnipotence, as opposed to coffee, which makes me feel fast, smart, and competent (unless I drink coffee when I'm fasting which makes me delusional). Humility is not low-self esteem but an accurate perception of my finitude. Humility magnifies my need for God and always leads me to Him. Fasting is a helpful aid in humbling oneself before God.

Third, fasting is a plea for help, a red flare sent up from the soul for a specific reason or cause. When I am in distress and desperate for God, I fast. But I fast with the caution that I am not attempting to manipulate God or make Him care more than He does. I'm not holding my breath in blueness until I get my way. Fasting is a vehicle allowing me to spend my passion and desire for deliverance, and I choose it instead of manipulating, yelling, or whining.

There is a lot I do not understand about the practice of fasting, or the tassels of the High Priest, but I have derived enough from its discipline to commend it to my disciples. I have at times suggested that they set aside a meal or day a week for fasting. On other occasions I have suggested a fast on things other than food, like television or video games (but never Playstation). Jesus seems to assume His disciples will fast and even if I never understand it fully I would practice it and commend it to my disciples for this reason alone.

CHAPTER THIRTY THREE

YOU DON'T GET THE GIST

On Scripture Memory

"A woman must not wear men's clothing, nor a man wear women's clothing, for the LORD your God detests anyone who does this" (Deuteronomy 22:5).

Strange as it may seem, this is the first verse of scripture I ever memorized. I mean I didn't put it on a 3 by 5 card or anything, I just thought it was amusing that this verse would find its way into the Bible and it stuck in my head.

Funny, I haven't found much use for it in ministry over the years. Seldom have I been in a situation where a rebuke of cross-dressing was called for. But should the occasion arise, rest assured, I'm prepared.

I'm the type of person who remembers ideas and concepts. I have never been drawn to the practice of Bible memorization because generally speaking, I generally know what the passage generally says and where to find it in the Bible if I need to, at least generally.

But in a variety of recently tempting circumstances, I have begun to rethink my earlier arrogance. There are times when the gist of a passage is not enough. Reread this account of the temptation of Jesus in the wilderness:

> "Then Jesus was led by the Spirit into the desert to be tempted by the devil. After fasting forty days and forty nights, he was hungry. The tempter came to him and said, 'If you are the Son of God, tell these stones to become bread.' Jesus answered, 'It is written: "Man does not live on bread alone, but on every word that comes from the mouth of God."'"
> *Matthew 4:1-4*

I think it's safe to assume that Jesus knew the gist of scripture. Yet He quotes God's Word itself to dispense with the temptation. While certainly a good reason in itself for memorizing scripture, I have found the exercise to go far beyond temptation in scope. Meditating on a passage is great for my mind helps me do something I have always been poor at—praising God. God's Word provides a jumping off point for praise and worship, which the gist of passages doesn't seem to do.

Bible memorization was standard training for most systems of discipleship a decade or two ago. But then came the emphasis on "real" life change, and the realization that memorizing verses didn't always equate to spiritual growth. The unfortunate result is that few people incorporate any form of Bible memorization into their discipleship.

Perhaps we overemphasized the role of knowing Bible verses in spiritual growth, but I'm convinced we've come to the point where we don't emphasize it enough.

Years ago, one of the great missionaries of our time, the late Bud Hinkson, was asked to give a talk to a group of missionaries returning from overseas. They were weary, discouraged, and desperately in need of spiritual nutrition. Though an important talk, Bud didn't invest a second in preparation. He didn't need to. He simply went up to the podium and from memory recited the book of 2 Timothy and sat down. No one will ever forget that talk. What he imparted was a confidence in the sufficiency of God's Word and a thirst to know it better. That's quite a memo to circulate to your disciples.

I'm sure there are a lot of good Bible memorization systems out there, but I have taught my disciples the simple system below and it seems to be adequate. Whatever you use, use something that gets them into the practice of taking the scripture off the page and into their minds.

On a closing note, I have not known many people to stay in the practice of Bible memorization who didn't have disciplers that modeled it, and lived it. This is a life practice that is passed on, transmitted from practitioner to learner.

- Read the verse through several times thoughtfully aloud.
- Using natural phrases, learn the topic, reference, first phrase and so on...
- Write out the verse as part of the learning process
- Review the verses frequently throughout the week. A good goal is two or three verses per week.
- Use a system like the sheet I've included to keep track of your memory verses. Start by working on a verse once a day for seven weeks. Then you will want to continue to review that verse once a week for seven months.
- Work on your memorization with someone

CHAPTER THIRTY FOUR

SPLIT THE DIFFERENCE

On Initiative And Relational Evangelism

When I came to Christ, I intuitively sensed that this was something I should share with my friends and family. It never occurred to me that I should be going door-to-door giving surveys. One of the greater challenges of personal discipleship is communicating the need to do initiative evangelism as well as relational. I have discovered that Colossians 4:3-6 allows me to get at this issue. Here is some of what I communicate.

"And pray for us, too, that God may open a door for our message, so that we may proclaim the mystery of Christ, for which I am in chains. Pray that I may proclaim it clearly, as I should. Be wise in the way you act toward outsiders; make the most of every opportunity. Let your conversation be always full of grace, seasoned with salt, so that you may know how to answer everyone" (Colossians 4:3-6).

Notice the natural division in this passage? Paul asks for prayer related to the type of evangelism he was doing: initiative evangelism. Then he addresses the Colossians on how they can be involved in relational evangelism. Both are essential because there are clearly two types of non-believers in the world: those who have a close Christian friend and those without any relationship with a committed Christian. Look first at what he addresses concerning initiative evangelism:

PRAYER AND LOOKING FOR AN OPEN DOOR

First the apostle Paul requests prayer for an "open door." He was always looking for one as a way to talk about Christ. Each day we make a decision whether we are going to be open to being used by God to share the gospel.

If I am open, I have a sense of expectancy that God is going to lead me and I view chance encounters as potential open doors. In essence, Paul is saying that random evangelism is never truly random, though the conversation might be with someone we have never met before. Integrated in Paul's request is his emphasis on the need for prayer.

SUFFERING

Paul notes that He is in chains for the gospel. Initiative evangelism and suffering go hand in hand. Feed the naked, clothe the hungry and everyone will adore you. Share the gospel, and you, my friend, are a lunatic. You cannot get around the difficulty of initiating a conversation about Christ with someone. Jesus said, "Unless a kernel of wheat falls to the ground it remains a single seed, but if it dies it becomes many seeds." Evangelism involves dying. Embarrassment is an emotional death. It is this act of dying that is fertilizer for the gospel. It cannot be avoided nor was it designed to be.

CLARITY MATTERS

The heart is critical to evangelism and of great value to God. Even if we are lousy evangelists God is pleased with our attempts.

The other side of this equation is that clarity matters. We live in a real world where people are moved and persuaded by real ideas. If Satan cannot keep the gospel from being spoken, he then targets clarity so that it cannot be understood. If we are going to proclaim the gospel, the immediate concern is for boldness and clarity.

Now we come to the transition in the passage. Paul has been asking for prayer related to his evangelistic efforts, and now he is going to transition to theirs. The Colossians live in a small town by today's standards, and therefore Paul is going to advise them concerning a relational mode of evangelism. There's no need to preach on a street corner because everyone knows each other; there's Marcus, Dorkus, Pontius, Augustus, heck, if you lived there, you'd know everyone. There are relational networks throughout the city and when you are doing relational evangelism you need to keep in mind the following skills:

BE WISE

First the apostle says to "be wise in the way you act toward outsiders."

A closer inspection shows what Paul means when he says, "be wise."

Paul is talking about being balanced. For example, when it comes to "Jesus talk," be balanced. Don't not speak about Christ, but on the other hand don't make it seem like you're double dating with him. Don't be too condoning of everything people say and do, but on the other hand don't be too judgmental. Be balanced.

BUY IT OUT

"Make the most of every opportunity" is a translation of a market phrase meaning to "buy out completely." It was used in the marketplace to refer to what you do when something comes on sale: you buy it out completely. Paul uses this phrase to illustrate that in the course of conversations with friends, eventually the opportunity is going to arrive for us to talk about Christ and when it does we need to be prepared to take full advantage of it. The gospel is now on sale; buy it out completely.

SALTY CONVERSATIONS

Last, he tells them to make their conversations seasoned with salt. Salt wasn't used as much for flavor in the first century as it was as a preservative. Salt kept meat from rotting. Like roast beef left out on the kitchen counter for an afternoon, conversations have a way of putrefying. They decay into gossip, sexual innuendos, or course jokes. Your job is to keep them from rotting through godly speech.

Now as you do this, the salt will make those with a God-hunger thirsty. This in turn will lead to conversations about Christ, and then you need to do what? Right, buy it out completely.

Having gone through the passage, I point out that both modes are biblical and critical. I come back to the point that wherever they go on campus there will be unbelievers who have close friends who are Christians and unbelievers who are outside of such relationships. Both need the gospel, therefore both modes have their place within the outreach of the church and our lives. They grow us and stretch us in different ways, use different faith muscles, and allow us to see God work in different ways. While most of us might prefer to do relational evangelism, the need to do missionary evangelism is inescapable.

CHAPTER THIRTY FIVE

DESIRE FOR DUTY

On Relational Discipleship

During my first year of STINT, I committed to formulating and following a "Personal Development Plan" for the year. As a part of that plan, I decided to inductively study every book in the New Testament. While I did not quite attain my goal by the end of the year (I only reached 2 Peter), I am still amazed by the way the New Testament books became so fresh and real for me. There is something incredibly stirring, almost revelatory, about studying the Bible while simultaneously engaging in full-time ministry. For me, I related to the context of the New Testament like never before, since I was serving in a closed country in the 10/40 window. About midway through the spring semester, I was starting to run out of gas. One area in which I was in need of some fuel was in that of discipleship.

Enter 1 Thessalonians.

Paul's letter was not written as a manual for discipleship. Most of the commentaries I have read agree that the purpose of this letter was to encourage the Thessalonian believers and to correct a few errors. However, Paul did set a remarkable example to be followed in Christian discipleship. After I finished my study of 1 Thessalonians, I understood what the book was about. I had compiled a ton of notes and read through various commentaries, but none of that seemed to matter because I was starting to see the story behind Paul's first letter to the church at Thessalonica.

BEING AN EXAMPLE: THE RELATIONSHIP HALF
OF DISCIPLESHIP RELATIONSHIPS

The story behind 1 Thessalonians is the amazing relationship that Paul had with the Thessalonians: his love, desire, care, and concern for them coupled with deep humility.

For some reason, many discipleship relationships are more mechanistic protocol than an actual relationship. Sadly, it was not until the end of my college career that I reflected on how I had been teaching and training others. I realized that those men with whom I had met one-on-one for weeks on end could recall little of the content of those Bible studies we had been in together. The things they did remember were the times we spent building relationships. Notice this in Paul's life:

> "...for our gospel did not come to you in word only, but also
> in power and in the Holy Spirit and with full conviction; just
> as you know what kind of men we proved to be among you
> for your sake. You also became imitators of us and of the
> Lord, having received the word in much tribulation with the
> joy of the Holy Spirit, so that you became and example to all
> the believers in Macedonia and Achaia."
> *1 Thessalonians 1:5–7*

It was not in "word only" that Paul taught the Thessalonians. He modeled for them a lifestyle. They became imitators of Paul. It had a snowball affect and before long, the Thessalonians became examples to the believers in Macedonia and Achaia.

During my first year serving in East Asia, there were two women on my team, Kel and Mary, who majored in this practice of "relationship over materials." My team was pioneering a campus ministry, and when we arrived on campus there was only *one* known Christian out of 17,000 students. Before long our ministry was seeing tremendous growth, particularly among the women. These girls did everything together. At times, I thought that Kel and Mary should have been charging rent for all the girls that would be lying around in their tiny foreign student dorm room.

In July of that year, we sent a summer project team out from our campus to another part of East Asia. Before they left, one of our students handed me a letter regarding their upcoming trip, in which she stated, "I do not know how I will raise the money to go. Maybe eat only two meals a day." In eight months, our campus went from only one known Christian to students willing to skip meals in order to share the gospel with others. In that same letter from that female student, two things jumped out at me: she mingled God's Word with her words and her references to the two women on my staff team—Kel and Mary. They had set an example by spending time with this girl.

DESIRE-FOR-DUTY DISCIPLESHIP

In discipleship relationships, we inevitably run into roadblocks. For many people, one common difficulty in discipleship is balancing the tension between duty and desire. This has been the focus of many books, seminars, and lectures over the past few years, and it is something that Paul seemed to handle with great ease. Paul commented:

> "But we proved to be gentle among you, as a nursing mother tenderly cares for her own children. Having so fond an affection for you, we were well-pleased to impart not only the gospel of God but also our lives, because you had become very dear to us." *1 Thessalonians 2:7-8*

Seeing this principle forced me to ask some questions: Do I genuinely care for my disciples and for those with whom I am sharing the gospel? Is this merely a job or work for me? Am I here in East Asia for strategic reasons or maybe because it seemed like the right thing to do? About the time I was dealing with these tough questions, a friend emailed me some prayer requests. She asked me to pray that God would bless her with disciples for whom she had a natural affinity. She wanted God to help her establish relationships with girls whose company she would enjoy and whom she would naturally love being around. I had never prayed anything remotely close to that prayer. I am not suggesting that your personality must line up perfectly with those you disciple, as I do not think that is what Paul was exemplifying either. Instead, my friend viewed this natural affinity concept as a heart change so that her relationships would be transformed to look more like love-relationships and less like work.

The problem with this dichotomy is that we have a hard time balancing two extremes. As soon as we gravitate toward the desire, or relationship part of discipleship, we inevitably neglect the hard work side of the equation in ministry. I have observed many people become rather lazy while focusing on the relationship part of this tension.

In 1 Thessalonians 2:9, Paul pointed out his "labor and hardship," reminding them how he worked "night and day so as to not be a burden to any." In verse eight, Paul also noted that had a fond affection for the Thessalonians and he was "well-pleased" to impart the gospel to them. There does not appear to be a duty/desire dichotomy for Paul. These were not inconsistent or mutually exclusive. Instead, Paul's desire was for his duty. He had such affection for the Thessalonians that he took great delight (desire) in working (duty) around the clock for them. If we could understand and harness this concept "desire-for-duty-discipleship," then perhaps our ministries would be more fruitful, enjoyable, and biblical.

CHAPTER THIRTY SIX

JUMP START

On Basic Follow-up

Imagine going to foreign country. In preparation for your trip you'd have two basic options to learn the language. One would be a thirty-day-crash-course-teach-me-how-to-say-bathroom curriculum. The other option would be to invest several years and really learn how to speak the language.

In the world of ministry there is a similar distinction made between discipleship and what is commonly called "Basic follow-up." Basic Follow-up is not a commitment to discipleship for the duration of life or even college life. For a variety of reasons, you may rarely meet with the individual again after you have gone through follow-up. Follow-up is the term used for grounding someone in the essentials of the Christian life, and giving them the basic tools and teaching they need to move forward in their faith.

Whenever you see someone come to Christ or someone new gets involved with your Bible study it is a good idea to initiate Basic Follow up, making sure their foundation has no major cracks. In Cru, Basic Follow-up is comprised of the following topics: assurance of salvation, confession and dealing with sin, prayer and how to have a quiet time, walking in the power of the Holy Spirit, and principles of spiritual growth. We typically addresses these subjects using the Campus Ministry resource called "*Life Concepts.*

You could argue that other topics should be included and you could certainly feel free to add them. For example in some countries, demon possession actually makes it to the top five. But if a person understands and applies these principles you have given them the basic ingredients to be able to cook for themselves (have a personal walk with God).

GET BACK

In C. S. Lewis's book *The Screwtape Letters*, the demon Wormwood learns lessons on human temptation from his uncle Screwtape. He is advised that if the man begins to ponder spiritual things too deeply it may have devastating effects and the man may become serious about his commitment and faith. A vexing problem for a young demon. The uncle advises him to bring him outside where the reality and busyness of life will distract his thoughts and the critical moment will be lost—nothing like a loud honking bus to bring one back to the material world.

If a person has trusted Christ or had agreed to go through Basic-Follow-up it can be a mistake to schedule the appointment for a week later though this is the common practice. This gives Satan seven days to steal the seeds that have been sown, arouse skepticism and distrust and to distract them from the choices they are beginning to make. Try to get back in touch with them in the next couple days. Many decisions for Christ actually take place in the first follow-up appointment, even if they have expressed a decision or claim to be a Christian already. This first appointment is really a matter of life and death and you need to be persistent in getting together because Satan will be persistent in keeping you apart.

FOLLOW-UP MADE SIMPLE

Life Concepts takes the foundational Christian concepts mentioned above and puts them into five lessons each centered on the study of one passage. All of the questions are right on the sheet. You don't have to be a genius or even a very mature Christian to share the *Life Concept* series (crupress.com). These are the lessons

- *Stepping from Uncertainty to Confidence*
  (teaching assurance of salvation)
- *Stepping from Feelings of Unworthiness to Forgiveness*
  (teaching forgiveness and confession)
- *Stepping from Being Unable to Empowered*
  (teaching about being filled with the Spirit)
- *Stepping from Being Unprepared to Equipped*
  (Walking in the Spirit)
- *Stepping from Being Undeveloped to Maturity*
  (principles of Spiritual Growth)

FIRST MEETING

First appointments can be kind of weird, and the person might think you're kind of weird (who goes around teaching Bible lessons?). The apostle Paul says that he, "became all things to all men," meaning he sought to find common ground with those that he ministered to. If you meet them in their room (which you should as there's a better chance they'll show up) scan around their room and look for some connection points, some non-spiritual issue on which to shoot the breeze. This cultivates a relationship and communicates that you are a normal person who also listens to music and watches movies.

Keep the time short—forty minutes, maximum. You could painlessly get talking and before you know it an hour and twenty minutes have gone by. No, she probably didn't mind, but next week when she must decide if she'll be around when you stop by, she'll remember that meeting could take up to an hour and half, and rationalize that she just doesn't have the time. Keep it to forty minutes.

BRING A GIFT

You can ratify their decision to follow Christ by bringing some kind of "gospel" gift to the appointment. I often bring a cheap journal and a Bible. In-between follow-up appointment two and three, I talk about having a Quiet time, suggesting they use the journal I brought to write down their thoughts, and bring mine as an example. A new Bible and journal is a tangible reminder that they have made a decision, and that their life is now different.

BRING A FRIEND

Depending on where the student lives I try to bring another Christian student with me who lives somewhere near by. I'm not thinking that they'll become best buds or tennis partners, but knowing there are other students who have made the same decision, who live close by, serves a purpose.

A BASIC SKILL

General Electric Phone Company: this is how I was taught to remember the order of Galatians, Ephesians, Philippians, Colossians. In the second or third follow-up, one of the most helpful things I have observed someone do is to quickly teach a system where a new disciple, by the end of the appointment, can learn the names and order of the New Testament books. This information makes them feel that they know their way around the Bible, and that they have learned a tangible skill.

AFTER FOLLOW-UP

You have pursued them for six weeks, and have done them an enormous service for which they can never repay: you have grounded them in their faith. But before investing more of your precious few ministry hours, you need to look for them to take a step toward you and God. During follow-up you should ask them to attend a weekly meeting or Bible study. If they've come, great. But now, as you come to the end of Basic Follow-up you need to explain that the next step for their growth is involvement in a Bible study. You really need to see some commitment on their part before continuing to invest weekly time. You are not a private tutor. You are a link and bridge to the Christian body and they must take some steps to join that body. You are a bridge not a doorstop.

CHAPTER THIRTY SEVEN

EVERYONE HAS LIMITS

On Discipling From Your Strengths

I am a reluctant discipler. I'd rather lay out to a team of leaders the vision and goals and then send them off with a command to "tell me how it went!" On Monday, I want to tell my team what to do. On Friday, I want to ask my team how it went. I don't like all that messy, people stuff that happens between Monday and Friday.

For me, Tuesdays through Thursdays on campus haven't always been so fun. I don't want to grab a coke and talk with a student about life, faith, girl problems, and his latest nuances about spirituality. I want to recruit a student to a team, give him a vision and an important task, and send him out to do it. Then I want him to report back to me, so I can celebrate whatever he accomplished!

Paul wrote, "By the grace of God I am what I am" (1 Corinthians 15:10). He was not like the other apostles. He wasn't with Jesus during His public ministry and had been a persecutor of the church of God. Paul describes himself as being "abnormally born." He had to come to grips with the fact that he wasn't like Peter, John, or any of the other original twelve.

When it comes to making disciples, we are committed to the same mission of turning lost students into Christ-centered laborers. We also have the same practices at our disposal that Christians have used for centuries: prayer, Bible study, confession, fellowship, worship, evangelism, service, etc. Every disciple needs to learn these practices to grow in Christ-likeness. But though the mission and the practices are the same, we have different strengths.

For example, Paul brought an intense focus to the task of discipleship. He had a compelling desire to get the gospel to the next unreached people group. He didn't have time for those who were distracted from the mission God gave him (Acts 15:36-41).

Barnabas must have had the gift of mercy. He had time for John Mark, who was distracted from the mission. He had time to help this hurting missionary (Acts 15:36-41).

Timothy had a gentle spirit. He must have loved the job of shepherding the church in one city for a long time, otherwise Paul wouldn't have given him that task (1 Timothy 1:3). Timothy came to Christ through the nurturing relationships of his mother and grandmother (2 Timothy 1:5), and it would be through nurturing relationships that he would teach others to follow Christ.

All these men rolled up their sleeves and made disciples, yet they brought different strengths to the task. Paul wasn't like the original twelve and he wasn't like Barnabas. Timothy and Titus brought a different gift package to the table than Paul.

My strengths are in directing a team to accomplish a significant goal. I've been this way since I was a kid. My mom got calls from the elementary school on occasion because "I was being bossy" again on the playground. In my grade school brain, getting two teams to play ball during recess was significant. With only ten minutes to play, I would become a self-appointed captain and then randomly choose another person to be the other captain. Teams were picked quickly when I was in charge. Maximum fun was experienced, I thought. I had my playground critics but more people were blessed than injured by me taking charge!

Assembling and directing a team of partners in the mission is what I'm good at. As believers roll up their sleeves and go after the mission on my team, they will be challenged to become more like Christ.

How about you? What are your strengths?

As you discover your strengths, you will also become aware of your limitations. I may have the gift of leadership, but that's about it. Any believer I disciple will also need others in the body of Christ to build them up. Others with gifts of mercy, shepherding, service, and hospitality will play a huge part in their development.

Not only am I limited by a gift or two, I am also limited by my weaknesses.

I am not a warm person by nature. People don't walk away from an encounter with me feeling warm and fuzzy. This can be a problem. A while ago, I watched a movie where the lead character realized that he is "good at friendship but bad at intimacy." It was the kind of movie that inspired me to think about my weaknesses and to seek to make some changes in my life. After the movie, I wrote down, "In the next five years, I don't need to get better at tasks, I need to get better at people."

One of the staff guys on my team is not like me. Before Monday is over, I will get more tasks done than he will in an entire week. But should he be like me? He will take long periods of time to get to know one freshman guy, make that guy feel appreciated, and consistently communicate that he is there to meet needs in his life. His vision is for guys to see him as their chaplain in the dorms. I can't do that. He does it every week. And his strengths are needed on this campus.

Always in a hurry. Accepting people for who they are. These are my weaknesses. It helps to know that. How about you? What are your weaknesses?

Weaknesses are not a cosmic accident. God has a plan and a purpose for them (2 Corinthians 12:9-10). The Lord uses our weakness to teach us solid spiritual truths to stand on and to lead from. Therefore, we should embrace our weakness because God will use them for His good purpose.

Yet as you seek to make disciples, don't get stuck on your weaknesses. Be aware of them and take a few steps to get better. But also be crystal clear on your strengths. Know how God has gifted you. Find out what you bring to the table. Let it rip in your strength areas. If it is teaching, major on teaching your disciples. If it is mercy, major on showing mercy to your disciples. If it is evangelism, be a model of evangelistic excellence to students and staff, and give all the glory to God because He gifted you in that way.

I need to give most of my energy to directing a team to accomplish a God-honoring vision. I should only spend a small amount of my energy working on the ability to show mercy and the ability to enthusiastically develop people. I should point staff and students to someone gifted in these ways.

Our staff and students need somebody who can meet that need. They also need somebody like you to help them be more like Christ.

CHAPTER THIRTY EIGHT

MULTIPLE MOVEMENTS

On Discipling Leaders Of Ministries

Occasionally you will disciple others who are either leading a small ministry or attempting to begin one. Let's say, for example, your disciples want to start a fraternity ministry or perhaps launch an Impact movement. They need someone to disciple them in leading or starting a ministry. Competency in this task is ultimately the key to developing multiple movements on the same campus or coaching ministries on several campuses concurrently. Your disciples will need coaching and direction in the following areas.

They Need a Plan

Show them how to do a strategic plan. Help them articulate an attainable goal, something that can be written out on paper. Practically speaking, together you are not planning out an entire ministry. You're helping them to start a specialized or contextualized small group that reaches one of the many separate and distinct campus communities. Only when multiple groups have formed will you need to think in broader ministry terms. The goal I usually move them toward is a contextualized small group with 12 to 15 members. It's tangible, and the steps to get there become fairly obvious.

With that as your north star, help them think through the logical steps that must happen to get there. There must be clear action steps and without you they simply will not be able to conceive of them. What follows are some of those key action steps.

Decide On the Particulars of the Small Group

The first step in launching this small group is to decide when, where, and what the small group should study. Content is shaped by two things: the audience you are targeting (African Americans, Greeks, a sorority, etc.), and topics that audience might find interesting. If you can not find specialized content, such as "Bible Studies for Greeks," then you must think in terms of topics that have drawing power: The DaVinci Code, Groups Exploring God, Revelation and the Middle East, etc.

Training On Leading a Small Group
Your disciples will need some training on how to lead a small group. Think through what you would want them to know, buy them *The Ultimate Road Trip*, and give them an opportunity to watch you lead your study.

Publicize the Small Group
Next, coach them in how to publicize the new group. Identify the target audience such as the Asian Christian Fellowship). You are seeking to gather Christians who are members of this community, because to get started you'll need a critical mass of people.

Then publicize the topic you decided would have drawing power to this audience—"Is Jesus Black, White, or Does It Matter?" If possible, include images of the target audience on the flyer.

Besides flyers brainstorm other ways to publicize this inaugural meeting: surveys, personal invitations, quarter sheets in mailboxes, etc.

After the First Meeting
You need to debrief with your disciples on what they did in their first meeting, but more importantly be a cheerleader, for they have taken a huge step of faith. Ask questions and give input where needed.

Gathering More
After they have had several small group meetings, revisit the original goals. How are they going to grow the group from five to 12 to 15 people? Brainstorm with them about where they can gather more people. Should they bring in a speaker, do a study on a hot topic, make personal phone calls, or do more publicity? The group needs to go on steroids and gather critical mass; by all possible means help them get the group to a stable dozen and get it out of intensive care.

Why is the goal 12 to 15 students? Realistically, at least half of these people will not return the following year. But if you can begin the next year with a handful of students, the fall influx will quickly bump the group up to 14 or 15 and now you have a ministry. A ministry is usually launched over two years.

Establish a Leadership Core
Now that the group is up and running, your disciple needs to assemble

a core of leaders to help him or her lead. It may be just one other student who has surfaced with a heart to help, but this step is critical. A leadership team allows for some of the more mundane tasks to be spread out, and breeds greater ownership and involvement in those brought into leadership. Give your disciples input on how to form, challenge, and structure the leadership of the small group. You might offer your assistance in meeting with the leadership.

Components of a Ministry

Starting a small group has its own unique path steps, which we have just reviewed, but once the group, which we might now call a ministry, is up and running, the group itself needs a plan to make sure it stays on track. Take your disciples to Acts 2:41-47, and pull out the following components of ministry: prayer, study of the Scripture, community, evangelism, and discipleship. Train them in how to make sure these components are being lived out in the small group, even if it is the lowest level of implementation.

Conferences

You know the value of a retreat in accelerating a ministry and building relationships. Teach this to your disciples. If they are able to get a handful of their small group to go on a retreat, a conference, or even an overnight function, the small group will become a community.

Discipleship

As your disciples gets new people popping in each week, train them on how to set up and conduct follow-up appointments. They need to get in touch personally with these visitors if they want them to return. Use this as an opportunity to share the gospel, or go through some basic follow up.

With all of this accomplished, your disciples will have the raw material to relaunch in the fall. With experience, a committed core of attendees, a few other leaders, and a whole new crop of incoming freshmen, this small group could very well become a movement which will have its own coaching concerns. But that's for another day.

CHAPTER THIRTY NINE

THE REAL WORK

On Praying For Our Disciples

As I started my career in fulltime ministry I was pretty uncertain how to do my job, but one thing I felt, was confident that I knew how to disciple women. I had been discipled by two godly women in college and was currently being trained by great role models. So I thought, "I can imitate what they have done with me," and women's lives will change just like mine did.

So, I set about the work of the ministry and discipleship, training my disciples in spiritual disciplines, praying with them, sharing my faith with them, leading them in the Word and memorizing scripture. Every week in Bible study they knew we would begin the evening by having them write their prayer requests on a 3x5 index card, so I could pray specifically for them throughout the week. I would pray for their up coming tests, family situations that concerned them, relationships with guys that they were in (or wanted to be in) but something was clearly missing.

I could be involved in, and pray for, the circumstances of their lives. I could train them in the "how to's" of ministry. But how was I suppose to make their character deepen and grow? Something seemed to not be working.

I asked the Lord, "How do *I* see change happen in their life? How do *I* move their hearts to the things of You? What do *I* need to do? There in was the problem—"*I*." Philippians 1:6 says, "For I am confident of this very thing, that He who began a good work in you will perfect it until the day of Christ Jesus." It wasn't me...I couldn't change them. But God could! God was more committed to their growth than I could ever be. Honestly, some of the biggest changes I've seen in my disciples hasn't happened because of what I said or did, but as I got out of the way and allowed God to work.

On campus, I would make prayer my first appointment of the day. Sometimes I would do it at my house, praying for my appointments and the disciples I was meeting that day. Sometimes I would go to campus and prayer walk, praying for my disciples as they came to mind, passing their dorms or classrooms. I would pray for their walks with God, their ministries and whatever else God brought to mind as I walked around campus. (I'm always amazed at how I think of more things to pray when I'm not sitting, but as I walk and observe the things happening on campus.) I also began to use my Bible more as I prayed for them, praying verses like Colossians 1:9-14; 3:12-17; Philippians 1:3-11; Ephesians 1:3-18; 3:14-21; 6:10-20; Galatians 5:16-26; Psalm 139... to name just a few. But I would also pray verses specific to them.

One day I was meeting with one of my disciples who shared with me that she had decided upon graduation to join staff with Cru. For a brief moment I was elated until she proceeded to inform me that she didn't really like evangelism and wanted to focus her ministry strictly on discipleship. Oops, that wasn't the second line I was looking for! Inside I was conflicted...so excited she wanted to be in the ministry but also concerned that she couldn't do the job without a heart for the spiritually lost.

Begging the Lord for wisdom, words somehow came out of my mouth. I knew that she was incredibly motivated by God's Word, so I encouraged her to look up verses about the lost and people's need to know Christ. I asked her to do this daily over the next month. I walked away praying, "Lord, would you develop a heart for the lost in her life, would you let her look at lost people the way You see them, would she still join fulltime ministry, but with a deep desire to see lost people come to know You." Every time she came to my mind I knew specifically what to pray for and would ask God to work in this area of her life. When I prayed the verses that I normally prayed for those without Christ, I began to pray that she, too, would have the same heart as the writers of those passages.

We met again at the end of the month and before I could even start the conversation, she pulled her Bible out, so excited about what she had learned over that month. She couldn't talk fast enough. She kept saying, "You wouldn't believe this," and proceeded to share with me what she had learned. Needless to say, I was incredibly grateful because God was changing her heart...real life change was happening.

She did end up joining staff and after her first semester on campus she called me up and started telling me stories about what was happening in her ministry. She shared her faith more that semester than I could have ever imagined and she saw several people trust Christ. I just kept thinking, "Is this the same person who told me she didn't really like evangelism?" What I loved is that she wasn't sharing her faith out of duty or obligation—because it was a part of her job—but because she truly had a heart for those without Christ.

Today, women I work with still get a 3X5 card to fill out with prayer requests, but my approach to prayer is different. I ask more questions about their requests to get to the heart-level issues in their lives. I want to pray for their real needs. The reality is we may be one of only a few people, if not the only person, praying intentionally for our disciples. Sometimes I still catch myself underestimating the power of prayer, thinking about what I can do to change someone or fix a situation. Prayer can be tedious; it can be hard work and I can get distracted doing it, but I'm convinced it is one of, if not the most, powerful things I can do for my disciples—the key to seeing life change.

CHAPTER FORTY

BLIND DATE

On The Question Of Dating

"I can't believe my luck!" exclaimed a jubilant Jack, flinging the door to his dorm room open. Startled, his roommate, Hal, looked up.

"What luck? What's going on?"

"Well," Jack began to explain, as he pulled up a chair. He was speaking quickly as the excitement seeped into every word and syllable. "You know that girl that comes to our weekly meeting – she sits on the right side of the room every week – she's the blond one with the really nice eyes."

Hal nodded. "You mean the freshman girl from across campus? Isn't she in Jana's Bible study?"

"That's the one. Well, I can't believe I'm even saying this to you..."

"Saying what?" interrupted Hal. "Out with it boy!"

Jack paused to catch his breath. "Ok, here's the deal.... We're dating."

Hal's eyes widened. "You mean like going out on a date? Or you mean like you two are now an item?"

Jack leaned back in his chair and clasped his hands behind his head, smiling broadly. "I mean like she's my girlfriend now. Simply amazing."

"Yup, pretty amazing," said Hal. "So, how exactly did this happen?"

"Pretty easy, really," replied Jack. "I thought she was really cute, so I asked her to come out with me to the coffee shop in the Union. We talked, and at the end of the conversation, I asked if she wanted to be my girlfriend. She said yes. Simple as that."

"Uh huh," Hal said softly, with a trace of doubt. "Hey, Hal, just how long have you known, um…"

"Stacey," Jack said, filling in the blank. "Well, this is really the first time I've had the chance to sit down with her alone, really. But we've talked on a couple of other occasions."

"So on a scale of 1-10, how well do you know her?"

"Probably about a 2, I guess. But that's what makes it so fun – I can't wait to get to know her better."

Hal nodded skeptically. "Not to seem negative, but I'm curious. Why did you start to date her exclusively?"

Jack looked back in surprise. "What do you mean why? She's cute, she's nice, and I want to get to know her better. What a ridiculous question."

"Jack, what do you think the Bible has to say about dating?"

"It says nothing about dating," replied Jack confidently.

"Well, can I ask you a few questions related to that?" Jack nodded, so Hal took the plunge. "Ok. Look at 2 Corinthians 6:14-15. It says, 'Do not be unequally yoked together with unbelievers. For what fellowship has righteousness with lawlessness? And what communion has light with darkness? And what accord has Christ with Belial? Or what part has a believer with an unbeliever?' What does that mean?"

Jack thought for a moment. "I always understood that to mean that a Christian should not marry a non-Christian, because it would create a spiritual imbalance in their relationship."

"Right," said Hal. "Do you think that should apply to dating?"

"I guess," replied Jack. "I haven't really thought about it."

"Ok then. What you have just done is agreed that a Biblical principle relating to marriage can be applied to your dating life. Which means that even though the Bible does not speak directly to dating, we can look at principles of marriage that would give us direction in our dating relationships."

"Sounds fair, but let's see where you're going with this."

"Alright. Now, let me ask you this. What is the purpose of dating?"

"Dating is where we get to know people of the opposite sex."

"But for what purpose?" Hal asked.

"Well, I guess ultimately to see if we might want to marry them."

"So is dating a way to make friends, or is it preparation of sorts for marriage?"

"Ok, I see where you're going," said Jack. "I guess if we see it as just a way to make friends, then it shouldn't be exclusive in nature. I mean, I can be friends with a lot of people without calling them my exclusive girlfriend or something."

"Exactly," replied Hal. "So what does that make dating all about?"

"Well, I guess it's safe to say that the primary purpose of dating is preparation for marriage. But," he said, pausing, "I don't think I'm ready to say I'm on the road to marrying Stacey."

"Why not?" asked Hal.

"Because I don't know her yet, really," admitted Jack. "I mean, I just kind of met her."

"But already you have this tag of exclusivity in your relationship, right? If you don't do that with other friends, why do it with her? I mean, doesn't that mean that you'd be upset if she went out with another guy?"

Jack nodded. "Definitely. I'd be ripped."

"But doesn't that mean that you're putting this friendship in some sort of a box, when the reality is that you don't even have a clue whether you guys are at all made for each other?"

"Yeah, I guess," said Jack. "So are you telling me I shouldn't date anyone, since dating anyone would do the same thing?"

"Not at all," replied Hal. "Here's what I'm getting at. You are dating Stacey exclusively when you don't know her, which seems to be putting the cart before the horse. I mean, why not become friends with her, like you become friends with other people, and if, once you get to know her, you both realize that your relationship has potential, *then* you make it more exclusive? Wouldn't that make more sense?"

"Interesting point," Jack conceded. "What are some benefits to doing it that way?"

"Let me list them," said Hal, ticking the points off on his fingers. "First, it allows you to develop a better foundation for a future relationship, which is your *friendship*. Second, it doesn't put your relationship into a premature box, and thus doesn't restrict either of you from pursuing other healthy friendships. Third, it means there is less of a chance for a broken heart. If you know someone really well, then you'll be going into the dating relationship with the firm foundation of a friendship, and you'll have a better understanding of each other from the get-go. And fourth, it minimizes the likelihood of sexual sin."

"Wait a second," said Jack. "How is that?"

"Well, it guarantees nothing, of course. But the attraction is primarily *physical* at this point. And if the attraction is primarily physical, and if you are investing lots of time alone in an exclusive manner, it seems like a recipe for trouble."

Jack nodded. "Yeah, I've already found it tough and were only in week one."

"That's a good warning that things could quickly spiral out of control. Look, I'm not saying that if youbecome friends first that you won't struggle sexually with her. I *am* saying that you will have built up other aspects of the relationship that are all part of what will make you attracted to her. Therefore, the physical doesn't become the primary attraction. And that lessens the danger."

"Good point," said Jack. "So the bottom line is dating is primarily a preparation for marriage, and I need to be purposeful about how I go about my dating relationships."

Hal smiled and clapped Jack on the back. "Jack my brother, that's exactly right. I am not at all saying we shouldn't date. I am saying that we need to think things through a little better than just, 'Wow, she's hot'."

"Yeah," Jack replied, "So why didn't you just say that in the first place?"

"Because," responded Hal, "This is an imaginary conversation for the sake of teaching a point."

"Right," said Jack. "Hey, are we imaginary too?"

"I'm afraid so," said Hal, as he vanished in thin air.

Foundations

SECTION SIX

& History

CHAPTER FORTY ONE

Discipling The Right People
(Adapted from the *Compass*)

SELECTION: DISCIPLINING THE RIGHT PEOPLE

Who should I disciple? Who should I invest my life in? The reality is that you can't disciple everyone. You're a full-time student or a busy staff member. Jesus didn't disciple everybody, and so we need to choose wisely. The most important decision you make at the beginning of each ministry year will be choosing which individuals you will pour your life into. Let's talk about why we must choose wisely, and then how to do it.

WHY MUST WE CHOOSE WISELY?

In Luke Chapter 6, observe how Christ chose to disciple, and the fact that He didn't disciple everybody. Luke 6:12 says, "And it was at this time that He went off to the mountain to pray, and He spent the whole night in prayer to God." The text doesn't say what Jesus prayed, only that He spent the whole night in prayer to God. You've got to wonder if at least some of the time was spent communing with the Father about the men that He was going to build the kingdom upon. Why? See verse 13, "And when day came, He called His disciples to Him and chose twelve of them, whom He also named as apostles." There you see the names of the guys: Simon and Andrew, Philip and Bartholomew, and all the gang. He chose twelve disciples.

Now watch what it says in verses 17-19, "And He descended with them, and stood on a level place; and there was a great multitude of His disciples, and a great throng of people from all Judea and Jerusalem and the coastal region of Tyre and Sidon, who had come to hear Him, and to be healed of their diseases; and those who were troubled with unclean spirits were being cured. And all the multitude were trying to touch Him, for power was coming from Him and healing them all."

When He descended with the twelve, there was a great multitude of His disciples—others who wanted to be followers and learners of Christ. Jesus had a whole lot of people He could have chosen. But He chose twelve. Did He love all those other people? Did He care about their needs? Did He have compassion? Of course He did. But He also knew, even as the very Son of God, that He could not do what we cannot do. He could not invest His life fully in hundreds of people, even though He was God in the flesh. For as a man He was limited in time and space and in how many people He could spend time with just like we are. So Jesus chose twelve.

WHY? FIVE REASONS TO CHOOSE WISELY

You can only disciple a few
As a student, it's just not possible to get deeply involved in ten, twelve, or fifteen people's lives. You can't do it. You simply don't have that much time to spend with that many people. You may have a dozen come to your Bible Study and hang out, but you can't give individual attention to that many people and also be a full-time student. Full time staff have a more time, but they too will need to make decisions, and draw lines based on capacity.

It's what Jesus did
Jesus invested in a few. We learn from Him because He's the Master.

Not everyone wants to be discipled by Cru
Here's the reality: there are a lot of Christians on campus and they don't all want to be discipled by Cru, nor has God called us to disciple everybody. There are other good ministries on campus, and we can't disciple everyone. We'll work with the people who want to be a part of what we're doing, and where God has called us to go.

Not everyone wants to move toward biblical discipleship
There are some believers on campus who don't want to be discipled by anybody. There are believers who are at a point in their lives where frankly, Jesus is not the Lord of their lives. Jesus is not their number one lover and deepest passion. There may be commitment issues,

priority issues and there are some for whom a boyfriend or girlfriend is more like the lord of their life. There are some Christians for whom GPA or resume is of higher priority than being a biblical disciple. Whatever the reason, there are believers who do not want to move toward biblical discipleship. They simply are unwilling to pay the price. That's why we've got to choose wisely.

Our long-term impact is critical

If you're going to invest your life in someone, if you're going to impart things that God has put into your life, don't you want to know that your disciple is going to take what you teach them and be faithful to apply it? This principle should inform all the discipleship decisions you make over the coming years. Obviously we don't have guarantees on anybody; no matter how promising someone may seem at the time, he may choose not to walk with God down the road and may not have the long-term impact we had hoped for. But by choosing biblical disciples wisely, our ministries will reproduce leaders who in turn will have impact on others.

HOW? FOUR WAYS TO CHOOSE WISELY

Carefully observe potential disciples

Ask questions about someone in whom you think you'd like to invest your life. There are several things to look for.

- **Do they have a heart for God?** Do they demonstrate a hunger to grow? Are they reading the Word? Are they having quiet times and showing a desire to get to know God? Are they asking you questions about their walk with God and spiritual growth? Are they dealing with sin in their life that the Holy Spirit reveals to them? Do they take advantage of opportunities to grow?

- **Are they FAT (Faithful, Available, Teachable)?** Faithful: Do they follow through on things? Do they attend Bible Study consistently? Do they want to be a part of the ministry? Available: Do they have time to meet? If you initiate getting together and they're always too busy with other meetings, it's going to be tough to disciple them. Teachable: You can know if someone is teachable by how they respond to what you try to impart to them. If you get a response like, "Oh, yeah, I've heard that before," "I know that," or "I was taught that before," that person may not be teachable. One of the biggest disappointments about discipleship is when you try to work with someone who thinks they've got it all figured out.

- **Are they socially and emotionally mature?** Everybody's got problems. We're all dealing with issues, and you're not looking for a perfect person who doesn't have problems. Emotional maturity means that the person acknowledges their problems, is growing in their ability to trust Jesus with those problems and is involved in biblical community continuing to function and grow. Sometimes you're going to get a person whose emotional needs are so deep that they're not freed up to minister to others. Some people may need professional help. In 2 Timothy 2:2, Paul tells Timothy, "And the things which you have heard from me in the presence of many witnesses, these entrust to faithful men, who will be able to teach others also." Notice the four generations of spiritual multiplication: Paul to Timothy, to faithful men, to others. Paul's implication is that Timothy should be teaching people who have the ability to teach others. Ask yourself if this person can relate well enough to others so that people will want to follow and listen to them.

- **Will they go where God has called us to go as a ministry?** As a campus ministry, we want to teach people to walk, communicate, and multiply their faith. If a person does not want to go in this direction, then it's probably not best for you to disciple them. We want to develop people, and if this person doesn't want to go in the direction of our ministry, it's not your place to twist their arm. There is no need to disciple someone who does not have a passion for the things God has called us to as a ministry.

Cast a vision for God's call to biblical discipleship
Sit down with the person you've observed and say, "This is where we're going. We're really committed to biblical discipleship. We want to help people to walk, communicate, and multiply their faith." Cast a vision so you can invite this person to come with you toward biblical discipleship. Consider the timeline of college: everything we want to build into a disciple's life during these four years involves equipping them to be a

biblical disciple for the next fifty years of their life. No matter what their vocational calling is, we want them to walk, communicate, and multiply their faith for the rest of their life. If they're a landscaper, wouldn't you love for them to know how to lead other landscapers to Christ?

Lay out the cost of discipleship

If this is a worthy vision you're casting, you'll have to explain what it takes to get there. You might say, "I would like to ask you to be committed to come to the Bible Study every week, not just when it fits into your schedule." Challenge this person to be discipled by you. You're going to make a commitment to their life, so ask them for a reciprocal commitment—coming to Bible Study, meeting individually for discipleship, attending the weekly meeting so they will be a part of the larger body of believers. Lay out the vision, and tell them that this is what it's going to take to get there. In Luke 14:25-35, Jesus encourages believers to count the cost before committing.

Ask that person to prayerfully decide if they will make a commitment Encourage them to ask these questions: Am I willing to count the cost? Am I willing to be committed? This way, you're not selecting them out; you're not determining if they're worthy of being discipled. You're casting the vision and saying to them, "Is this where you want to go?" They can decide, "Yes, that's where I want to go," or "No, I don't really want to go there. I'd rather give my life to something else." You may select who you'd like to work with based on your observations of that person, but they make the decision. It's up to them to count the cost and respond, "Yes, I'm in."

Finally, when you do start a Bible Study for the first time, realize that there will be new people who are young in their faith, and that they may not have those qualities we look for in a potential disciple: they may not be teachable or come each week. Realize that they may not be ready yet. You're not challenging the whole group to discipleship. Start out with a large number of possible people: six to eight potential disciples. Over the course of time, you will be able to discern which of these really have a heart to become a biblical disciple. Then give them a specific challenge. You may end up with just three faithful disciples, but if chosen wisely, they will multiply and impact eternity.

CHAPTER FORTY TWO

SPIRITUAL MULTIPLICATION

SPIRITUAL ADDITION VS. SPIRITUAL MULTIPLICATION

Spiritual addition in ministry is when someone wins other people to Christ, but does not disciple, train, and deepen those converts to go out and do likewise. While we will review the biblical basis for spiritual multiplication, for now let it suffice to state that in Matthew 28:18-20, we are commanded to go and make disciples, not simply converts.

"Then Jesus came to them and said, 'All authority in heaven and on earth has been given to me. Therefore go and make disciples of all nations, baptizing them in the name of the Father and of the Son and of the Holy Spirit, and teaching them to obey everything I have commanded you. And surely I am with you always, to the very end of the age'" (Matthew 28:18-20).

If you led a thousand people to Christ every year for 36 years (taking each one through basic follow up), how many people would you have reached with the gospel? Answer: 36,000. However, if you led three people to Christ, discipled them, and trained each one to reach three other people, and everyone that was discipled in turn reached three other people each year, then when we multiply the process out over 36 years the number of disciples becomes 1,048,576. That's exponential growth. That's spiritual multiplication.

This seems to be what the Lord had in mind in the Great Commission, as it makes the completion of the task feasible as it's doubtful that Jesus expected His disciples to keep up a case load of one thousand disciples a year.

THE BIBLICAL PRECEDENT FOR SPIRITUAL MULTIPLICATION

We have already alluded to the precedence of the Great Commission in the book of Matthew, but there is other biblical support for this model. What follows is a brief survey.

Colossians 1:28; Ephesians 4:12-16

Colossians 1:28 states, "We proclaim Him and admonish every man, and teach every man that we may present every man complete in Christ." That's every man, complete in Christ. The goal is not conversion but completion, or as Matthew 28:19 states it, "teaching them to observe all that I have commanded you." Not just some of what Jesus had commanded, but all. And in Ephesians, we read:

> "To prepare God's people for works of service, so that the body of Christ may be built up until we all reach unity in the faith and in the knowledge of the Son of God and become mature, attaining to the whole measure of the fullness of Christ. Then we will no longer be infants, tossed back and forth by the waves, and blown here and there by every wind of teaching and by the cunning and craftiness of men in their deceitful scheming. Instead, speaking the truth in love, we will in all things grow up into him who is the Head, that is, Christ. From him the whole body, joined and held together by every supporting ligament, grows and builds itself up in love, as each part does its work." *Ephesians 4:12-16*

These passages underscore that it is God's will that all who come to faith should grow into maturity in Christ and become full in the true knowledge of Him, fulfilling God's desire for their character and their ministry. In verse 12, it mentions that the saints are to be equipped "for the work of service, to the building up of the body of Christ." We are to do this "until we all (there is that word again!) attain to the unity of the faith."

Again, mere conversion is not what God prescribes.

> "And the things you have heard me say in the presence of many witnesses entrust to reliable men who will also be qualified to teach others." *2 Timothy 2:2*

The emphasis in this verse is on multiplication. Notice the connection between the teacher, his students, and his students' students. There is a long-range view to discipleship versus a terminal one.

Teaching does not simply start with a teacher and end with his students. It is to go on to the students' students, their students and so on. The idea of one generation teaching the next is explicit here in the text. It supports the view of spiritual multiplication as opposed to mere spiritual addition.

> "From him the whole body, joined and held together by every supporting ligament, grows and builds itself up in love, as each part does its work." *Ephesians 4:16*

This idea of connection is explicit in this text. Look at the language the Holy Spirit has Paul employ: "the whole body, being fitted and held together by that which every joint supplies." This runs counter to the more modern, Western view of rugged individualism wherein we have lone rangers doing ministry while others are on the sidelines watching. A ministry of addition leads to this kind of mentality.

If one person is doing all the evangelism, or all the discipleship, and there isn't any plan for delegation, we're swimming against the tide of the New Testament. God intends there to be spiritual multiplication in our ministries.

OLD TESTAMENT PRECEDENT

There is also an emphasis upon spiritual multiplication in the Old Testament. Look at Exodus 18. In this passage, Jethro confronts Moses for trying to lead Israel single-handedly, teaching the Law and implementing its particulars on his own.

First, Jethro displays his concerns for Moses:

> "What is this thing that you are doing for the people? Why do you alone sit as judge and all the people stand about you from morning until evening? You shall surely wear out, both yourself and these people who are with you, for the task is too heavy for you; you cannot do it alone." *Exodus 18:14, 18*

The indictment of "doing it alone" has a sting to it, and it's obvious that Moses ought to delegate. But, before we get to the solution, notice it says not only that Moses the leader will be worn out if he doesn't change his ways, but, also, the "people who are with [him]." What does this mean?

Can we surmise that it is wearisome to those around us when we don't include them in the work of God's kingdom? Is it because a leader is hoarding the task and has marginalized those around him? This makes for some very interesting conjecture.

Second, Jethro outlines his solution to Moses:

> "Now, listen to me: I shall give you counsel, and God be with
> you. You be the people's representative before God, and
> you bring the disputes to God, then teach them the statutes
> and the laws, and make known to them the way in which
> they are to walk, and the work they are to do. Furthermore,
> you shall select out of all the people able men who fear
> God, men of truth... and you shall place these over them,
> as leaders of thousands, of hundreds, of fifties and of tens."
> *Exodus 18:19-23*

Again we see delegation and multiplication—leaders who in turn teach leaders, who in turn teach leaders, and so on. This strongly supports the notion that spiritual multiplication is biblically prescribed for us as the way in which God intends His kingdom to function. This is something we see in both the Old and New Testaments.

TIPS FOR DEVELOPING AND EXCELLING IN
SPIRITUAL MULTIPLICATION

We first looked at a comparison between spiritual addition and spiritual multiplication. We then briefly explored the biblical precedence for spiritual multiplication. Now, we want to examine some ways that we can excel in the task of spiritual multiplication. While there are many ways to go about this, I will give you my top eight suggestions.

Tip 1—Leaders start and stay focused with the end in mind.
Stephen Covey in his book *The Seven Habits of Highly Effective People* popularized the notion that effectiveness is linked to viewing a worthy goal before one begins working on the task. Certainly spiritual multiplication is a worthy goal. When a leader works toward that end, a view of it must be in her mind at all times as she pursues it.

A great suggestion is made by Sherm Brand of Here's Life America, a ministry of Cru, to help us in this arena. He encourages leaders to have a vision to multiply out to four generations. He bases this on 2 Timothy 2:2: "And the things you have heard me say in the presence of many witnesses entrust to reliable men who will also be qualified to teach others."

Brand advises this: "If a leader begins to strive toward that goal [of four generations, beginning with himself as Timothy and his leader as Paul], it will serve to keep him on track and will help him to know if he is truly building multiplying disciples. If he is not eventually multiplying to four generations, he knows that he is weak in some aspect of building disciples. Once he does reach to four generations... his goal then becomes to help his people reach to four generations and so on. Again, we start small, but always think big. It will take time to see four generations develop but that is the best visible measure of how well we are building disciples."

So, we start by focusing upon the end in mind: spiritual multiplication. We are not simply thinking of our discipleship, or even their disciples, but a step further. We communicate with the expectation that what we teach will be handed down a line or chain of disciples. This informs what and how we disciple.

Tip 2—Leaders seek to be servants.
One of the more significant paradigms a leader needs to embrace is the concept of servanthood, not only to be obedient to the Lord, but to be effective in spiritual multiplication.

Leaders need to see that their disciples have been entrusted to them. We are to help them live fruitful lives, and serve them toward this end, never selfishly seeking the expanse of our own ministry.

Tip 3—Leaders think deeply about the content they are exposing to their disciples.
There are whole libraries on the subject of spiritual growth. It would be presumptuous to think that a few paragraphs could do justice to this topic. So, let's look at the outline found in Ephesians:

"It was he who gave some to be apostles, some to be prophets, some to be evangelists, and some to be pastors and teachers, to prepare God's people for works of service, so that the body of Christ may be built up until we all reach unity in the faith and in the knowledge of the Son of God and become mature, attaining to the whole measure of the fullness of Christ. Then we will no longer be infants, tossed back and forth by the waves, and blown here and there by every wind of teaching and by the cunning and craftiness of men in their deceitful scheming. Instead, speaking the truth in love, we will in all things grow up into him who is the Head, that is, Christ. From him the whole body, joined and held together by every supporting ligament, grows and builds itself up in love, as each part does its work" (Ephesians 4:11-16).

The "menu" has five major headings:

> **Training** "Equipping the saints" (v. 12)
> **Doctrine** "Unity of the faith, knowledge of the Son of God" (v. 13)
> **Character** "Mature man, the fullness of Christ" (v. 13)
> **Team Effectiveness Skills** Relational effectiveness,

communication skills, team building skills, personality and temperament awareness. "Speaking the truth in love, fitted and held together by that which every joint supplies" (vv. 15-16)
Unique Contribution "The proper working of each individual part" (v. 16)

Select material or experiences that balance the above to ensure a balance of growth in your disciples.

The other major category under the heading of content is assessment—selecting material and experiences based on the needs of your disciples. This is in contradistinction to a simple, generic formula given out to each member of the group. You should have a unique development plan for each of your disciples.

This leads to a third category of content—monitoring multiplication. This means that the leader is not only thinking about the content in his group, but the content in his disciples' groups and even his disciples' disciples' groups. This accountability is crucial to ensure that multiplication is happening beyond a generation or two.

Tip 4—Leaders know content isn't the only focus.

Leaders know that if they only focus on the content of what is being imparted (teaching, experiences, training, etc.), the process of spiritual multiplication will abort or be immature.

So much of discipleship and spiritual multiplication is dependent upon relationships. There needs to be an atmosphere of grace, time to just hang out together, and opportunities for the leader to model the Christian life—not just talk about it.

Tip 5—Leaders continue in evangelism.

In discipleship, it is easy to let evangelism slide into the background. But, it must remain front and center, because this is where the future disciples are going to come from.

This is also the whole point of the Great Commission—"go and make disciples." Sometimes, in the effort to make disciples, unconsciously, evangelism takes a secondary role instead of discipling in the context of evangelism. Content apart from the practice of the ministry becomes seminary, not discipleship.

Tip 6—Leaders rely on praying to a Sovereign God.

Leaders instinctively know that given God's sovereign rule and reign, nothing will happen apart from Him (John 15:5). So, they are vigilant in prayer, in their planning, their teaching, their evangelism, and their selection of disciples. God is the author of it all and unless the Lord builds the multiplication chain, they labor in vain who build it (a paraphrase of Psalm 127:1).

Tip 7—Leaders pay heed to the importance of selection.

We have looked at 2 Timothy 2:2 quite a bit in this chapter. It warrants another look as we consider selection (the process of deciding who to invest your life into). When Paul uses the expression "able to teach others also," it is implies that we are to make judgments as to whether or not a potential disciple is indeed "able to teach." In other words, is the potential disciple someone who not only has the intellectual capability but the character as well?

A helpful acrostic is S.T.A.F., which stands for social, teachable, available, and faithful. In the mode of selection, the leader ought to be looking for disciples who are:

- Able to relate well enough for people to follow
- Willing to learn
- Free enough from scheduling demands (e.g. school work, job, family)

Selection can seem partial and a leader needs to be able to address such critiques. One criticism of selection is that it feels elitist. What about those that don't fit the mold? Aren't they vital to God?" We would vehemently agree. So much so that we think it makes a case for why selection in spiritual multiplication is so very crucial.

Consider a jigsaw puzzle as an illustration to answer this critique. Let's say you are putting together a jigsaw puzzle of a farm scene. To begin, you look for the corner pieces first. When in place, the edge pieces are pursued feverishly. Then, as the puzzle box is examined, certain colored pieces are hunted for, perhaps those that make the barn. Slowly, painstakingly, the middle, more elusive pieces are brought into the picture and the puzzle is completed.

Now, does the pursuit of the corner pieces imply that the person putting the puzzle together is bias in favor of "corners"? Does he like "edges" better? Are "corners and edges" more valuable, more likable, more important? Are the "middle pieces" something to pass over, ignore, unvalued and unloved?

The answer to these rhetorical questions is obvious. But, here is the irony. It is precisely because the middle pieces are so important—that is where the main focus of one's eye will be when the puzzle is finished—that one pursues the corners and edges so earnestly. They are strategic to getting the middle pieces in place. Go after the middle pieces first, and the puzzle takes years. Start with corners and edges and it is done in a few hours.

It is because each and every student on that campus is so vital that we start to build a multiplication chain with men and women who are "S.T.A.F." These are the edges and corners.

Tip 8—Leaders remember to bake all they do in encouragement
Taking on the colossal task of spiritual multiplication brings with it challenges from within and without. There is criticism, attacks of the enemy, and loads of self-doubt. So being planted in rich, vital fellowship with other leaders is critical for encouragement.

CHAPTER FORTY THREE

DISCIPLESHIP PLAN

Developing A Personal Plan For Every Disciple

My wife developed "The Personal Vision Plan" from a desire to encourage and motivate her women to greater growth. It is used to reinforce the disciple's strengths. It can be used to identify needs and perhaps share a blind spot that is holding this person back from further growth. It captures a dream or vision of this person's potential in Christ. And it pinpoints long and short-range goals to help the disciple take purposeful steps toward maturity in Christ.

How do you begin? Let me walk you through my own thought process. First, I need to become a student of my disciple. I start listing recognizable strengths. I will ask him to list his strengths. I observe him and check with people who have worked with him. I will ask his friends to describe him. What are his positive qualities? If he is married, I will seek to gain insight from his wife, the person who knows and loves him best. How does he handle school? What is he like in a social setting? What role does he take when he plays a sport? What does his room look like and why? What kind of a leader is he? I take a sheet of paper and write down strengths in seven major categories; 1) relational, 2) task, 3) walk with the Lord, 4) biblical abilities, 5) leadership, 6) character 7) mind. After recording my thoughts, I ask more questions to deepen and broadens my thinking.

THEIR STRENGTHS

Let's say I wrote that my disciple is very enjoyable to be with. I want him to know specifics as to why that is true. Is it because of his sense of humor? Or is it because he is so accepting? Maybe it is because he asks great questions. Maybe it is a combination of all of these. Write these reasons down.

If I cannot see his strengths and believe in his potential, then I question if I should be working with him. I would be cheating him and someone else might do a better job discipling him. We also need to be working with the right people, individuals who are faithful, able, available, and teachable. If there is one issue that hinders ministry growth, it is discipling people who really don't want to be discipled. We need to disciple those who truly have the potential to multiply their faith. Become a student of your student. Look at the questions and lists that follow. Initially it takes time but you'll get better at it.

NEED TO BE DEVELOPED

Look at the sample in this chapter. On one half of the paper list the strengths. On the other side list the needs to be developed. As you can see, we have included questions that help you think through a disciple's needs. I ask questions such as, "What needs to be developed in this person's life? What is preventing him from taking the next step of leadership?" Answers may range anywhere from "He needs to develop an ability to be more open or more personal" to "He needs to use his time better or be a better student of the Word." Is there anything that hinders him from taking on additional responsibility? Write these areas under the "needs to be developed" section. Also cover in your thought process additional aspects like character or social skills development.

THE VISION

Next develop the "personal vision" for this individual. Dream before the Lord about this person and pray, "Lord, with these unique strengths and with the minimization of his weaknesses, what special contributions or role will he play in your kingdom?"

What kind of individual is this? What motivates him? Is he a shepherd? Is he a motivator of God's people? Is he a pioneer, an individual who finds ways to open doors? Is he a hill charger? Maybe he's an innovator.

What I am trying to do is to figure out his natural and spiritual gifting. If he maximized his strengths, what would his potential be? Isn't that what Jesus did with Peter? One day he is shifting sand but soon he would be solid rock.

It's not necessary or even wise to plan a career for your disciple. But, you can recognize abilities that can be used in many scenarios. For example, you may have a disciple who is a gifted shepherd. You could explore that role with him in full-time Christian work, or in many different places. This is dreaming about how the Lord uses a life yielded to Him and living out his strengths. I am not determining God's will for him. I am trying to discover intrinsic motivations.

As I have shared with disciples how wonderful their strengths are and their potential for the King, I have seen their faces light up. They are delighted that what they hope is true about them has not only been identified but the deep longings of their hearts are being encouraged. They feel deeply believed in. They want to hear about the areas in their lives that hold them back. They are highly motivated to meet. We have purpose and direction and a plan to get there.

From the sample discipleship plan you can get an idea of how your disciple might move from the strengths and weaknesses to derive a vision. I sit down across from my disciple and share with him this plan. If I do nothing more than share these strengths, that alone will have a tremendous impact on his life.

THE PLAN

After I ask the Lord to help write a vision plan, the next step is to translate this into a long-term plan. In what areas does my disciple need to develop in order to move toward this dream? As you look at the example, you can see how the vision, strengths, and weaknesses are addressed in the long-term plan. There is a general lifetime plan to address their development in the Scriptures. This is targeted to this individual.

My next step is to take each long-term goal and establish a short-term objective that I can focus on for a summer, a school year, or a college career. The last step is to get this into the schedule using a week-by-week plan.

Before I learned how to do this, my discipleship was not well planned. It was all so thrown together. I realized that I had a thirty-week school year. At best that meant about fifty hours of personal time with my disciple in a year. It might take me three to five hours to plan out a year or semester for my disciple, but that investment saves me enormous amounts of wasted time, and it benefits my disciple.

Below is a sample of how my wife, Janet, has set up her week-by-week schedule. Notice how she has a variety of activities and places where they meet. Notice the balance. There is no sense of rush or being overworked or pressured. Janet would add this, "What we have accomplished is we have gone sharing six times, we have done an evangelistic meeting, and we have had four meals together for fun. There has been a lot of variety. We have met all of her short-range goals. We have done follow up, and personal Bible study. We have challenged people to her Bible study, and worked on her testimony. It has been well paced. All of this occurred during our personal times of discipleship."

SAMPLE VISION PLAN

MARY

STRENGTHS	NEEDS TO BE DEVELOPED
• Good people skills	• Stronger self image
• Loves people	• Can be a people pleaser
• Strong socially	• Has trouble saying "no"
• Attractive personality	• Fear of failure
• People want to be with her	• Procrastinates
• Warm and caring	• Can be undisciplined
• Gift of mercy	• Has trouble confronting others
• Good communication and speaking skills	• Lacks training in discipleship
• Positive spirit	
• Enthusiastic	
• Desires to multiply her life	
• Influences others for Christ	
• Loves the Lord	
• Has a consistent walk with God	
• Shares Christ effectively	
• Woman of growing conviction	

VISION

A loving, caring woman who is a natural leader and influencer of women. Her positive spirit sees the best in people and draws that out in them. As women are drawn to her attractive personality and heart for God, the Lord will use her ability to communicate (through speaking, teaching, and discipling) to build faith and convictions in them, and express His warmth, love, and personal care for them.

LONG-RANGE GOALS

1. Develop a strong self image based solely on her relationship with Christ, not people or performance
    a. Learn to express her love for others without being a people pleaser
    b. Learn to confront in love
    c. Find her significance in Christ, not success or failure

2. Develop her natural leadership and people skills so that she might reach her potential in Christ
    a. Develop discipleship skills
    b. Develop speaking skills
    c. Give opportunities to lead

3. Build strong biblical base from which to minister

SHORT-TERM GOALS

1. a. Have her read *The Search for Significance* and discuss what she is learning
    b. Look for opportunities for her to confront or say "no." Help her through it. Reinforce what she's learning in 1.a

2. a. Share her faith four times this semester
    b. Help her pull together a Bible study on her floor
    c. Discuss the basic "whys" and "hows" of discipleship
    d. Help her think through what to do with her disciples. Learn to think like a discipler

3. Think through some basic doctrinal topics to study personally. Take her through weeks 9 through 11 in *The Compass*

1 - 3: Go on a summer project this summer.

SAMPLE APPOINTMENTS FOR THE QUARTER BASED ON VISION PLAN

MARY

WEEK 1
• Go sharing
• Get to know her better
• Ask questions about her

WEEK 2
• Lunch at my house
• Share my vision and goals for her
• Encourage her in who she is
• Give her the book Search for Significance

Week 3
• Go sharing
• Talk about her quiet times and personal Bible study
• Go through lesson 9 in *The Compass*

Week 4
• Meet with two women about being in her Bible study

Week 5
• Go out to lunch
• Share with her about summer projects
• Discuss discipleship and how to start her Bible study

Week 6
• Go sharing
• Discuss her progress in her book (Search...) and Bible study

Week 7
• Go through lesson 10 in *The Compass*
• Follow up a new believer or go sharing
• Come over for dinner this week

Week 8
• Set up an evangelistic meeting together in her dorm
• Discuss her disciples. How is her Bible study going?

Week 9
• Go sharing
• Go through lesson 11 in *The Compass*
• Lead an evangelistic dorm program

Week 10
• Come to my house for a special lunch
• Review our progress in her goals
• Rejoice together in what God has done in and through us!

CHAPTER FORTY FOUR

RELATIONSHIP, SCRIPTURE AND MINISTRY

The Components Of Biblical Discipleship
(Adapted from *The Compass*)

What makes for quality discipleship? What are the things within a discipleship relationship that produce real growth and make for an enjoyable, satisfying discipleship experience?

The four Gospels offer fascinating answers when you consider two things: What did Jesus impart to His disciples, and how did He do it? He imparted to them His compassion for the lost, and the necessity of servanthood. He demonstrated the importance of His relationship with the Father, and even how to pray. Now consider how He did that – how He imparted these things while teaching in a large group setting; how He told stories to illustrate the kingdom of God; and how He modeled ministry at the very feet of His disciples.

Mark 3:13-14 describes Jesus' method of discipleship: " ... He went up to the mountain and summoned those whom He Himself wanted, and they came to Him. And He appointed twelve, that they might be with Him, and that He might send them out to preach." Jesus selected these twelve to spend the next two and a half years with Him, to go wherever He went, and to eventually be sent out into the ministry. Jesus' example is the very nature of discipleship we hope to model. Here are three components of quality discipleship.

1ST COMPONENT – RELATIONSHIP-BUILDING

The number one thing that Jesus did was get involved in people's lives. When you disciple someone, you're not taking on a project, you're investing in a person. Look at 1 Thessalonians 2:7-12, a classic passage where Paul talks vividly about his heart for the people in whom he invested in the city of Thessalonica. "Having thus a fond affection for you, we were well-pleased to impart to you not only the Gospel of God but also our own lives, because you had become very dear to us" (v. 8). These believers at Thessalonica weren't just a crowd of people; they weren't just objects or a project. These were people who Paul deeply loved. No matter how spiritually gifted you may be or how much theology you may know, "People won't care what you know, until they know that you care."

While ministering at University of Miami – Ohio, I worked with a guy named Eric, an African-American man who had grown up in inner city Cleveland dealing drugs and hating white men. I was twenty-five years older than Eric, Caucasian, and grew up on a farm in rural Pennsylvania. Eric had met the Lord, and the Lord changed his whole life. I began discipling Eric his junior year, and Eric became like a son to me. I'll never forget the day, as we sat in the dining hall where Eric was an RA, when he said to me, "Hersh, I want you to know something. Our weekly time together, our discipleship appointment is my favorite time of the week.'

"Really?" I said. "Why is that?"

"Because when we get together every week, I realize this is the safest place I have to be on campus all week long because I know you love me, you believe in me, you'll encourage me, you'll listen to all my junk, and you'll walk me through my failures and sins, and I know you care."

Race, age, background, it doesn't make a difference. When you move into someone's life, when you love them and they know it, they will respond.

2ND COMPONENT – THE WORD OF GOD

Quality discipleship involves getting the Word of God into someone's life. People don't change unless the word of God changes their thinking and changes their perspective on life. Life transformation comes from the Word.

God's Word also builds convictions. We don't want students who have been discipled to do it just because they're involved with Cru while they're in college. We want them to see that these things come from the Scriptures and to have the Word of God build a deep, internalized conviction to live out biblical discipleship for the rest of their lives.

Most powerfully, God's Word is the truth. Every one of us has lies in our belief system, and those lies can only be replaced with the Truth of God's Word.

3RD COMPONENT – DOING MINISTRY TOGETHER

Training your disciple in how to have a ministry involves more than simply talking about how great it would be to reach out to people who don't know Christ. Doing ministry together means planning outreaches together, and actively sharing your faith with others. Look what Jesus did. He took His disciples and went throughout Galilee and Israel, ministering to people. He spoke to the masses; He healed; He cast out demons; He taught. For two and a half years, Jesus went about ministering, and He took the disciples with Him.

When Paul challenged Timothy in Acts 16, he did not say, "Timothy, let's hide away for three years. I'll teach you everything I know from the Old Testament, give you a crash course in theology, and then you'll be ready for ministry." Instead, Paul said, "Timothy, just go with me," and Timothy joined Paul on his missionary journeys. Timothy learned how to have a ministry by hanging out with Paul. For you and your disciple, ministry may be talking with guys at the basketball court where you're playing hoops. Maybe it's modeling to your disciple how to initiate with a person, build a rapport with them, and transition into the Gospel. Modeling ministry in these ways, allows the disciple to see your heart for the lost.

Four things happen when you are in ministry together:

- **Our view of God develops** When you and your disciple are sharing your faith and following up with a survey contact, your disciple's view of God will grow because the Lord shows up and even if that that person doesn't come to Christ, you may have a great spiritual conversation, where your disciple walks away saying, "Wow, that is cool! Look what God did!" God shows up and works in someone's life when you're doing ministry. Not when you sit around and talk about it, but when you get out and do it.

- **Compassion develops for the lost** Compassion for lost people only develops when we're eyeball to eyeball with someone, hearing the hurt and pain in their life. Even when we meet someone whose life seems all

together, who is as happy as can be dismissing God as
totally irrelevant, our compassion grows as we realize
how lost and without purpose their lives truly are.

- **Our confidence that God will use us grows** When you
go out and share your faith and see God use you to
bring someone comes to Christ, or when you simply
have a great conversation during which the Holy Spirit
gives you things to say, you experience God's leading.
He brings Scripture to your mind, and recalls the answers to things you learned in the past. You walk away
saying, "Wow, God used even me!" Confidence in God
grows as you're involved in ministry.

- **Ministry builds vision and passion** When disciples
are out sharing their faith, it's all they can talk about.
There's a passion, a zeal, an excitement. Because when
you're involved in a ministry, your disciple is getting
in on what God is doing, and that naturally brings
excitement. As a discipler, you must love your disciple
enough to model ministry in a way that prepares them,
increases their confidence that God can use them, and
helps them to develop true compassion for the lost.

Healthy discipleship involves all three components—building relationships, studying the Word of God, and doing ministry together. The
challenge is to balance all three and periodically evaluate which component needs improvement. There is no perfect discipler. You learn to disciple by doing it. Building relationships and studying God's Word may
be easy for you. Ministry is usually the most difficult because it means
stepping out in faith and bringing another person along with you. But if
we do not embrace all three, we rob people of the privilege of growing,
of seeing God show up, of watching God work.

BASIC DISCIPLESHIP RESOURCES

Most of the discipleship resources mentioned in the book can be found by going to crupress.com.

Life Concepts
Basic Follow-up series to take a new or young Christian through 5 lessons:

Stepping from Uncertainty to Confidence (Assurance of salvation)

Stepping from Feelings of Unworthiness to Forgiveness (Forgiveness and confession)

Stepping from Being Unable to Empowered (Being filled with the Spirit)

Stepping from Being Unprepared to Equipped
(Walking in the Spirit)

Stepping from Being Undeveloped to Maturity
(Principles of Spiritual Growth)

The Compass
A two-year campus discipleship curriculum containing over 40 discipleship appointments. On CD.

Cru.Comm
90 Bible studies grounded in scripture and Crusade ministry distinctives. Everything you would want a student to learn in their four years on campus. On CD.

Transferable Concepts
Bill Bright's booklet series on foundational concepts of Christian growth (The Holy spirit, Confession, Evangelism, etc). 10-booklet series.

Satisfied
A booklet for sharing the ministry of the Holy Spirit.

Flesh
A book for men, dealing with sexual purity and pornography, a critical issue of discipleship.

I Am a Tool
Written by Shelby Abbott, *I'm a Tool* tackles the many challenges of Christian dating, particularly within Cru.

Four Sevens
Showing someone how to have a daily devotion is an essential part of personal discipleship and this resource was specifically designed to help you do that.

Thirsty
Thirsty is a two-week devotional that expands and develops on all the concepts of the Spirit Filled Life.

One Story
The *One Story Guidebook* helps you teach your disciple how to study the Scripture, and to learn to see Christ in all of Scripture.

Discipling Women
There are significant issues that can hinder a woman as she grows in Christ. *Discipling Women* will help you to navigate through these sensitive topics with your disciple.

You'll find a number of other helpful resources in the Discipleship section at CruPress.com